Iran and Christianity

Iran and Christianity
Historical Identity and Present Relevance

Mark Bradley

continuum

Continuum International Publishing Group

The Tower Building
11 York Road
London SE1 7NX

80 Maiden Lane
Suite 704, New York
NY 10038

www.continuumbooks.com

British Library Cataloguing-in-Publication Data
A catalogue record for this book is available from the British Library.

ISBN-13: PB: 978-1-4411-1167-8

Library of Congress Cataloging-in-Publication Data
A catalog record for this book is available from the Library of Congress.

Typeset by Newgen Imaging Systems Pvt Ltd, Chennai, India
Printed and bound in Great Britain by Biddles Ltd, King's Lynn, Cornwall

For my wife

Contents

Foreword   ix

Part One: Iran's Identity
Chapter 1 Iran's Religious Identity   3
Chapter 2 Iran's Cultural Identity   28
Chapter 3 Iran's Political Identity   45
Conclusion to Part One   63

Part Two: Impact of Revolution
Chapter 4 The Revolution   69
Chapter 5 War   81
Chapter 6 Economic Hardship   100
Chapter 7 Cultural and Political Authoritarianism   113
Conclusion to Part Two   132

Part Three: Christianity
Chapter 8 Christianity Before 1979   137
Chapter 9 The Church and the Islamic Republic   164

Conclusion   186

Bibliography   188
Index   191

Foreword

Many years ago I had the good fortune to be invited to tea by a gregarious Scotsman with long black curly hair called Bill Raeper. I don't remember the tea, but I remember a room covered in books, some on shelves, some on tables, many on the floor. 'I don't read them all', he said, 'I just like to dip into them to get what is interesting . . . I read very few books from cover to cover . . .' Bill had a brilliant mind and went on to write an outstanding biography of George MacDonald. By now he would have written many more books, but tragically he died in a plane crash in 1992.

I am reminded of Bill because there is a lot of history in this book, and history books should certainly be dipped into. Part One gives a general overview of the Iranian identity; Part Two assesses the impact of the Revolution; and Part Three gives the history of Christianity from its arrival in Iran to the early twenty-first century. As well as history though there is a central thesis that has grown on me in the past 25 years as I have observed Iranians engaged in presenting the Christian Gospel to their fellow countrymen. Early on I noticed that Iranians were willing not to just give Christians a hearing, but some were ready to actually become Christians. As someone who wants people to respond to the Christian Gospel this was of course encouraging. But it was also intriguing for the simple reason that then, in the 1980s, there were very few reports of people becoming Christian from a Muslim background anywhere in the world. Over 25 years later there are more reports, but still virtually top of the list are the Iranians. For those in the church caught up in the work of sharing the Gospel and building up new Christians there has understandably been much talk of a sovereign move of God. He is certainly sovereign and in Jesus' own words 'the wind blows wherever it pleases': but my reading regarding Christian mission, especially Donald McGavran's *Understanding Church Growth*, and David Bosch's excellent *Transforming Mission: Paradigm Shifts in Theology of Mission*, also suggested that this wind sometimes blows more strongly along valleys shaped to be more receptive by human history. So I read much more about Iranians, seeking to discover whether there were any obvious characteristics in their historical background that would make Christianity attractive to them, that would give the essentials of this faith a ring of familiarity. These themes were not hard to discover, and are worked out in Part One of the book.

The fact that there is much in the Iranian identity that relates to Christianity was only a part of the answer as to why many Iranians are now open to the Christian Gospel. The blunt truth is that despite this identity, Iran has largely ignored the Christian message since the Arab invasions of the mid seventh century. This is seen by the fact that Muslim converts to Christianity were extremely rare, even in the late nineteenth century and early twentieth when missionaries were very active. It would seem that however much their identity had links with Christianity, Iranians were content with their religion – Shia Islam and Sufism. This then obviously pointed to the 1979 revolution and its aftermath as being the monumental event that impacted the Iranians' reaction to the Christian message. So my reading moved to the Ayatollah who claimed to be the 'Velayat-e Faqih', the guardianship of the jurists, and establised a regime where his and his successor's interpretation of the Shia religion had absolute power. Till 1979 the Shia leadership were generally quietist, so they could never be blamed for any of the political ills Iran faced. Since 1979 Shia Islam and the rule of the government have been one, so Shia Islam's reputation was bound to be weakened, as Christianity's has whenever it has been too close to a throne. But the relationship between Iran and Shia Islam has more than weakened: it has suffered, even been dislocated. For however favourably one wants to write about the Islamic Republic it is impossible to ignore the fact that most people have endured the impact of war, economic mismanagement and authoritarianism: this is looked at in Part Two of the book.

The argument that Iran's relationship with her religion has been so wounded that Iranians are looking at other faiths then made all the discussion about the Iranian identity in Part One very relevant, for this would suggest that if indeed Iranians were looking for another spiritual home, Christianity would be the natural faith for them to turn to. To flesh this out I felt it was important to first outline the history of Christianity in Iran up to the revolution, to see what sort of image the faith already had before that cataclysmic event. Two things were very clear: on the whole Christianity had a very positive reputation in Iran, but it was normally thought of as being foreign. Then it was time to write perhaps the most difficult, but also perhaps the most interesting chapter of the book – the history of Christianity since 1979. This would be the chapter that would find out whether all the talk of Iranians being open was just personal impressions, hearsay and the hype of reports from excited Christians, or whether there really had been significant growth. There is no doubt it is the latter. This means that the central thesis of the book that Christianity is the natural religion for Iranians to turn to once their relationship with Shia Islam was wounded has some validity.

However my research for this chapter became much more intriguing when it became clear that since at least 1996 the main arena of activity for Christianity was no longer with the historic churches with their foreign connections, but with the house churches where most were from an ethnically Iranian Muslim background. This brought me back to Donald McGavran and his seminal studies on church growth: it seemed like for the first time in Iran's church history a situation might well be developing that would could be recognized as one of those valleys where that wind will be able to keep on blowing.

MB, 2008

Part One

Iran's Identity

Chapter 1

Iran's Religious Identity

Large numbers of Zoroastrians, Jews, Buddhists, Christians, Gnostics, Sunnis and Bahais have all worshipped under Iran's vast skies: but it is Shias and Sufis who dominate the religious landscape. Not only is 90 per cent of the population Shia, but Iran is the only country in the world where the state religion is Shiism. Ever since the 1979 Iranian Revolution the very word Shia in Western minds has conjured up images of crowds clad in black chanting angry slogans. It would seem unlikely they would have a religious identity that easily relates to Christianity. However when one looks closely at the Shia faith, as practised in Iran, one notices there is a passionate devotion to a suffering saviour figure; a fervent belief in the invisible presence of a guide; and an ardent expectation a prophet will return to rule the world with justice. Though from the church's point of view these beliefs are directed towards the wrong men, nevertheless they are still similar to central Christian doctrine.

This points to the Iranian religious identity having bridges with Christianity, but there is more. To the visible eye Iran is officially Shia, but unofficially it is Sufi. For, from the humblest mullah in the smallest village, to the most learned Ayatollah in Qom – mysticism is practised. Furthermore Iranians revere their poets, and three of their most famous, Attar, Rumi and Hafiz, were Sufis. So Shia doctrines, close to what Christians believe about Jesus, are immersed in a religious tradition which believes in experiencing God in mystical ways, just as many Christians do. To fully understand the impact of the Shiism and Sufism on shaping Iran's religious identity, we need to look at these two entwined religious movements in more detail.

Shia roots

In the 1960s, when the economy was booming and rich Iranians could buy the latest Paris fashions, the casual observer could easily assume the country did not take religion very seriously. Iranians seemed thoroughly worldly, and the very pro-Western Shah, Mohammad Reza, was encouraging people to relate to their pre-Islamic history rather than their Islamic heritage. However Al e-Ahmad, a 1960's writer likened to Marx in terms of his literary impact,[1] rejected the Shah's promotion of ancient kings and warned his countrymen to be wary of

'Westoxication' instead, though not religious himself, he urged Iranians to
return 'to our Islamic, especially Shiah roots',[2] for outside the fashionable cafes
of Tehran, '90 per cent of the people in this country live by religious values and
criteria . . .'.[3] To understand Iranian's religious identity we must look at these
Shia roots.

The Shia sect of Islam began in 656, but initially only had support around
Kufa in Iraq (110 miles south of Baghdad). In the middle of the tenth century
two Shia tribes, the Buyids and Hamdanids, seized control of Baghdad and
parts of Northern Iraq respectively, and the Shia faith began to spread throughout the Middle East. Then in 1501 Ismail, the founder of the Safavid dynasty,
declared Iran to be Shia and it has been the country's national religion ever
since.[4] At the emotional centre of the Shia faith stand the stories of Muhammad's
son-in-law, Ali, and grandson, Hussein. Ali was Muhammad's cousin; the husband of Muhammad's only living child, Fatimah, and the father of Hasan and
Hussein. Shias claim that just before his death, Muhammad designated Ali as
his successor. According to their sources Muhammad is reported to have twice
said, 'He whose master I am has also Ali as his prophet.'[5] Furthermore they
claim that Muhammad made all the Muslims come up and honour Ali as his
successor in his tent.[6] However Ali was only 33 years old when Muhammad died
in 632, and it was not normal in the Arab tribal culture for a young man to
become the overall ruler. Rather the custom regarding succession was to have a
large meeting and one of the elders of the tribe would be chosen. This is exactly
what happened after Muhammad's death. The elders chose Abu Bakr, a man in
his sixties from the powerful aristocratic tribe of the Quraysh, as their leader, or
Caliph. He had been one of Muhammad's senior advisors and was also the
father of Muhammad's favourite wife, Aisha.[7]

While Fatimah was alive, Ali did not support the new leadership, but when
she died, just 6 months after her father, he swore allegiance to Abu Bakr
and became one of his unofficial counsellors. Ali was overlooked twice again –
Umar, also from the Quraysh tribe and also a father-in-law to Muhammad,[8]
became the Caliph after Abu Bakr, and then by a vote of three to two against Ali,
Uthman, from the powerful Umayyad clan, became the next one. It was only
after Uthman's assassination by rebels that Ali finally became Caliph – some
25 years after Muhammad's death. Shia writers always remind their readers
that Ali was cheated out of his inheritance and refer to the first three Caliphs as
the 'usurpers' who ignored the will of Muhammad.[9]

Though Ali lived in Medina and certainly benefited from his relationship
with the first three Caliphs, Shia writers like to distance Ali from the wealth and
military conquests of the ruling party. They wrote of a short, balding, and white-
bearded scholar who had a formidable knowledge of the Koran. When asked
how he knew so many traditions, Ali replied – 'Whenever I asked the Prophet
anything he revealed it to me, and when I kept silence he would begin telling

me things.'[10] Ali taught a growing number of disciples social justice, backed up by a simple lifestyle. One historian, Ibn Athir wrote:

> They [Fatimah and Ali] had no bed save a ram skin to lie on at night and to feed their camel from in the daytime. They had no servant. When he was Caliph, Ali wore a tunic too thin to protect him from the cold. Once when asked to describe the proper condition of a Muslim, he replied – 'Pinched with famine, dry with thirst, blear-eyed with tears.'[11]

This was certainly not the image most Muslims had of the ruling circle in Medina during the rule of Uthman, the third Caliph. This was when many Arabs chose to enjoy the luxurious lifestyle of armed dictators in the newly conquered territories such as Egypt, Syria and Persia. Their arrogant dominance caused intense resentment among the subject peoples, which was directed against Uthman. Inevitably these malcontents, made up of the new non-Arab Muslims, began to look for an alternative leader and Ali, as a member of Muhammad's family and a teacher of social justice, was a promising candidate. In 656, with Uthman refusing to reign in the greed of his governors, the malcontents marched on Medina calling on Ali's name, for they were partisans (Shias) of Ali. They hacked Uthman to death and Ali became the next Caliph. He made his home in Kufa, the power base of the rebels and faced fierce opposition from both the Quaraysh aristocracy in Medina and their cousins, the Umayyads in Damascus. They had supported Uthman, and despised the non-Arab support that Ali relied on.

Ali also faced hostility from a group of separatists known as the Kharajites, mainly made up of Bedouins, who felt left out by the Arab establishment and Ali's party. The Kharajites demanded that the leadership be open to all Muslims, regardless of tribe or family blood. At a meeting in Mecca they vowed to kill Ali and the leader of the Umayyads, Muawiya.[12] Ali was cut down by his assassin in on 19 Ramadan 661 on the way to morning prayer in Kufa. He died 3 days later from the wound, having been Caliph for less than 5 years. There is a tradition that Ali's last request was for his body to be slung on a camel which should then be allowed to wander in the desert. Wherever the camel first knelt – this was to be Ali's burial place. The camel knelt a few miles East of Kufa in Najaf, which then became a holy place for all Shias. On hearing of Ali's death, Muawiya, Uthman's brother and the leader of the Umayyads, claimed the Caliphate and marched on Kufa to deal with the Shias. He met little resistance from Ali's first son Hasan, who, after a few skirmishes, readily surrendered and lived in retirement in Medina till he died in his forties of tuberculosis. To secure power permanently for the Umayyads, Muawiya made the Caliphate hereditary, so on his death in 680 his son, Yezid, succeeded him and he expected homage from everyone, including Hussein. But Hussein refused, escaped to Mecca and from there he sent his cousin, Muslim, to Kufa, the Shia power base, to find out the strength of his support. Muslim sent word back to Hussein that up to 18,000 men were ready and urged Hussein to come to Kufa.

On the way to Kufa, near a place called Karbala, just south of present day Baghdad, Hussein's small party of 500 horsemen, was met by an army of thousands led by Abu Wakkas for Yezid. Despite the impossible odds Hussein chose to fight, though he allowed anyone in his party to leave if they wanted to: most did and just 72 remained.[13] Knowing certain death awaited him, Hussein put on a white funeral gown the night before the battle. The next morning Hussein's party was butchered. Hussein's body was trampled under the feet of Abu Wakkas' horsemen. The mutilated body was then buried at Karbala, which has since become the spiritual centre of Shiism, while Hussein's head was sent to Yezid in Damascus. One tradition says that Yezid struck the lips of the head with his staff and said, 'We have taken the lives of those who were dear to us, but who became rebellious and unjust'. He was then rebuked by a shocked colleague who said 'Withdraw your staff, for have I not seen the mouth of the Prophet on this mouth with a kiss.'[14]

With the shedding of Hussein's blood, there could be no peace with the supporters of Yezid. They became known as the Sunnis, which literally means 'one of the path', traditionalists. The Sunnis accepted the first three Caliphs and then the Umayyad dynasty, while the Shias only acknowledge Ali and his descendents. For the Shias the first Caliphs are just mere politicians, while Ali almost takes on a semi-divine role, as do the Imams that descended from him.[15] Most Shias believe in Twelve Imams,[16] and in the popular mind all have miraculous powers. A typical example is a story told about the Tenth Imam, al Naqi who after listening to the financial problems of a friend he, 'thrust his blessed hand into the ground and gave him a handful of sand and stone' which turned into gold.[17] For Iranians, Imam Reza is especially important because he died in East Iran and is buried in Iran's second city, Mashad. Reza's sister, Fatimeh is also special for the Iranians as she died in Qom, just south of Tehran which is second only to Najaf as a centre for Shia scholarship. The shrines of Reza and Fatima attract millions of pilgrims and many come hoping for a miracle.

As well as the miraculous, the Imams had something else in common: violent deaths. Of the eight coming after Hussein, six were poisoned, one was murdered, and one 'died mysteriously'. It was as if the drama of the attacks on Ali and Hussein, of evil against good, were endlessly repeated. Until we come to the Twelfth Imam, Mahdi in the ninth century: he was neither poisoned, nor murdered, nor killed in battle. Mahdi disappeared as a young boy aged 7 or 8. Though he disappeared, Shias believe that Mahdi, the Master of the Age, is very much a spiritual presence. In their writings there are many instances of when he showed himself to believers, when they prayed or were in need. So though concealed, sincere believers can make contact with him. This is especially true of pilgrims. It is said that Mahdi is always at Mecca during the Haj and though the pilgrims cannot see him, he can see them. Pilgrims can also write him short letters that he will definitely receive when put on the tomb of any Imam. There is also a legend that Mahdi is hidden at the bottom of a well at the Jamkaran mosque near Qom and every year thousands visit this site to pray to him. There was even a rumour that at President Ahmadinejad's first cabinet meeting in 2005 he asked all his ministers to sign a letter to Imam Mahdi which they then posted down this well.[18] Not only can Mahdi be contacted today, but at the end of the world, it will be Mahdi who will return, with Jesus, to end all corruption and establish universal justice.

The justice of Ali, the martyrdom of Hussein, the authority of the Imams and the presence of the hidden Mahdi who will return at the end of time, these beliefs are at the heart of the Shia version of Islam. And it was the Shia religion that was adopted by Iran in the sixteenth century and despite the Pahlavis using all the power of the state to weaken its appeal, this religion has remained dominant. To appreciate the Iranian identity, it is important to understand how the Shia faith relates to Iran's national character.

Iran and the Shia faith

Ismail (1487–1524), the founder of the Safavid dynasty, radically promoted the Shia faith. Coming to power in 1501 he demanded that the first three Caliphs be publicly denounced throughout Iran, and threatened to kill any Iranian who did not become Shia. His reasons were political as he was establishing a new dynasty in the face of fierce opposition from the Ottomans in the West and the Uzbeks in the East who were both Sunni. He needed his subjects' exclusive religious loyalty. Iran initially became Shia through compulsion; since then the religious narrative of the Shia story has so successfully merged with Iran's national story that Al e-Ahmad is quite correct to emphasize the importance of Iran's Shia roots. It fused well with Iran's story for three reasons: it enabled the nation to reassert its own identity; it mirrored the people's experience of injustice; and it was in tune with the country's political system. As a great civilization whose language, literature, music and art continued to dominate the Middle East, despite the Arab invasions, Iran always needed a national religion to assert its identity. The Shia sect was suited to meet this need as the leading heroes of the sect, Ali and Hussein, were the challengers of the ruling Arab elite and so they were the perfect icons for any nationalist Iranian ruler wanting to resist either Arab or any foreign imperialism. This is exactly what Ismail, the founder of the Safavid dynasty wanted to do. He brilliantly exploited the perception that Ali and Hussein were semi-detached from the Arab elite and effectively made them into virtual Iranians. With breathtaking confidence he claimed that Ali when searching for a wife for his second son, Hussein, did not go to the Arabs. He went to the Iranians. And the girl he found was none other than Shahrbanou, the daughter of the last Iranian Sasanian king, Yazdegerd. With one alleged marriage Ismail achieves a lot for Iranian nationalism.[19] First of all by having Ali come to the Iranians for his son's wife he underlines the perception that Ali was more comfortable with the Iranians. Then with the actual marriage Ismail combines two of the most revered genealogies in the popular Iranian mind: the Sasanians and Muhammad's family. And of course now all the Imams after Hussein have Iranian blood in their veins, so the Shia faith has in a way become an Iranian religion.[20]

The second reason the Shia faith has merged successfully with Iran is because it mirrors – and continues to mirror – the national story of Iran. So Hossein Derakhshan wrote that the symbols around the story of Hussein are 'more Persian than Islamic . . . he is our icon of struggle against inequality and tyranny . . . and this is how we have infused our Iranian culture inside this Islamic body, and built this Shia faith of ours'.[21] At the heart of the Shia faith is a burning injustice and violent outrage and ever since the demise of the Persian empire, Iranians have felt cheated of their birthright to be a regional power and, worse, their soil, like Hussein's body, has repeatedly been trampled on by invaders – the Arabs, the Moguls, the Turks, the British, the Russians, the Americans and most recently the Iraqis. The story of Hussein has provided the perfect cathartic outlet for Iran's national grief[22] and his tragic end has become by far the most memorable event about the Shia faith for Iranians. The battle of Karbala is constantly referred to in sermons and books, the whole month of *Muharram* (the first lunar month) is given to mourning for Hussein and on the tenth day, *Ashura*, the actual anniversary of the death, thousands of Shias will march, beating themselves with chains and sticks. In Iranian cities this whole drama of Karbala is re-enacted every year the only live street theatre most Iranians will ever see. This is really where the merging of Iran and the Shia faith happens. Writing in 1871 Matthew Arnold noted how there was no space between the actors and the audience; rather the whole community re-lived the tragedy together.[23] And when the actor of Hussein puts on the white funeral shroud on the eve of the battle, it is then the crowds cry in anguish.[24] Ayatollah Khomeini understood how deeply this religious theatre was rooted in the Iranian mind; so in 1978 when the Shah's troops were using live ammunition against demonstrators, he told them to wear white funeral shrouds to be true sons of both Hussein and Iran. And it was during the month of Muharram in December 1978 that the revolutionary movement erupted out of control.

The third reason why the Shia faith has merged well with Iran is because it is much more in line with Iran's political character which looks to semi-divine monarchs.[25] These ideas of kingship did not disappear when the Arabs arrived in Iran and this partly explains why Iranians found it so easy to support the Shias' condemnation of the first three Caliphs who were chosen by mere men in a council. And this also partly explains why Ali and Hussein are so popular among Iranians – both were from Prophet Muhammad's family, both had charisma, and Ali, like the Zoroastrian kings before him, understood the importance of a contract with the people. So in 'The Sermons of Ali' we read – 'God has given me a claim over you by making me the trustee of your affairs; and you too have a claim over me, like mine over you.'[26] Ali insisted that a ruler be just. He told the governor of Egypt –

> You must be just and serving the common man must be one of your prime objectives; the gratification of the aristocracy is insignificant. Look after the deprived who need food and shelter. They deserve your help . . . Be kind to those you rule.[27]

Given that Ali has both divine charisma and a concern for social justice, it is no wonder that Iran has absorbed the Shia faith where so much devotion is lavished on Ali, the champion of the poor. Finally the Shia faith is very well suited to Iran politically because it gives the rulers freedom from outside interference. Until the early twentieth century there was always a Caliph in Sunni Islam who was never Iranian and so could dilute the nationalistic loyalties of the masses. But in the Shia faith there are just the Twelve Imams, and the last one, Mahdi, disappeared in the ninth century. This is ideal for any political ruler who can govern without outside interference and claim the support of the hidden Mahdi, as both the kings and the Ayatollahs have done.

For the past 400 years it is the Shia faith that has provided most Iranians with a spiritual and moral framework. Furthermore it is this faith that has allowed Iran to reassert her own culture and still remain a part of an Arab religion; it is the Shia faith that has so successfully mirrored Iran's own national tragedies; and it is the Shia faith that is in tune with Iran's political temperament. Iran and the Shia faith have obviously suited each other. What has not been so obvious is that the Shia faith is also well suited to share its symbols with Christianity.

Christianity and the Shia faith

The distinguishing symbols of the Shia faith are so close to Christianity that some scholars are reasonably sure that Shia Islam has drawn on the influence of Christianity that was widespread in Iran before the Arab invasion.[28] It is not very difficult to see where Christianity, particularly Roman Catholicism,[29] and Shia Islam are very close. Most importantly Iranian Shias relate to Hussein as a suffering sinless hero whose death is more than voluntary sacrifice in the face of injustice: it also has redemptive power. There are continual references to this in the annual passion play. When Ali speaks sadly of the woes that are coming on his family, Hussein replies – 'Father, there is no occasion to call these things trials since all refer to the salvation of our sinful followers.'[30] There is even reference to Muhammad recognizing his grandson's redemptive power – 'He shall die for the sake of my people.'[31] And his sacrifice was pure, because in the Shia mind all the Imams are sinless. So Majlisi writes: 'All agree that belief in the sinlessness of the prophets is one of the necessary beliefs of the Shia faith.'[32] It is often said there is no concept of the cross in Islam. That is true for Sunni Islam: it is certainly not true for Islam in Iran. There Hussein is the most beloved Imam, and he is also the nearest figure in Islam to a righteous, sinless, suffering Saviour.[33] The Shias also relate to Hussein, and all the other Imams as risen Saviours, for it is only through their intercession that people can get to heaven – 'The Imams are the mediators between God and mankind. Except by their intercession it is impossible for men to avoid the punishment of God.'[34] Or as the Muslim scholar Mahmoud Ayoub writes – '(Shia Islam) has developed its own quasi-soteriological Christology in the doctrine and the role of the Imams . . .'[35] This partly explains the power of pilgrimage for the Shias, for when they visit the tomb of an Imam, his intercession for the pilgrim increases in strength. Though in this sense the Imam's resurrection is only spiritual, it is still very similar to the teaching in Hebrews[36] regarding Jesus who in his heavenly state can plead for mankind. As with Jesus' resurrection, there is also a very physical side to the Imam's resurrection, in that the Twelfth Imam never experienced physical death. So we have a physical death with Hussein, but we have a physical escape from death with Mahdi. Here is the resurrection hope, the belief shared with Christians that evil will not always win. And with Mahdi's return, this resurrection hope turns into certain victory.[37] While for the Sunni it is not required belief, the return of Mahdi is absolutely central for the Iranian Shias, as the return of a Saviour was important for the Zoroastrians.[38] The Shias rely mainly on the traditions rather than the Koran,[39] so according to Majlisi[40], Muhammad said – 'O ye people! I am the Prophet and Ali is my heir, and from us will descend al-Mahdi, the seal (i.e. the last) of the Imams, who will conquer all religions and take vengeance on the wicked.' And the first people to be saved are those who have faithfully followed the Imams. In other traditions there is also an Antichrist figure, a Jew called Sa'if ibn Sa'id who by spurious signs will deceive the thoughtless to follow him. The closeness of all this to Christian teaching needs no comment.

Iranian Muslims also have a belief, similar to the Christian belief in the 'Paraclete', the Comforter, whom Jesus promised would come to guide believers into all truth.[41] For the main role of Mahdi, in his concealment, is to –'guide mankind towards that which the Apostle of God has revealed', and to lead men in worship. The reason why he is hidden is that if he came most men would not accept him. So it is as the hidden Imam his 'grace and blessing can still reach the earth'.[42] Finally there are two aspects of the Shia faith that are especially close to Roman Catholicism. There is intense devotion towards Mary in Catholicism, as there is towards Fatimah, the daughter of Muhammad in Shia Islam. And secondly, just as Roman Catholics see ultimate authority for their church flowing from the apostle Peter through the bishops of Rome, so too the Shias claim authority flows from Ali through the first Twelve Imams.[43]

This closeness of the Shia faith to the central truths about Christ means there is an almost instinctive understanding and love for Christianity freed from its Western trappings at the heart of the Iranian identity. So when the Iranian hears of a dedicated, sinless, Saviour who deliberately chose to suffer death rather than compromise with evil, this is not an alien concept. When they are told that God raised Jesus from the dead, they already know that God spared the Twelfth Imam from death. When they are told that though they cannot see this Saviour, he is still ever present by His Spirit – this reminds them of the hidden Mahdi. And the fact that history will end when this Jesus returns in glory, Shias already believe this.

Al e-Ahmad was correct when he reminded Iranians in the 1960s that a return to their roots would mean a return to their 'Shia roots'. However though Iran is indeed a Shia state, nevertheless Al e-Ahmad could have added that these Shia roots grew up in a land soaked in Sufism. Indeed Sufism is so prevalent that one cannot state that the nation's religious identity is just Shia. It is both Shia and Sufi, and the Sufi element enables the religious identity of Iran to have even more bridges to Christianity.

Sufism

Sufism began as an ascetic way of approaching God within Islam, probably during the reign of the Umayyads (AD 661–749) when the pious felt the religion of Muhammad was being overrun by worldliness. These ascetics took to meditating on verses from the Koran that dealt with the Day of Judgment, spending many hours at night in prayer, and some of them wore simple white woollen garments. The Arabic word for wool is *suf,* so they were known as Sufis.[44] Henry Corbin, the world famous expert on Islam, defines Sufism as 'the realization of the Prophet's spiritual message, the attempt to live the modalities of this message in a personal way through the internalization of the content of the Quranic Revelation.'[45] Though rooted in Islam, there is also a universal edge to Sufism, so Idries Shah, a leading authority on mysticism writes – 'Sufism is the essence of all religions'.[46]

To become a Sufi, the seeker must find a guide known as a *Shaykh* or a *Pir.* For a Sufi not to have a Shaykh was unheard of, as Bistami, an early Iranian Sufi said, 'He who does not have a Shaykh, his Shaykh is Satan.' The guide would normally be teaching a small group of fellow travellers who completely submitted to his authority to learn how to walk the mystic path. All teachers agreed that repentance was the first step the new devotee had to take, and this had to be much more radical than Muslims involved in formal religion. Sari as-Saqati, a famous ninth-century Sufi teacher, makes this contrast – 'The way of the multitude is this that you observe prayer five times daily behind the imam, and that you give alms. The way of the elect is that you thrust the world behind you altogether. These are the two ways'.[47] Though after repentance, there are variations on the subsequent stages, nearly all teachers agreed on the importance of *Dhikr*[48] and *Fana*. In the *Dhikr* the Sufi aims to constantly remind himself of God. To do this he continually repeats either the name of Allah or a phrase of praise about Allah. This repetition is to go on – either individually or in a group – till the mind becomes aware of nothing else and so the devotee falls into a trance, or *fana* (a passing away, or annihilation), and this ideally should lead to a place of seeing in the devotees' inner being.

Sufism and Iran

Though there is much scholarly dispute over the movement's exact origins[49] there is general agreement that the movement soon owed much to Iran. Henry Corbin who wrote extensively on the links between Zoroastrian and Shiite spirituality[50] believed that mysticism flourished in Iran because of 'le genie iranien . . . la vocation imprescriptible de l'ame iranienne'. Another expert, Learnord Lewisohn writes that this idea 'represents the opinion of a wide spectrum of Islamicists, literary historians, religionists, and historians'.[51] And so the scholar Fereshteh Ahmadi concludes – 'Few will dispute the fact that the development of Sufism owes much to Iranian mystics.'[52] Two of Sufism's earliest leaders, Hasan Basri (d. 728) and Rabia al Adaqiyah (d. 801) were from Basra, and are considered Iranian by some scholars.[53] Basri, belonged to the mourning group of Sufis, but Rabia exalted in the love of God. 'I love God', she declared 'I have no time left in which to hate evil'.[54] Not only were these early leaders connected to Iran, but also the first martyr of Sufism was Iranian. As the original ascetic movement turned into a more mystical one, so Sufis began to talk about experiencing God in ways that seemed blasphemous to Muslims. By far the most famous 'blasphemer' was Mansur al-Hallaj (858–922) from Southern Iran. As a young man he became a Sufi and learned the Koran off by heart. He later travelled widely teaching Sufism, as well as making several pilgrimages to Mecca with his students. He eventually settled in Baghdad where he became very popular and gained a reputation for being able to lead men back to God. He also became famous for going into trances. It was during one of these that he uttered the fateful words, 'I am the truth.' This was too much for the Islamic authorities. They put him on trial for blasphemy and sentenced him to a cruel execution on 26 March 922. He was first crucified, then beheaded, then maimed, and finally his torso was burnt. For many Sufis, Hallaj was no blasphemer, but a seeker who had experienced what all genuine mystics desire, reunion with God. He believed that through *fana,* God could become incarnate, and the example he cited for to support this doctrine was not Muhammad, but Jesus. This might explain why the Muslim authorities began his execution with crucifixion.[55]

Sufism and Iranian philosophers

As well as Sufism's first martyr, Iran also gave the movement her greatest philosophers. So the concept of *fana* was introduced by the Iranian al Bistami (d. 874),[56] from Bastan, about 300 miles East of Tehran. His grandfather was a Zoroastrian, and this might have influenced him towards mysticism and the 'light of Allah'. Initially he was a serious Islamic scholar, and rigorous ascetic, but then spiritual frustration led him towards Sufism where, through experience, he declared the self had to be annihilated. He prayed fervently to know nothing except God, 'This opened to me a vision that I was no longer in existence and I vanished completely from myself into Himself' which meant he had reached *fana*.[57] Bistami later in life testified as to why *fana* was the best approach to God. 'I stood with those who pray excessively and those who fast excessively and I didn't make a footstep of progress. Then I said, "O Allah, what is the way to You?" and Allah said, "Leave yourself and come"'.[58]

Bistami was a respected Sufi thinker, but probably the greatest Sufi philosopher was another Iranian, al Ghazali (d. 1111). According to one scholar, Duncan Macdonald, he is 'the greatest doctor of the Muslim church'[59] and another, Roy Mottahedeh, says he 'is perhaps the greatest moral thinker of the Islamic tradition'.[60] Like Bistami, al Ghazali was from the north of Iran. He began his career as an academic and was an outstanding student of canon law, theology and dialectic science. In 1091 he was appointed the head of Nizami Academy in Baghdad, but shortly after taking up the post he experienced a crisis of doubt, not just in religion, but in whether a human can have any certain knowledge. He came out of this crisis, not through 'a systematic demonstration or marshaled argument', but through 'a light that God most high cast into my breast'.[61] In other words, he could only 'know' through mysticism. He continued to teach at the prestigious university, but constantly felt a true Sufi should renounce all worldly attachments. For a while he resisted this inner prompting, but then one day in July, 'the matter ceased to be one of choice and became one of compulsion'.[62] He was seized by a pain in his chest, and his tongue became so dry he was unable to lecture, and he knew he had to leave his comfortable position in Baghdad. For 2 years he lived the ascetic life in Syria, then went on several pilgrimages, and finally returned to his home town of Tus. Here he wrote at least seventy books, two of the most significant being *The Incoherence of The Philosopher*, and his Magnus Opus, *The Review of The Religious Science*. Through his life and writings, al Ghazali changed the course of both Sufism and Islam. In the *Incoherence of the Philosopher* he refuted the idea that there was a necessary link between cause and effect – 'The connection between what is customarily believed to be a cause and what is believed to be an effect is not necessary . . . but each of the two is independent of the other.'[63] He uses the example of a blind man regaining his sight and so thinking that all he can see is due to his healed eyes. In fact, all he can see depends on the sun giving light.

As well as wanting to stress that the cause of all immediate events is solely God, al Ghazali is also attacking his fellow Iranian philosopher, the renowned Ibn Sina (Avicenna) who emphasized the importance of reason in determining 'the fate of the rational soul'. For al Ghazali this approach is incoherent, and in that some of this thinking was inspired by Aristotle and Plato, Greek unbelievers, it is 'pure abomination'.[64] By refuting the centrality of reason and condemning any dependency on Greek philosophy, al Ghazali established mysticism as man's most important endeavour. This thinking has impacted all of Islam to the present day. However his greatest legacy was to firmly put Sufism within the boundaries of orthodoxy. He relentlessly condemns antinomianism, arguing that first the true Muslim must learn the normal religious disciplines, before moving on to master mysticism. After al Ghazali there was no question that Sufism had a recognised place within Islam.

Another great Iranian Sufi philosopher who went on to ensure mysticism stayed at the heart of the country's religious identity was Al-Suhrawardi (1154–1191),[65] the founder of the Illuminationist (Ishraq)[66] School. He was born less than 50 years after al Ghazali, and was also from the north-west of Iran. As a young man he was attracted to Sufism, and would give himself to solitary retreats, and ascetic practices such as just eating a few ounces of food each week. After his schooling he began to travel looking for a mystic guide. He was never successful, and while becoming outwardly more eccentric, sometimes dressing as a Muslim learned man, sometimes as a Sufi, sometimes as a beggar, he developed and wrote out his mystic philosophy of light. Agreeing with al Ghazali that mystical knowledge is the only true knowledge, he then went on to argue that the only valid nature of existence was light, but then developed a system that, contrary to al Ghazali, incorporated Greek ideas. Light is the primary reality in Suhrawardi's scheme of things. Then, similar to neo-platonic thinking, lesser lights emanate from the primary light; this is followed by an intermediary world of horizontal lights, full of angels with Zoroastrian names whose role is similar to Plato's forms. It is these angels who control our mundane world where the human soul is a 'focus of luminosity more intense than its surroundings, a distant but recognisable flash from the original and supreme light'.[67] This is why a human being, when he or she becomes self aware of this natural link to the light, can begin to experience a mystic journey towards the Light of Lights. Suhrawardi was clearly a genius, but not all his contemporaries appreciated this and when he arrived on his travels in Aleppo, Syria, his eccentric reputation had gone before him. The Muslim authorities were especially outraged at his poetry which used images of wine and the union of lovers to convey the delights of the soul reaching God and in late July 1191, Suhrawardi was executed on the orders of Saladin who having just captured Jerusalem was in no mood for schism.

Though he died when he was just 38, Henry Corbin says regarding Suhrawardi's Philosophy of Lights, 'the entire spiritual life of Iran has been marked with its imprint.'[68] For his insistence on light both draws on Zoroastrianism with its battlefield between light and darkness ultimately won by a Saviour from the forces of Light and it agrees with one of the most loved verses of the Koran memorized by millions –

> God is the light of the heavens and the earth; and His light resembles a niche in which is a lamp; and the lamp is within a crystal glass, and the crystal is as it if were a bright star; it is lit from a blessed tree, an olive, neither of the East nor the west . . . *Light upon light!*[69]

It also brings in the universal ideas of Plato with its references to emanations and forms controlling the world.

Though Iranians deeply appreciate the work of Suhrawardi, it is likely they feel closer to another great philosopher, Mulla Sadra (1571–1640). Born in Shiraz, the son of the governor of Fars, Mulla Sadra received the finest education both in his home city, and the Safavid's new capital, Isphahan, where he was taught by Iran's greatest philosopher of the day Mir Damand.[70] Mulla Sadra had many opportunities before him, but after his studies he was spiritually frustrated and withdrew to a village near Qom where for 15 years he practised extreme asceticism in the pursuit of the 'illumination' that Suhrawardi had taught. It was here that he wrote most of his books, his masterpiece being *Asfar* which was an encyclopaedia of philosophy divided into four journeys, modelling the journey a Sufi takes. Though Mulla Sadra had philosophical disagreements with Ghazali and especially Suhrawardi, he greatly furthered their mystic cause. Indeed his impact on Iran's religious life was decisive. He reconciled into one system (he called it a metaphilosophy) all the insight of the previous masters and showed in his life and writings how to practise *irfan* the seeking after light. By insisting on the primacy of experience whereby only the initiated were allowed to teach *irfan* to seekers, he really set up a system for spreading the technique. In recognition of Mulla Sadra's impact, Roy Mottahedeh refers to the 'victory' of his teaching which brought about 'the domestication of mysticism among the Shiah mullahs'. This is still true today, and Mottahedeh refers to 'the honeycomb of ties of erfan that run through the community of mullahs in Qom.'[71]

Perhaps the names al Bistami, al Ghazali, al Suhrawardi and Mulla Sadra are not so familiar to Western ears, but mention them to an Iranian and he will immediately recognize them as fellow country men who have shaped their country's religious identity.

Sufism and Iranian poets

If Iranians are rightly proud of their philosophers, they are passionate about their poets. And it is the poets, even more than the philosophers, who have made Sufism a part of Iran's soul, for though not every Iranian is a devout Shia, every Iranian loves their national poetry. Of the six recognized giants of Persian poetry – Ferdowsi (*ca* 935–*ca* 1020), Khayyam (1048–1131), Attar (1130 (?)–1221 (?), Saadi (1183–1290), Rumi (1207–1273) and Hafiz (1310–1325) – it is relevant here to note that at least three of them are Sufis, including the most popular Hafiz.

Attar, from Nishapur in the north-east of Iran, was so affected by the suffering of the people he treated as a pharmacist that he abandoned his career and took to travelling. On the road he met a number of mystics and returned home to promote their teachings and write poetry. By the time he was murdered by the invading Mongols he had penned over thirty mystical poems, the most famous being *The Conference of the Birds*. Well known both in the East and West the poem tells the story of 30 birds (*Simorgh*) led by a hoopoe who have to travel across seven valleys to meet the great *Simorgh* a mysterious bird in Persian mythology, similar to the Phoenix in the West. The story is a brilliant allegory of the journey Sufis need to make with their guide so the last valley they have to cross is the valley of *fana*. When they arrive in the land of *Simorgh*, they only see their reflection in a lake, underlining the Sufi idea that God is not separate from existence, but is rather the totality.

The Mongols also nearly devastated the family of Rumi who had to flee their home in Balkh, now western Afghanistan, and came to Nishapur. There is a story that Rumi's father, mystic Walad, sought out Attar here who gave him a copy of one of his poems. If true, Attar's gift certainly bore fruit because Rumi went on to become Iran's greatest mystical poet.[72] From Turkey to Tajikistan Rumi's official title is Mawlana Jalal al Din – the Master of the Glory of Religion. He is usually simply referred to as Mawlana – *Our Master*. He is given this title not just because of the outstanding beauty and sheer amount of poetry, 70,000 couplets, but also because he managed to take the philosophy of Sufism and make it easily accessible to ordinary people. Rumi's aristocratic refugee family finally settled in Konya in Central Turkey where Rumi became the head of the religious school when he was 25. He might have lived the rest of his life as a devoted scholar, however in his late thirties he began a relationship with a wandering mystic, Shams Tabrizi who became his 'grand student'. For 2 years they were inseparable, with Rumi even giving his young 15-year-old stepdaughter to Shams who was in his sixties. She tragically died and her death either caused Shams to leave Rumi's home, or as many others believe, to be murdered by Rumi's youngest stepson, Alleidin. The impact of his departure on Rumi was electrifying. His grief erupted into mystical verse which flowed for the next 25 years. So, as one of his translator's says, we have to recognize that 'Rumi without Shams would not have been known to history.'[73] And Rumi made sure that however disliked this wild holy man was, Shams also was never lost to history. His first major work is called, *The Works of Shams Tabrizi* and at the end of hundreds of his love poems he used Shams as a pen name. Rumi's most famous work is called *Masnavi Ye*

Manavi (Spiritual Couplets), which some call the Persian Koran, and Rumi himself called 'the roots of the roots of the roots of the (Islamic) Religion'.[74] It took 43 years to write and with nearly 30,000 rhyming couplets it is like the size of a Bible and contains all that is needed for a seeker to reach God after the Sufi fashion.

The Sufi teaching of the *Masnavi* is apparent in its opening lines –

> Listen to the reed-flute, how it complains
> Lamenting its banishment from its home
> Ever since they tore me from my osier bed
> My plaintive notes have moved men and women to tears
> I burst my breast striving to give vent to sighs
> And to express the pangs of my yearning for my home
> He who abides far away from his home
> Is ever longing for the day he shall return[75]

The opening line is a call to all seekers to listen to Rumi's favourite musical instrument the reed flute which symbolized the soul that had emptied itself of ego and could be played through by God's spirit. The flute is sighing about its separation from the osier bed, the reed field, and this is the complaint of all seeking souls. They have been taken from their original homeland with God where they lived in peace, are now separated, and long to return. Rumi is renowned not only in the East, but also in the West. Till recently this was because of the famous Dervish dances of the Mevlevi Sufi order he founded in Konya. Still active, they perform a swirling dance in slow circles and take up special postures which allegedly help them enter into an ecstatic trance. However in recent years his poetry has enjoyed great popularity in the West. He is now one of the most widely read poets in the United States, some of his supporters include celebrities such as Madonna and Goldie Hawn[76] and UNESCO declared that 2007, the eight-hundredth anniversary of his birth year should be Rumi Year.

Apart from the beauty of his poetry which engages the emotions and that wistful part of human nature, there are three characteristics that make his appeal so universal. First of all there is an emphasis on hope. The reed flute longs to return to its homeland and throughout Rumi's poetry there is the expectation that this can happen. One of his most famous verses sums this up with the wonderful declaration – 'Ours is not a caravan of despair.'[77] Secondly, like all Sufis, he believed the primary essence of man was love which leads him to describing God in a very intimate, personal, almost sensual way –

> Suddenly the drunken sweetheart appeared out of my door.
> She drank a cup of ruby wine and sat by my side.
> Seeing and holding the lockets of her hair
> My face became all eyes, and my eyes all hands.[78]

Finally his emphasis is truly tolerant. Whereas both Christianity and Islam are over shadowed by a frightening Day of Judgment when infidels are cast into an eternal hell, Rumi insisted that all religions lead to God –

> Because He that is praised is, in fact, only One.
> In this respect all religions are only one religion.
> Because all praises are directed toward God's Light,
> These various forms and figures are borrowed from it.[79]

His insistence on this was sometimes deliberately provocative, stressing the central Sufi doctrine that God must be experienced. So in his *Rubi'yatt* he wrote –

> If the image of our Beloved is in the heathen temple
> Then it is flagrant error to walk round the Ka'ba[80]

At his funeral in December 1273 it was fitting that Muslims, Christians and Jews all carried his coffin. He had begun his life running away from the racial horror of the Mongol invasions and ended his days as the religious tribalism of the 'Christian' Crusades spread violence in Palestine. In such a context he surely pointed to a better hope and deserves his honoured place in history.

If you ask an Iranian who is more important, Mawlavi (Rumi) or Hafiz they will frown, hesitate, and in the end say it is an impossible question – both were so great. However when asked if they would bring a book of Rumi's or Hafiz's poems to a desert island where only one book was allowed – most choose Hafiz. He is called Hafiz because as a young boy he learned the whole of the Koran by heart, *hafiz* meaning, memorizer. He was born in 1319 in Shiraz and despite the violent political upheavals that swept over that city during his lifetime he managed to die there, an old man, in 1410. He lost his father, a coal merchant, as a child, and was brought up by his uncle who sent him to work in a drapery and a baker's shop.[81] There is a story that Hafiz's uncle was trying to compose a poem for a local poetry group but, not being very gifted, he gave up and asked his young nephew to have a go. Hafiz brilliantly completed the verse, and his career as a poet began which took him to the court of the local Sheikh and to lecturing at a college started by one of his patrons. By the time of his death he had written some 500 Ghazals (Sonnets), 42 Rubaiyees (Quatrians, verses of four lines) and had achieved national fame. The popularity of his poetry rests not just in its exceptional lyrical beauty, but also in the way he somehow manages to sum up what it means to be a true Iranian. As the great nineteenth-century English translator and orientalist Edward Fitzgerald said – 'Hafiz is the most Persian of the Persian. He is the best representative of their character . . ..'[82]

And though doubted by some, a part of that character is Sufism. Some take Hafiz's references to wine and women literally, rejecting the idea he used Sufi symbols.[83] They also like to call attention to the controversy that surrounded the poet's funeral because Hafiz's reputation was so questionable that the mullahs of Shiraz were unwilling to give him a Muslim burial. His supporters vociferously protested and it was decided the matter should be settled by a young boy randomly consulting one of his poems. Perhaps the boy was given some help, because the verse he found was decisive and the poet was buried properly – 'Fear not to follow with pious feet the corpse of Hafiz for though he was drowned in a ocean of sin, he may find a place in paradise'.[84] Like earlier mystics, Hafiz wrote verse that deliberately challenged orthodox Islam, but though he certainly enjoyed his wine, and complained in verse when Shiraz suffered a prohibition, his lifestyle was not hedonistic. We know from his poetry that his wife died, so for most of his adult life he was single, but there is no evidence he was a womanizer. However there is definite evidence he was a mystic and so it is quite proper to also give symbolic meaning to his references to wine. Some claim he was a follower of the mystic Sheikh Mahmud Attar[85] and the poetry itself constantly deals with familiar Sufi themes. So, as with Rumi, there is great emphasis on union with the beloved, and there is a brave willingness to dispense with orthodoxy to gain an experience with God. In one Ghazal he provocatively brings together the tavern and the mosque – 'The purpose of the Masjid (Mosque) and the Tavern is union with you'.[86]And shockingly in the first and famous Ghazal, he writes 'Dye your prayer-carpet in wine/If the "Magian Teacher" command it.'[87]

Dr Arley Loewen[88] in his MA dissertation 'The Pir-i[89] Mughan in the Divan of Hafiz' notes that there are 80 references to this figure, and to understand his role, 'we are compelled to take a close look at Islamic Sufism.[90] Dr Loewen shows that Hafiz's insistence on having a pir, a spiritual mentor, means he initially followed an orthodox Sufi route. However there is an unconventional twist. For Hafiz is not content with the normal Sufi pirs, indeed he pours scorn on their hypocrisy. He only accepts the Pir-i Mughan who in Hafiz's poetry becomes much more than a usual Sufi Master: he becomes a manifestation of The Perfect Man, a redeemer figure, dispensing joy and pleasure through wine. So we read in another Ghazal:

> Last night I carried my problem to the Pir-i Mughan who with but a glance of his eye solved the riddle I had.
>
> I saw him joyful and laughing with a glass of wine in his hand and that mirror of the wine glass he was watching the manifold secrets of the universe.[91]

It is perfectly clear that the glass of wine is more than a pleasant drink for it holds 'the manifold secrets of the universe' which links it to the "The Jam of Jamshid", the legendary wine-glass of the ancient king of Iran who is said to have invented both fire and water.'[92] In some sonnets this mystical Pir-i Mughan comes from an invisible universe, but in another, Hafiz finds the Pir inside himself.

'For years my heart was searching everywhere for the Goblet of Jammshid
And that what I had within myself I was groping from strangers

The Pearl which is out of the shell of both worlds was searching among the
lost ones scattered along the shores of the ocean of life.'[93]

Hafiz's Pir then is much more than a usual Sufi guide, nevertheless the symbolism still belongs firmly in the world of Iranian mysticism. The concept of the
Perfect Man 'runs through the fibre of Islamic Sufism'; it was the Sufis who took
the legend of Jamshid's wine glass and developed mystical interpretations
around it; the belief that certain special students could have invisible angelic
Pirs was a Sufi tradition, and the fact that Hafiz could find the Pir in his own
heart takes us all the way back to Attar and his play on the *Simorgh* (30 birds)
who found what they were looking for when they saw their own reflection in
the lake.

Once he was safely buried, an elaborate mausoleum was built for Hafiz, the
pilgrims started to come, and they have never stopped. Like his own Pir-i
Mughan it seems that Hafiz has taken on a role that goes beyond that of a
respected poet. Not only will nearly every household in Iran have a copy of
Hafiz's poetry, not only do millions quote his verse every day, but some of those
pilgrims who come to Shiraz will pray at his tomb, others will have their fortune
told by specialists after they have blindly chosen a verse from a poem; and
during Iran's most important festival, No Ruz (New Year), some Iranians will
place a copy of Hafiz's poems on a special table they display, along with photos
of departed loved ones. Indeed for many Iranians, Hafiz is their invisible Pir-i
Mughan and it is he and the other Sufi poets, especially Rumi, who have taken
the work of the great Iranian Sufi philosophers and made mysticism a part of
Iran's religious soul. For unlike Westerners who struggle to even quote a few
lines from their national anthem, Iranians can spend entire evenings reciting
poetry to each other, and they will constantly sprinkle their daily conversations
with verse, using it to show ordinary events on a broader, more enigmatic canvas. The mosque gives the Iranian a very black and white world to live in, but, as
many observers, including Roy Mottahedeh points out, the Iranian soul is more
at home in an ambiguous setting and poetry meets this need: 'Persian poetry
came to be the emotional home in which the ambiguity that was at the heart of
Iranian culture lived most freely and openly'.[94] And in this ambiguous world the
symbols are not necessarily hostile to Christianity.

Iranian Sufism and Christianity

Sufism is not Christianity: not only is it rooted in Islam and so rejects the divinity
and cross of Christ, but it also has the concept of a universal Spirit whereby
the 'many is one, and the one is many.'[95] However it would be a mistake to

assume there can be no relationship between Iranian Sufism and Christianity on the grounds of doctrinal difference. For the whole point of Sufism is that it operates beyond rigid religious rituals and doctrines, this is why Hafiz tells his reader to stain his prayer mat with wine if your Pir (which can be your inner voice) tells you to. So one clear message of Sufism is this – be ready to tear up tidy tribal religious ideas if you want to experience God. This does not mean that Iranian mysticism has a direct link with Christianity, but it does mean that all Iranians who have soaked their minds in Sufi poetry are ready to open a door to a symbolic world that speaks of spiritual experience. And in this symbolic world there is much that is similar to Christian teaching. There is the shared sense that human beings are not completely at home in the present world, to remedy this the seeker needs to submit to a guide, a shepherd; there is then the shared motif of a journey which begins with the all important step of radical repentance, continues with repetitive prayers of remembrance and ends with the denial of self (fana); on this journey there is a shared hostility for outward ritual and doctrine, and an insistence on the primacy of experience. And finally there is the expectation of present reunion with God which both Christianity and Sufism share. And both insist that the God the seeker reunites with will be like a 'beloved', or will be 'love' or 'light'. Theologically Sufism and Christianity live on different continents; but, apart from Christ's cross, experimentally their paths seem to share similar sign posts. John Gilchrist, an authority on Islam confirms this. He writes that though 'Islam can hardly be regarded as a stepping-stone to Christianity . . . *Sufism definitely is*.[96]

Conclusion

Iran then is both Shia and Sufi well illustrated by the country's greatest twentieth-century icon, Ayatollah Khomeini. For more than a quarter of a century he was the severe face of the Shia religion. Yet behind those uncompromising eyes was a committed Sufi who wrote fine mystical love poetry.[97] Arriving in Qom in the 1920s he sought out masters to teach him Sufism, and by 1929 he was writing with confidence on the subject and became a teacher of *irfan*. He was particularly respected for his mastery of Mulla Sadra and the subject of man's journeys towards God.[98] Ayatollah Khomeini was no friend of Christianity. To him and all his fellow revolutionaries this was a religion that had been superseded by Islam, and was being used by the West to oppress Muslims. Yet before his revolution hardly any Iranian Muslims had become Christian; now it is Iranian Muslims, more any other Muslim group, who are turning to Christianity. One very likely reason for this is that the dual religious identity Khomeini has enforced has many bridges to Biblical Christianity. The Shia faith instils the importance of a just Imam, who is willing to die for his people, yet still present to guide, and certainly determined to return in victory; and the philosophy of Sufism invites everyone to move beyond rigid religion, and embark on a journey where they deny themselves to experience the light. As disillusionment with the Islamic Revolution has spread, so the appeal of a religion which shares so much with Shiism and Sufism has increased – especially when shed of its Western externals. Rather than being the enemy of Christianity in Iran, the dual religious identity of Iran might prove to be its best friend.

Notes

[1] One critic, Reza Baraheni, said the impact of Al e-Ahmad's work 'Gharbzadegi', Westoxication, in clarifying 'the duty of colonised nations vis a vis colonialist nations' was comparable to that of Marx's manifesto which clarified economic relations. See *Iranian Intellectuals and the West* by Mehrzad Boroujerdi, Syracuse University Press, Syracuse, 1996, p. 67.

[2] Quoted by Roy Mottahedeh in *The Mantle of the Prophet*, Oneworld Publications, Oxford, 1985, p. 331.

[3] Quoted from Euromania by Mottahedeh in *The Mantle of the Prophet*, p. 300.

[4] See below for a full discussion of the Safavids' coming to power.

[5] This was first reportedly said when Muhammad returned back from an expedition to al-Hudaibiya, and is found in the source Mas'udi, who is considered to be the Heroditus of Islam; the statement was repeated according to historians such as Mulla Bakir al Majlisi (d. 1700) shortly after the death of Muhammad's son, Ibrahim. For an excellent discussion of Ali's claim to be Muhammad's legitimate successor see chapter one of *The Shi'ite Religion* by Dwight Donaldson, published by Luzac, London, 1933, p. 3.

[6] This was also recorded by Mulla Muhammad Baki-I-Majlisi (d. 1699), the greatest theologian of the Safavid period (1501–1736), see *The Shi'ite Religion* by Donaldson, pp. 5 and 6.

[7] Aisha had a long-standing personal grudge against Ali because, according to Yakubi (classical Arabic historian, d. 891), Ali had advised Muhammad to put Aisha away because she had got left behind during an expedition and had arrived later on a camel, led by a young Kurd. This caused so much gossip that Muhammad turned to Ali for advice, which he then did not accept. Instead Muhammad received a revelation which said that you had to have four witnesses of the actual act to prove adultery. See *The Shi'ite Religion* by Donaldson, p. 29.

[8] Muhammad had 20 wives, so it is not surprising that a number of fathers-in-law are hovering around the court.

[9] Such is the hatred of the Shias for the usurpers that at the festival of Ghadir, the name of the watering hole where Muhammad first designated Ali, three images of the usurpers are filled with honey and then stuck with knives. The honey drips out symbolizing their blood and is sipped by the Shias. See *The Shi'ite Religion* by Donaldson, p. 4, from *Hughes' Dictionary of Islam*, p. 138.

[10] The source is Ibn Sa'd, Tabakat, II, p. 101. See *The Shi'ite Religion* by Donaldson, p. 19.

[11] *The Shi'ite Religion* by Donaldson, p. 17.

[12] Muawiya was the son of Abu Sufyan, a leading companion of Muhammad.

[13] Others sources say it was not 72, but 87.

[14] See *The Shi'ite Religion* by Donaldson, p. 85. There are various stories about Hussein's head. Other traditions claim the head first went to Ascalon and then on to Cairo where there is the mosque of Hussein.

[15] 'The Shias have carried their veneration for Ali so far as to raise him to the position of a divine person and most of the sects (i.e. Shias) make their Imams partakers of the divine nature.' T. P. Hughes, *Dictionary of Islam*, quoted by Donaldson.

[16] (1) Ali, the son-in-law of Muhammad; (2) Hasan, the son of Ali; (3) Hussein the son of Ali; (4) Abidin, the son of Hussein; (5) Baqir, the son of Abidin; (6) Jafar, the son of Baqir; (7) Musa, the son of Jafar; (8) Reza, the son of Musa; (9) Mohammed at-Taqi, the son of Reza; (10) Ali an-Naqi, the son of Mohammed at-Taqi; (11) Al Hasan al Askari, the son of Mohammed at-Taqi; (12) Imam al-Mahdi, the son of al Hasan al Askari.

[17] See *The Shi'ite Religion* by Donaldson, p. 214.

[18] See www.iran-press-service.com/ips/articles-2005/october-2005/jamkaran_211005.shtml [last accessed 6 June 2008].

[19] This claim was made popular by the Safavids who liked to link the Shia faith with Iranian nationalism. See Eileen Humphreys' *The Royal Road*, Scorpion Publishing, London, 1991, p. 194.

[20] Abbas Milani argues that this adoption and absorption into the Persian culture is a characteristic of Iranians. 'Persians freely adopted aspects of other cultures, but always did so only after creatively transforming what they wanted to adopt into something that was uniquely Persian.' See his *Lost Wisdom*, Mage Publishers, Washington, DC, 2004, p. 15.

[21] Quoted in Nasrin Alavi's *We Are Iran*, Portobello Books, London, 2005, p. 128.

[22] The story also serves as an outlet for private grief and guilt, the latter because the people of Najaf did not come to help Hussein.

[23] It is of course very similar to the Christian Passion play performed in Oberammergau, and might well have received some inspiration from Medieval Christian theatre.

[24] See Roy Mottahedeh's *The Mantle of the Prophet – Religion and Politics in Iran*, Oneworld, Oxford, 1985, pp.176–179 for a fuller discussion of this.

[25] See Chapter 3 for a full discussion on Iran's political identity.

[26] See Mottahedeh's *The Mantle of the Prophet*, p. 279.

[27] Quoted by Sandra Mackey in *The Iranians*, Plume, New York, 1996, p. 53.

[28] For a full discussion of Christianity in Iran before the Muslim invasion see Samuel Hugh Moffett's *A History of Christianity in Asia*, Orbis Books, New York, 1998, especially Sections Two and Three.

[29] For a full discussion of the relationship between Roman Catholicism and Shia Islam see *Roman Catholics and Shi'i Muslims: Prayer, Passion, and Politics* by James A. Bill and John Alden Williams, University of North Carolina Press, Chapel Hill, published August 2003.

[30] Ali goes on to say – 'Thou, Hasan, and I, together with our mother the Virgin, will accept sufferings according to the best of our ability.' See *The Shi'ite Religion*

by Donaldson, p. 342. The reference to Fatimah being a virgin is clearly due to the influence of the church's teaching about Jesus' mother Mary.

[31] See *The Shi'ite Religion* by Donaldson, p. 341.

[32] Sunnis do not believe in the sinlessness of the prophets.

[33] Referring to the Hussein story the Islamic scholar Stanley Lane-Poole commented – 'One may see it as a Christian side to Islam. In the dry severity of the Arabian faith there is too little of the self-giving love which renounces all, even life itself, for the sake of others; there is more of the stiff necked pharisaical pride which holds up its righteous head on its assured way to Paradise. The death of Hussein, as idealized by after ages, fills up this want in Islam.' Ordinary Iranians still refer to this, so the blogger Hekayat writes 'Imam Hossein said: "I will die to reform my followers."' Quoted in Alavi's *We Are Iran*, p. 128.

[34] Majlisi, quoted in *The Shi'ite Religion* by Donaldson, p. 344.

[35] Quoted by Anthony Mahoney in 'The Image of Jesus and Christianity in Shi'a Islam and Modern Iranian Thought' p. 261 of *A Faithful Presence: Essays for Kenneth Cragg*, Melisende, London, 2003.

[36] See Heb. 2.16–18; also consider Isa. 53.12 generally believed to be prophecy about Jesus Christ: 'He was numbered with the transgressors; and he bare the sin of many, and made intercession for the transgressors.'

[37] The author was in conversation with some young people in a taxi in Iran who were generally complaining about their lives. At the end one of them sighed and said – 'It will all be made right when Mahdi returns'.

[38] The name of the returning Zoroastrian saviour was Saoshyant.

[39] See *The Shi'ite Religion* by Donaldson, pp. 228–229.

[40] See www.irshad.org/islam/prophecy/mahdi.htm for information about Majlisi's teaching about Mahdi [last accessed 6 June 2008].

[41] Jn. 16.13.

[42] See *The Shi'ite Religion* by Donaldson, pp. 306–314.

[43] See Shawqi Talia, 'From Edessa to Urmia', *Bulletin of the Royal Institute of Inter-Faith Studies*, Autumn/Winter, 2005, p. 55 for a very useful paragraph on Roman Catholicism and Shia Islam.

[44] Some argue these ascetics were copying the Syrian cave monks who apparently wore similar garments. See *Islam: A Christian Perspective* by Bishop Michael Nazir-Ali, p. 60. And the Muslim Professor Saeed Sheikh writes 'the woolen dress fashion among the early Sufis . . . was surely of Christian origin.'

[45] Quoted by Fereshteh Ahmadi in *Iranian Islam*, St Martin's Press Ltd, Basingstoke, p. 56.

[46] See *The Sufis* by Idries Shah, Doubleday and Company, Garden City, NY, 1964 p. 49.

[47] John Gilchrist, *Mohammad and the Religion of Islam*, Vol. 1, Chapter 9, 'Sufism in Theory and Practice'. Available on Answering Islam website: www.answering-islam.org/Gilchrist/Vol1/9a.html [last accessed 6 June 2008].

[48] The famous Dervish dances still performed in Turkey are a development of this idea.

[49] Idries Shah notes that different scholars have argued for Christian, Hindu, Shamanism, Buddhism, Neoplatonism and Manichaeism influences. See *The Sufis*, p. 41.

[50] Most famously in his work *Spiritual Body and Celestial Earth: From Mazdean Iran to Shi'ite Iran*, published by I. B. Tauris, London, 1990.

[51] Quoted by Ahmadi in *Iranian Islam*, p. 39.

[52] Ahmadi in *Iranian Islam*, p. 39.

[53] See *Spirituality in the Land of the Noble* by Richard Foltz, Oneworld Publications, Oxford, p. 130.

[54] See http://spiritualityandpractice.com/books/books.php?id=8514 [last accessed 6 June 2008].

[55] See *Sufism: An Account of the Mystics of Islam* by A. J. Arberry, Dover Publications, New York, 1950, pp. 59–60.

[56] For example, 'Many Muslim scholars in his time, and many after his time, said that Bayazid al-Bistami was the first one to spread the Reality of Annihilation (fana')'. See www.naqshbandi.org/ [last accessed 6 June 2008]. See also 'The Relation between Buddhism and Sufism: Response to Majid Tehranian' by Alexander Berzin, November 2006. www.berzinarchives.com/web/en/archives/study/islam/general/relation_between_buddhism_sufism.html [last accessed 6 June 2008].

[57] See www.naqshbandi.org/chain/6.htm [last accessed 6 June 2008].

[58] See www.naqshbandi.org/chain/6.htm [last accessed 6 June 2008].

[59] See *The Life of Al-Ghazali, with Especial Reference to His Religious Experiences and Opinions* by Duncan Macdonald, Professor in Hartford Theological Seminary, Hartford, Conn. www.ghazali.org/articles/dbm-gz.htm [last accessed 6 June 2008].

[60] Mottahedeh, *The Mantle of the Prophet*, p. 198.

[61] See www.ghazali.org/articles/gz2.htm [last accessed 6 June 2008].

[62] See www.cis-ca.org/voices/g/ghazali.htm [last accessed 6 June 2008].

[63] See wttp://mdhd.tripod.com/ghazali4.html [last accessed 6 June 2008].

[64] Al Ghazali was particularly incensed by the philosopher's assertions regarding the eternity of the world; the denial of God's knowledge of particulars via perception; and the denial of the bodily resurrection. See *Islamic Philosophy* by Professor M. Saeed Sheikh, Octagon Press, London, 1962, p. 89.

[65] For a detailed account of Al Suhrawardi's impact see Mottahedeh's *The Mantle of the Prophet*, pp. 149–156.

[66] Ishraq literally means 'rising', but is associated with the rising of the sun – hence light.

[67] Mottahedeh's *The Mantle of the Prophet*, p. 156.

[68] See Corbin's *Spiritual Body and Celestial Earth*, p. 111.

[69] Koran Sura 24 v. 35; my italics. http://i-cias.com/e.o/texts/koran/koran024.htm [last accessed 6 June 2008].

[70] In the mid-seventeenth outright mysticism could arouse hostility, so Mir Damand would write in a very complicated fashion that could only be deciphered by the initiated. There is a story that on his death the angels Nakir and Monkar came to question him. When they asked him 'Who is your creator' he replied in a mixture of Arabic and Greek with 'an element above all elements'. The angels returned to God complaining they could not understand his creature. 'Don't worry', replied the Almighty, 'Nobody in the world understands him.' See *Khomeini: Life of the Ayatollah* by Baqer Moin, Thomas Dunne Books, New York, 1999 p. 45.

[71] Mottahedeh's *The Mantle of the Prophet*, pp. 179, 182.

72 Another story says that Rumi saw the father walking ahead of his son and said, 'Here comes a sea followed by an ocean'. See *Rumi, Poet of the Heart* by Laz Slamovits, www.crazywisdom.net [last accessed 6 June 2008].

73 See essay on Rumi's life by his translator Shahram Shiva, www.rumi.net/rumi_by_shiva.htm [last accessed 6 June 2008].

74 See 'Jalaluddin Rumi' by W. Chittick, www.rumi.org.uk/chittick.htm [last accessed 6 June 2008].

75 Book 1, *The Prologue of the Masnavi I Ma'Navi*, translated by E. H. Whinfield 1898, published by Yassavoli Publications, Tehran, 1999.

76 'The talk is that Jelaluddin Rumi, born 1207, died 1273, is not only back in fashion but has become the best-selling poet in America, with a range of admirers including Madonna, Goldie Hawn, Donna Karan, the composer Philip Glass and the celebrity new age guru Deepak Chopra.' John Ryle, *The Guardian*, February 1999.

77 From the poem, *Look, This Is Love*. See www.sfusd.k12.ca.us/schwww/sch618/Literature,%20Poetry/Literature3.html [last accessed 6 June 2008].

78 Translated by Coleman Barks and Shahram Shiva, see http://peacefulrivers.homestead.com/Rumilove.html [last accessed 6 June 2008].

79 See www.fordham.edu/halsall/source/1250rumi-masnavi.html [last accessed 6 June 2008]. From: Charles F. Horne (ed.), *The Sacred Books and Early Literature of the East*, Parke, Austin, & Lipscomb, New York, 1917, Vol. VIII: *Medieval Persia*, pp. 111–130.

80 See *Music of a Distant Drum: Classical Arabic, Persian, Turkish, and Hebrew Poems* by Bernard Lewis, Princeton University Press, Princeton, 2001, p. 121.

81 See www.iranchamber.com/literature/hafez/hafez.php [last accessed 6 June 2008].

82 Quoted in an essay on Hafiz by Gertrud Bell, an early translator (1897) of Hafiz.

83 Richard Le Gallienne an early translator (1903) of Hafiz wrote that this symbolizing came from a 'type of mind . . . with a holy horror of flesh and blood . . . (that) loves to dehumanize literature, and prove our great warm-hearted classics cryptograms of fantastic philosophy or speculation.' A less extreme view is that of A. J. Arberry who believes that Hafiz's reference to wine symbolize 'the intoxication of the intellect'.

84 See www.hafizonlove.com/bio/index.htm for a good summary of this story [last accessed 6 June 2008].

85 See www.1902encyclopedia.com/H/HAF/hafiz.html [last accessed 6 June 2008].

86 Dr Loewen's translation – see footnote 38.

87 See 'The Pir-i Mughan in the Divan of Hafiz' by Dr Arley Loewen, MA Dissertation for University of Toronto, 1990. His translation of the verse is on p. 8.

88 For my discussion on the Pir-i Mughan in the thought of Hafiz, I am grateful to have had access to Dr Arley Loewen's unpublished MA research dissertation on 'The Pir-i Mughan in the Divan of Hafiz'.

89 Pir means a spiritual mentor or teacher.

90 See 'The Pir-i Mughan in the Divan of Hafiz' by Loewen, p. 3.

91 See 'The Pir-i Mughan in the Divan of Hafiz' by Loewen. His translation of the verse is on p. 13.

[92]   Loewen, 'The Pir-i Mughan in the Divan of Hafiz'.

[93]   Loewen's translation, see footnote 38.

[94]   Mottahedeh's *The Mantle of the Prophet*, p. 64; my italics.

[95]   For a full discussion of Sufism's emphasis on the Unity of Existence see *Iranian Islam* by Nader Ahmadi and Fereshteh Ahmadi, Macmillan Press, Basingstoke, 1988, pp. 73–87. This phrase is used in the conclusion.

[96]   Gilchrist, 'Sufism in Theory and Practice'; my italics. Available on Answering Islam website.

[97]   For example, this verse from 'Lover's Rapture'.

> If you are an traveller of lover's path
> Shun prayer-carpet, cloak then
> No guide's there but love alone
> In love thyself soak then

See www.geocities.com/ahlulbayt14/khom-poem.html [last accessed 6 June 2008].

[98]   See *Khomeini: The Life of an Ayatollah* by Moin, pp. 49–52.

Chapter 2

Iran's Cultural Identity

Some countries, such as Saudi Arabia and Pakistan, rely more on Islam for their identity than their own history and culture. Not so the Iranians: for their historical and cultural identity is very strong. This is partly because of the power of the country's royalist past,[1] and partly because their Shia religion is more Iranian than Arab.[2] However the main reason for Iran's vibrant self-assured cultural identity is the passionate love affair Iranians have with their national language, Persian.

An ancient language

A part of this passion is its vintage. The Persian (not Farsi)[3] spoken today can be traced back to Cyrus the Great who used an ancient form of the language to give the world its first declaration of human rights in 539 BC. His successor Darius also left us inscriptions both on the walls of his palace at Persepolis and at the nearby Behistun monument.[4] Though their alphabet cuneiform is no longer used, it is still recognisably the same language, and so gives Iranians a link back to their ancient civilization. After the fall of the Achamenians, the language continued to develop in and around Persepolis in the province of Pars, and so was known as Parsi, while the script used which was derived from Aramaic was known as Pahlavi.[5] This was the language of the Sasanid Empire which made Zoroastrianism Iran's official religion. Much of the Pahlavi literature reflects this. However, as well as most of the Avesta being still extant,[6] there are also manuscripts on geographical and sociological subject, and fascinatingly, there is even a seventh-century Psalter extant in Pahlavi.

Though disputed by some scholars,[7] Iranian writers tend to argue that the scarcity of Pahlavi literature with us today is due to the rampaging tendencies of the invading Arab armies, and blame them not only for the destruction of the great library at Alexandria in 642, but also the library in Ctesiphon.[8] However violent the Arabs might have been, nevertheless the Persian language not only survived, but also enjoyed a revival under their rule. For the new rulers relied heavily on the administrative experience of the Iranians, they copied the Sasanid forms of government and later moved their capital to Baghdad which was formerly a suburb of Ctesiphon. With Iranian influence in the corridors of power, so much so that soon some regions were ruled by Persian speakers, a script for Persian developed using the Arabic alphabet. This became the basis for the modern language and not surprisingly it incorporated many Arabic words. In the far east of Iran, local rulers keen to garner support from their Persian speaking subjects used their patronage to encourage poetry. So Rudaki and Daqiqi both wrote lyrical nationalistic verse in the Samanid court in Bukhara. And one of Iran's most famous sons produced a poetic epic for Mahmud of Ghazna. This was Abdul Qasim Mansur from Tus in north-eastern Iran, better known as Ferdowsi. His masterpiece *Shahnameh* (King of Kings) is still found in every educated Iranian's home.

Ferdowsi's nationalism

Over 35 years, Ferdowsi (*ca* 935–*ca* 1020) drew on Pahlavi texts and oral traditions to re-create 1,000 years of Iran's pre-Islamic history. His aim was to revive the soul of Iranians in the aftermath of the Arab invasions. He achieved this first of all by writing his 60,000 line epic in Persian, and secondly by focusing on the story of Iran's pre-Islamic kings. The great hero of the work is Rostam, the mighty defender of Iran who epitomizes all the manly virtues of courage in the face of his country's enemies. There is however a tragic twist in the story: Rostam is called to fight a duel with the champion of Iran's traditional enemy, Turan, to decide the outcome of their war. During the combat Rostam fatally wounds his younger opponent, but then recognizes a distinctive arm band he had left years ago with a Turan girl to give to his child if she had become pregnant by him. Rostam had slain his own son, Sohrab. This then is not just a tale about manly honour, a crucial part of Iran's cultural identity,[9] but also what Ferdowsi calls, 'hunchback fate'.[10] A fate which in *Shahnameh* always favours Iran; it is the chosen nation. And so even though he is Rostam's son, Sohrab is sacrificed, for the nation. As he lays dying Sohrab recognizes this –

> This was the fate allotted me.
> The heavens gave my key into your hand
> It's not your fault. It was this hunchback fate
> Such is decreed by the stars
> That I be slain by my father.[11]

The agony of the drama is exquisite, but there is still this acceptance that fate or God ultimately knows what is best for the higher good. This belief in 'hunchback fate' enshrined in the *Shahnameh*, has remained at the heart of Iran's cultural identity, and helps explain why Iran has so fervently adopted the story of Ali at the battle of Karbala, where again an honourable man was sacrificed for a higher cause. It might also explain why Iranians are generally not instinctively repulsed as some Muslims are when they hear about a Father allowing his Son to be sacrificed for the salvation of His people. They have grown up with this story.

Though Ferdowsi is never outrightly anti-Arab or anti-Islamic, indeed he writes as a Muslim for a Muslim court, there is no doubt that his main passion was Iran, well summed up by his famous line, known by almost every Iranian, 'Let not this body live, if there is no Iran.' His great achievement was to revive the Persian language and reconnect his people with their ancient culture. Ferdowsi, like the writers of Israel's history, created a unique and immortal cultural identity which inspires and unites all the different tribes of the Iranian plateau. Since its publication in around 1000, this is exactly what Shahnameh has done. The author Sandra Mackey once attended a conference on nomadic people sponsored by the present government. In a hall hung with portraits of the then leaders of the Islamic Revolution four nomads from different tribes recited the Shahnameh in turn. The audience clapped and cheered and 'on the first word of a recognizable verse voices within the crowd joined in unison. Together, reader and audience spoke of their commitment to the Iranian nation and to their assurance of their uniqueness among the peoples of the world'.[12]

Ferdowsi unfurled a banner of Iranian poetic genius that has flown now for over a thousand years. Of the seven great medieval poets, Rudaki and Ferdowsi were fervently nationalistic, and as we have seen Attar, Rumi and Hafiz were Sufis. This leaves Khayam and Saadi, who are sometimes pushed into the mystic camp, but really they belong to a worldlier one.

Khayyam's cynicism

From Nishapur in north-eastern Iran, Khayyam achieved fame in his lifetime as a mathematician.[13] He conceived the theory of general cubic equations, he accurately measured the length of the year as 365.242198 (today it is 365.242190 days) and he corrected the Persian calendar. His fame as a poet came later, especially after the Englishman Edward Fitzgerald published his very free and open translation of his Rubaiyat in 1859. His tone is much more hedonistic than other writers. Whereas both the nationalists and Sufis lead their readers on to a higher goal, Khayyam is much more pessimistic. He has no clear answer as to why we are here, or where we are going: so there is mockery for Iran's great kings – 'They say the Lion and the Lizard keep/ the courts where Jamshyd gloried and drank deep'[14]; and disdain for the pious and the philosophical who proclaim dogmatic answers when the only certainty is death – 'Like foolish Prophets forth; their Words to Scorn/ Are scatter'd and their Mouths are stopt with Dust'.[15] As death renders life meaningless, the only sensible philosophy is to enjoy life by drinking wine. 'And Lip to Lip it murmur'd – 'While you live/ Drink! – for once dead, you never shall return'.[16]

In a land where organized religion and informal mysticism have always flourished it is perhaps strange that a poet such as Khayyam should enjoy respect. Certainly he is not as popular as Ferdowsi, Rumi or Hafiz, but he is accepted as one of Iran's great poets. This means his cynical view of life forms a part, albeit a small one, of the Iranian cultural identity. And the fact that he has not been denounced as a dangerous heretic by the Islamic authorities or his work expunged from the nation's literary canon proves that ultimately, when all the nationalistic and religious fervour has died down, there is room in Iran for people to shrug, sigh, and with resigned pessimism say

> While the Rose blows along the River Bank
> With old Khayyam the Ruby Vintage drink.[17]

Saadi's Proverbs

For those who like their poetry to be practical, Saadi, another famous son of Shiraz, has much to offer. Some argue that he too is a Sufi, but his verse is much more didactic, practical, and down to earth than the mystics. Or, as the son of one religious leader said – 'Saadi was a horizontal man; Hafiz was vertical'.[18] Much of his two major works, *Bustan* and *Gulistan*, are filled with anecdotes punctuated with moral observations from characters in the drama, which are in many ways similar to Solomon's Proverbs. So for example Chapter One of the *Gulistan* titled 'The Manners of Kings' is all about a band of brigands who are captured and sentenced to death, except for a young boy whom the king has mercy on after intercession from the chief minister. At the time, the king was uneasy with this decision saying –

> He whose foundation is bad will not take instruction from the good,
> To educate unworthy persons is like throwing nuts on a cupola.[19]

After being brought up by the chief minister, the boy makes a secret pact with a criminal gang. Together they kill the chief minister and his son, make off with lots of booty, and the boy establishes himself as the gang's leader. The king again underlines the moral of the story – *To do good to wicked persons is like doing evil to good men.*[20] – a line often used today. Even when Saadi introduces a philosopher into his stories the contribution is very practical. There is a frightened boy on a boat whose cowardly cries infuriated the king, so on the philosopher's advice the boy is plunged into the cold, rough sea and then pulled back to the stern by his hair. After that he sat in corner quietly, with the philosopher commenting –'Before he had tasted the calamity of being drowned, he knew not the safety of the boat; thus also a man does not appreciate the value of immunity from a misfortune until it has befallen him.'[21]

Due to its beauty and breadth of subject matter, Saadi's poetry has been immensely popular in Iran, for whatever the topic of conversation; there is usually a verse from Saadi that will give pithy insight. If Ferdowsi has given the Iranians their own national story, like the Biblical writers of Kings and Chronicles,[22] and Attar, Rumi and Hafiz, their own spirituality, like the writers of the Psalms, and Khayyam has given even the devout space to be pessimistic, like the writer of Ecclesiastes, then Saadi, like the writer of Proverbs, has given Iranians the assurance that their culture has wisdom to live by.

Modern poets

By the time Hafiz was safely buried at the end of the fourteenth century, Iranians were spoilt for choice when it came to feeding their literary soul. The diet was rich and plentiful, quite enough to keep both the serious student and the dilettante satisfied. And the food was so delicious there was no reason to taste new fare. Not surprisingly would be poets felt overawed by these masters and intimidated by the intricate rules of rhyme, rhythm and meter classical poetry demanded. It was only with the arrival of modern poetry in the early twentieth century that this spell was broken. A new generation of Persian poets arose and like their classical predecessors they too gained celebrity status. This was clearly seen by the estimated crowd of 30,000[23] who poured out onto Tehran streets to bid a final farewell to Ahmad Shamlou in the summer of 2005.

The acknowledged father of modern Persian poetry is Nima Yushij (real name Ali Esfandiyari) who according to one scholar 'single-handedly challenged and systematically changed almost all the traditionalistic tendencies in Persian poetry'.[24] As a child Nima soaked in the stories of the shepherds and farm workers around camp-fires in the north of Iran, but when he was 12 he was sent to a French Roman Catholic school and it was here, encouraged by one of his teachers, he started writing poetry. He first tried to write in the style of Hafiz and Saadi, but his experience of a city and the new ideas encountered in his school, were not easy to relate to the strict rules of classical poetry and their traditional symbols of birds, moons and taverns. So, influenced by the Belgian poet Emile Verhaeren (1855–1916), he began to experiment with free verse and let the length of a line depend on the thought he wanted to express, rather than the dictates of a stanza with a fixed pattern of rhyme and rhythm.

For Yushij, the heart of all poetry was not form, but sincerity – 'The more sincerely you express yourself' he advised others, 'the more poetic you become . . .'. And this means the poet must 'be the essence of his time, without pretense, without falsity . . .'.[25]

So to sincerely reflect his time, Yushij not only changed the poem's form, but also brought in everyday language and images. The result was, not surprisingly, a focus on pain. 'The main theme of my poems is pain. I write poems for my and people's pains, and words, rhythm and rhyme are all tools which I had to change them to accord with my and people's pains.'[26] Also, to reflect his own time, his poetry was political and he gave conventional symbols a contemporary meaning. So 'night' came to mean the political oppression under the Pahlavis; 'morning' the awakening to freedom; the 'lark' the intellectual who refuses to remain silent. This willingness to use poetry politically was taken up enthusiastically by his successors. Yushij's radical innovations in both style and content aroused some hostility which he himself acknowledges ironically in a poem where he used the classical form –

> With my poetry I have driven the people into a great conflict;
> Good and bad, they have fallen in confusion;
> I myself am sitting in a corner, watching them:
> I have flooded the nest of ants[27]

However, both Yushij's poetry and his reputation survived this 'great conflict'. His work is still published and admired, and he is acknowledged as the man who refused to be dwarfed by the great names of the past or be confined to their form or content. This stuck a chord with the public, and opened the door for others to walk through. Many did – the most famous being Ahmad Shamlou (1925–2005), Sohrab Sepehri (1928–1980), Mehdi Akhavan Saless (1928–1991) and Forough Farrokhzad (1935–1967).

All of the above made their own distinctive contribution to literature and Iranians will struggle to say who their favourite is. Sohrab Sepehri, also a painter, is well known for the visual dimension to his poetry, the revival of the Sufi theme and his experimentation with abstract images ('a throat in the cool thickness of wind'[28]). Mehdi Akhavan Saless is greatly admired for his excellent knowledge of Persian literature and the fact he could write both first-class classical poetry and free verse. He is best known for his haunting collection of poems called *Winter* (1957) whose tragic tone well suited the colder political climate that developed in Iran after the ousting of Mossadeq in 1953. Even if they have never read her work, nearly every Iranian knows of Forough Farrokhzad, one of Iran's few female poets.[29] As well as the beauty of the verse, there is genuine sincerity about matters rarely discussed in public.[30] She dealt with the frustration of Iranian women coping with chauvinist traditions. Having married at 16, only to be soon separated from both her husband and son, this was very real for her. And shockingly she wrote about her sexual experiences. Not surprisingly this unconventional divorcee had her critics, but when she was tragically killed in a car crash in 1967, thousands mourned her death, and fellow poets such as Sohrab Sepehri wrote their own laments.

Another poet who grieved in verse over her untimely death was Ahmad Shamlou who perhaps most of all epitomizes modern Persian poetry. A political rebel, indeed for a while a signed up member of the communist party, he developed Yushij's linking of poetry to politics and wanted to use verse as a weapon to awaken the masses to revolution. This produced the brilliant allegory *Fairies* which established his fame in 1956. Disillusionment soon set in when the new Shah began to crush the communists and many of Shamlou's friends were executed, betrayed by other 'comrades'. After this he no longer trusted the 'people', and his bitterness is clearly seen in his famous poem *The Death of the Nazarene* (1966) where even Lazarus, who owes his life to Christ, walks away. 'From the tumultuous ranks of the onlookers, Lazarus, / Pacing, went his way'. [31] As an atheist Shamlou believed the only god was man, and that religion was the 'sin' of his times. He was particularly angry at the way he saw, even in the 1960s, that Iranians would probably turn to a religious messiah figure. In an almost prophetic poem he warns of what will happen in a poem called the *Tablet* (1965):

> I knew that they were awaiting
> not a clay tablet but a Gospel
> a sword and some constables
> to ambush them with whips and maces
> to drop them to their knees
> before the heavy steps of the one
> who will descend the dark stairway
> with a sword and a Gospel. [32]

When Ayatollah Khomeini did finally arrive and descend the stairway of his Air France plane, Shamlou became even more depressed, and wrote of an aborted dawn. He spent his final years working on a book of colloquial language, resigned to the fact that his poetry had failed to inspire the people in the way religion had. [33] However he had had much more impact than he realized, and would have been surprised to have seen the 30,000 who lined the streets of Tehran, many quoting his poetry from memory, when he made his final journey that summer's day in 2005.

Poetry's ambivalence

There is no other country in the world where so many would turn out for a poet's funeral, for when it comes to poetry, Iran is unique as Elaine Sciolino writes – 'No other people I know takes its poetry so seriously.' [34] Certainly other literary forms – the novel, short stories, essays – play a role in Iran's cultural identity, as does music and especially cinema. But these are all dwarfed by the power of poetry in Iran: it is at the heart of the nation's cultural identity.

And here there is a problem, for while the poetry is steeped in Islamic symbolism there is really no concentrated engagement with Islam. The fact that orthodox Islam is not a central theme for any of Iran's poets is in itself very significant. It would be like having the canon of English literature with no John Milton, John Donne, George Herbert, Gerald Manley Hopkins or T. S. Eliot who all engaged intensely with Christianity, their country's national religion. But there is more. Not only is there this lack of interest in Islam among the Iranian poets, but some of their verse has issues with orthodox Islam. Ferdowsi's whole focus is on the glory of pre-Islamic Iran; Rumi insists that all religions lead to God; Hafiz tells his readers to pour wine on their prayer mats; Khayyam mocks those who think they can deliberate on the after life; and the atheist Ahmad Shamlou, for the moderns, was infuriated that people were willing to bow before 'the book and the sword'.

This presents the outsider with a puzzle. For if poetry is a central pillar to the Iranian cultural identity but her poetry is not very focused on Islam, then this would indicate that essential culture is not Islamic. Yet with mosques on every corner and an entire government bound by Islamic rules, that is absurd, even though, as seen in Chapter 1, Iran's Islam is very different from other countries. Perhaps it is best to say though that the poets reveal that at the heart of Iran's cultural identity there is ambivalence towards Islam. At root this ambivalence is not just the message of the poetry, but also the passion Iranians have for Persian, which in Islamic theology must have second place to Arabic. Iranian Muslims respect Arabic, but very few would ever prefer it over Persian. This is the language of their hearts and history whose legendary glory was shining long before the advent of Islam. So every time they hear the language of Islam, this ambivalence is awakened.[35] At one end of this spectrum of ambivalence are those who, for a variety of reasons, are hostile to Islam and for them the poets are the heroic authors of what amounts to alternative Scriptures. In the middle are those who accept Islam as a way of approaching God, but they are not dogmatic, and they are very happy to imbibe the message of the poets as well, especially because they reinforce Iranian nationalism. And finally there are the devout Muslims who might know their Koran in Arabic off by heart, and indeed love the Arabic language, but because of Sufism they are very open to experiencing poetry. So we have Ayatollah Khomeini, the stern leader of an Islamic Revolution, yet at the same time, a writer of mystic Persian verse. Wherever the Iranian is on this spectrum, poetry gives an awareness that there is another dimension beyond Islam to explore what is more enigmatic, more open ended, more tolerant.[36]

Poetry and Jesus Christ

And in that more mysterious world that the poets open up, there is room for Jesus Christ. It is intriguing to note how sympathetically He is treated.

Ferdowsi mourning the loss of Iran to the Arabs, brought to life the ancient epics of his country and he compared this to how Christ raised the dead –

> These tales which relate to the monarchs of old
> In volumes of elegant verse I have told
> Time swept them aside and death stilled heart and brain
> But here in my verses they live once again
> Like Jesus whose voice called the dead back to life
> I've wakened dead heroes of struggle and strife[37]

While Ferdowsi reminds his readers that Jesus could raise the dead, Rumi refers to the joy Jesus brings to the afflicted, and how he heals the sick.

> The house of Isa (Jesus) was the banquet of men of heart
> O afflicted one, quit not this door
> From all sides the people ever thronged
> Many blind and lame, halt and afflicted
> At the door of the house of Isa at dawn
> That with his breath he might heal their ailments[38]

Saadi narrates his own version of the parable of the Publican and Pharisee found in Lk. 18.:9–14, happily acknowledging that the story happened 'in the time of Isa (on him be peace)'.[39] And Hafiz expresses yearning for Jesus's miracles –

> And if the Holy Ghost descend
> In grace and power infinite
> His comfort in these days to lend
> To them that humbly wait on it
> Theirs too the wondrous works can be
> That Jesus wrought in Galilee[40]

And in another poem he urges his many readers to imitate Christ in lines that all Christians would be happy to meditate on –

> If thou like Christ be pure and single-hearted
> Who once ascended far beyond the sky
> Thy life will shine with beams of light, whereby
> The sun will brighten by thy light imparted.[41]

Of the many ghazals Hafiz wrote, it is this one that has been inscribed in large letters on the eastern wall of the walled garden where his tomb lies.

Lesser known classical poets such as Nezami, Shabistary, Sanaie and Khaqani made reference to Christ as well, and as we have already seen, the modern poets also turned to Christian symbols, especially the cross, which became a symbol of unjust suffering for the moderns. So Akhavan Saless writes –

> As my enemy's desire, a lonely soul
> And the pen on my back, a cross
> Has fate mistaken me for Mary's Jesus?[42]

Ahmad Shamlou in *The Death of the Nazarene*, a poem already referred to, uses the story of the cross to depict the cruelty of man's betrayal, and in, *Moments and Always* he uses the cross to portray his own inner conflict –

> Lo, there am I, having traversed all my bewilderments
> Up to this Golgotha
> There am I, standing on the inverted cross
> A statue as tall as a cry
> There am I
> Having plucked cross-nails out of the palms with my teeth.[43]

Even Forough Farrokhzad whose poetry is so immediate and sensual, is unable to completely forget Christ –

> In night's refuge, let me make love to the moon,
> let me be filled
> with tiny raindrops,
> with undeveloped hearts,
> with the volume of the unborn,
> let me be filled.
> Maybe my love
> will cradle the birth of another Christ.[44]

The curious point here is that when she wants to convey the idea of love giving birth to a greater love, she turns to Christ as her symbol. And this point is significant in all these Christian references in Persian poetry, old and new. For though of course they do not indicate that any of the poets were followers of Christ, these references do show these poets have warmth towards Him and are comfortable using symbols from the Christian story. This underlines the overall conclusion that poetry in Iran constantly moves beyond the sharper dogmatic lines of orthodox Islam and offers an 'enigmatic' more where, as said, there is certainly room for Christ.

Cinema

Nothing can compare with the role of Persian poetry in Iran, but if there is any competition, with 20,000 coming out for the funeral of the film star Ali Fardin,[45] it has to be from cinema. There was a time when few saw cinema as a serious cultural force. In the postwar period cinema was swamped by Hollywood movies; and then when the Islamists took over in 1979 it looked as if it was funeral time for film. Ayatollah Khomeini personally hated cinema, considering it as sinful as dancing and mixed swimming. His fiery rhetoric against superficial and sensualist Western entertainment literally set on fire or demolished nearly 200 cinemas during the revolution.[46] However from these ashes cinema arose as powerfully as any other phoenix of the East. Once the fundamentalists had won power, like the Soviets before them, they realized that film was far too influential a medium to be ignored, especially when the country was at war. They argued that their hostility to cinema had been on account of its subservience to Hollywood. So in 1982 Mohammad Khatami, the then Minister of Culture and Islamic Guidance, set about making sure post-revolutionary cinema would be Islamic – and successful. Rules were laid down to ensure films would be Islamic and generous funding was made available.[47] Though some of the restrictions are irritating, people especially complain about women having to wear scarves even in the home, the generality of their purpose, such as not being allowed to encourage wickedness, corruption and prostitution, has given directors plenty of room for manoeuvre[48] These restrictions have in fact helped Iranian cinema. For the regime's hostility to Hollywood has forced directors to draw from Iran's own cultural inheritance and the result has been very successful with Iranian cinema attracting a huge domestic audience, and gaining an international reputation. It is certainly worth briefly assessing what it tells the outsider about Iran's cultural identity.

New Wave Films[49]

It is the neo-realist Iranians directors such as Bahram Bayzai, Abbas Kiarostami, Majid Mahini, Mohsen Makhmalbaf and Jaffar Panahi who have a huge international following, all of them having won awards at international film festivals. What has undoubtedly attracted Western audiences is the way their work is so refreshingly different. It is not just the lack of packaged background music, special effects or clichéd story lines that makes them so, it is the whole approach. Most noticeable is the focus on one insignificant image or event which is used to open up the audience's emotions and imagination. So Makhmalbaf has an entire film, *The Cyclist*, about an old man who agrees to ride a cycle constantly for 7 days as a circus act to raise money for his sick wife's treatment. And Kiarostami, probably the best known Iranian director, has made minimalist plots and blurring reality with film in titles such as *Close Up* and *The Taste of Cherry* the hall mark of his work. This focus on what Hamid Dabashi calls the 'universalization of the Iranian particular'[50] goes first back to Sohrab Saless the father of this new wave cinema, and ultimately to Iran's poetical and mystical inheritance which has long accepted layers of meaning for outward 'ordinary' things. Another common theme is that of people, such as in Kiarostami's *Life Goes On* set after the Gilan earthquake, struggling to make a difference in impossible situations they have not created. Like Sohrab of old, they are dealing with 'hunchback' fate.

Popular films

So great has been the success of these new wave films on the international circuit that it can be easily assumed that they represent Iranian cinema. This is a mistake and there is a very vocal part of the Iranian film industry that accuses these directors of producing pseudo-artistic films to pander to the patronizing Western desire to see Iran as exotic, a 'National Geographic' story.[51] This is harsh: of much more significance is the fact that these new wave films are simply not so popular in Iran. Most people go to the cinema to be entertained and films about an old man riding a bicycle do not immediately meet this need.

So though these new wave films shed some light on Iran's cultural identity, it is the films that people queue to see that tells us more. In the 1980s and early 1990s the popular films tended to be action and war films, but in recent years the films that have broken all box office records in Iran are the comedies. In 2004 people were queuing round the block to see *Marmulak* (Lizard) about a thief who has to pretend to be a Mullah until it was eventually banned. In 2005 the popular film was *Maxx*, another wonderful story of mistaken identity when an Iranian rapper from Los Angeles is invited to be the guest of honour for the Iran Institute of Culture in Tehran. In 2006 it was *Atash Bas* (Ceasefire) about the childish pranks of a feuding married couple, and in 2007 it was *Ekhraj-ha* (The Expelled) where some town buffoons prove themselves to be braver heroes than the pious in the war.

While the new wave films underline the same point as poetry, that Iranians are concerned more with the universal than the particular, a common theme in the popular films is that the supposed sinner often ends up having more righteousness than the hypocritical establishment, and can change for the better – favourite themes in Jesus' teaching. Superficially there is nothing remotely Christian about Iranian films, however, as a 'window into the soul of a nation', it reveals again that the culture is concerned not with the rigid dogmas, but a much wider canvas, where there is little room for hypocrites, but much for the theme of grace.

New Year Celebrations

If Iran's poetry and cinema point to a world beyond the mosque, so too does the country's most important festival, No Ruz (New Year), celebrated at the time of the Spring Equinox. For weeks before Iranians will be spring-cleaning their houses, literally called 'a house shaking', and then on the Wednesday of the old year there is *Chahar-Shanbeh Soori*. This is when Iranians light small bonfires and jump through them shouting – 'My yellow for you and your red for me', a poetic way of exchanging weakness for strength for the New Year. As the old year ends there is more preparation. New clothes must be bought, fish and many other dishes must be cooked for the festal day, brand new notes and coins must be got from the bank for the 'eidi', for older people to give to children and the Haft Seen (Seven Ss) table must be made ready. This is a table where seven items are put which all begin with the Persian letter 'Seen'. The usual items are a *seeb* (apple), *sabze* (green grass grown specially in the house), *serke* (vinegar), *samanoo* (a meal made out of wheat), *senjed* (a special berry), *seke* (a coin) and *seer* (garlic). A mirror with a candle is also put on the table, as is a bowl with a few fish. And finally a special book. Most Muslims put a copy of the Koran; Christians put a Bible; and some put a copy of Hafiz.

The exact second of the equinox is known as *Saal Tahvil*, and it is announced by official astronomers in Tehran. So rather than looking at a clock, as with the Western New Year, Iranian families sit in front of a TV, or around a radio, waiting for this announcement. When it comes, the festivities begin, and the country closes down for about two weeks as families visit each other. On the thirteenth day of the New Year, every one tries to leave the house to have a picnic to throw away the *sabzeh* (grass) that was grown for the Haft Seen table, usually into a river. There is also a tradition that says if an unmarried girl ties together the grass into a bundle, then she will get married that year.

The origins of No Ruz stretch back to the Sumerians. They had a 'martyred god' who was killed in the autumn, and then brought back to life in Spring, then it is likely the Zoroastrians influence the ceremony, seen in items on the Haft Seen table and the reverence for fire on *Chahar-Shanbeh Soori*. However there is nothing overtly Zoroastrian about No Ruz. It is a celebration of universals – new life, spring conquering winter, the strength of fire – not religious dogmatics. It is difficult to overemphasize the cultural importance of No Ruz in Iran. It has survived all the invasions that have trampled over the Iranian plateau, as well as one of the most extreme religious governments in the world for at the start of the revolution Ayatollah Khomeini declared the whole affair unIslamic and banned it.[52] However as it was for the Puritans in seventeenth-century England trying to ban Christmas, it proved impossible. This then brings us again to the same puzzle we met after looking at poetry. The culture is clearly dominated by Islam, yet, apart from a Koran that might or might not be on the Haft Seen table, the country's most important festival has no relationship with Islam. And again the answer to the puzzle is the same: that beyond her religion, there is an engagement in Iran's cultural identity with a broader, more enigmatic, universal canvas.

Conclusion

There are many other art forms and festivals that make up the Iranian cultural identity like calligraphy, carpet weaving, miniatures and music. This chapter has only looked at poetry, cinema and No Ruz because they are the most popular. And what they all reveal about the Iranian identity is that Iranians are not mentally chained into viewing the world solely through the eyes of religious dogma. Indeed in their poetry and their cinema, there seems to be ambivalence towards Islam. It is accepted, sometimes happily, sometimes with reservation, as a part of their context, but it is the universal human condition which is the central focus. So a thousand years ago in *Shahnameh*, Ferdowsi moved beyond any Islamic context to look at the universal themes of honour and fate. In both poetry and cinema this pattern has remained. There is a context which might or might not feature religion – but the heart of their art deals with universal themes. This does not mean that the Iranian cultural identity rejects Islam in anyway at all, but it does mean that Iranians do not see themselves as just being Muslims. The No Ruz festivities underline this. To sum up, the Iranian cultural identity gives Iranians the experience to perform on the world stage, not just the Islamic one. And on that world stage, as seen with her poets, there is certainly room for Iranians to engage with the teachings of Jesus Christ.

Notes

[1] See Chapter 3 for a full discussion of Iran's Royalist Past.

[2] See Chapter 1 for a full discussion of Iran's Religious Identity.

[3] English speakers sometimes wrongly call Persian 'Farsi', which is the Persian word for their language, though originally it was called Parsi, but changed to Farsi as the Arabs did not have a letter for 'p'. For an English speaker to use the word Farsi is as inconsistent with normal English usage as it would be to ask someone if they spoke 'Fronsay' or Doitch when long-established English equivalents – i.e. French and German – are in common usage.

[4] Europeans discovered these in the seventeenth century but they were not successfully translated till 1846.

[5] Reza Shah in 1926, wanting to free Iran from what he saw as backward medieval religion, deliberately chose Pahlavi as the name of his dynasty to remind his country men of the glories of their pre-Islamic past.

[6] For a complete survey of Pahlavi literature see – 'Pahlavi Literature', E.W. West at www.sacred-texts.com/zor/sbe05/sbe0503.htm [last accessed 6 June 2008].

[7] For example, the Islamic expert Bernard Lewis see www.nybooks.com/articles/3517 [last accessed 6 June 2008].

[8] See 'Translation Movements in Iran' by Massoume Price at www.iranianchamber.com for a full discussion of this [last accessed 6 June 2008].

[9] For a more in-depth discussion of the concept of manliness and reputation in *Shahnameh* see 'Reputation in the Epic of Shahnameh' by Dr. Arley Loewen, Elam Review 2001.

[10] For a full discussion on fate in *Shahnameh* see 'Hunchback Fate in the Tragedy of Rostam and Sohrab' by Issa Dibaj, Elam Review 2001.

[11] See 'The Tragedy of Sohrab and Rostam' translated by Jerome W. Clinton, University of Washington Press, 1996, p. 151.

[12] See *The Iranians* by Sandra Mackey, p. 64.

[13] Iranians have constantly excelled in this subject, so Richard N. Frye writes – 'The contributions of Iranians to Islamic mathematics is overwhelming.' He also notes that most of the mathematicians and astronomers at the court of the Caliph al-Ma'mun were from Eastern Iran. See his *The Golden Age of Persia*, Phoenix, London, 1975, p. 162.

[14] *The Rubaiyat of Omar Khayyam* translated by Edward Fitzgerald, v. 19. www.persia.org/Literature/Poetry/Omar_Khayyam.html [last accessed 6 June 2008].

[15] *The Rubaiyat of Omar Khayyam* translated by Edward Fitzgerald, v. 28.

[16] *The Rubaiyat of Omar Khayyam* translated by Edward Fitzgerald, v. 39.

[17] *The Rubaiyat of Omar Khayyam* translated by Edward Fitzgerald, v. 48.

[18] Amir Mahallati, son of Ayatollah Mahallati of Shiraz in conversation with Elaine Sciolino see *Persian Mirrors: The Elusive Face of Iran*, Free Press, New York, 2000, p. 156.

[19] See www.saghaei.net/gulistan/index.php?id=4 [last accessed 6 June 2008].

[20] See www.saghaei.net/gulistan/index.php?id=4 [last accessed 6 June 2008].

[21] See Story 7, 'The Manners of Kings', www.saghaei.net/gulistan/index.php?id=7 [last accessed 6 June 2008].

[22] Christians would argue that with Rostam living 400 years there is a lot more legend in Ferdowsi than in these Biblical books, however the point of creating a national identity remains.

[23] According to an eyewitness in an email sent to Iranian.com, www.iranian.com/Features/2000/August/Funeral/index.html [last accessed 6 June 2008].

[24] See 'A Well amid the Waste: An Introduction to the Poetry of Ahmad Shamlu'. An essay by Ahmad Karimi-Hakkak, www.shamlu.com/Shamlu-1.doc [last accessed 6 June 2008].

[25] Quoted by Karimi-Hakkak in 'A Well amid the Waste, – www.shamlu.com/Shamlu-1.doc [last accessed 6 June 2008].

[26] Quoted by the writer Shakeri in an essay on the Contemporary Poetry of Iran found at www.cppll.com/content/view/16/27/lang,en/ [last accessed 6 June 2008].

[27] Quoted in an essay on Nima Yushij the Farhangsara website at www.farhangsara.com/nimayushij.htm [last accessed 6 June 2008].

[28] Quoted by Mahmud Kianush in 'A Summary Introduction to Persian Poetry' found at www.art-arena.com/book.htm#Sohrab_Sepehri [last accessed 6 June 2008].

[29] Parvin Etesaami and Ghorat-ol-ein are also well known.

[30] One comment from many on her website illustrates this well – 'My name is Golnaz and I am 21 years old. From a very young age I was infatuated by Forough. I love her and her poetry. She has had such an impact in my life that I can't even begin to describe.'

[31] Quoted by H. B. Dehqani-Tafti in *Christ and Christianity in Persian Poetry*, Sohrab Books, Basingstoke, p. 12.

[32] Tablet by Ahmad Shamlu translated by Ahmad Karimi-Hakkak, found at www.angelfire.com/rnb/bashiri/Poets/Shamlu.html [last accessed 6 June 2008].

[33] Though no friend of religion, curiously he offered to translate the whole Bible for the Bible Society that was then open in Iran. As he was not a Christian, they turned him down. He did though translate the Song of Songs.

[34] *Persian Mirrors*, p. 157.

[35] Sciolino in *Persian Mirrors*, p. 158 captures this – 'But I often feel that if there were to be a contest between Koranic recitations in Arabic and poetry recitations in Persian, the poetry recitations would win out.'

[36] Azar Nafisi's fascinating *Reading Lolita in Tehran*, Fourth Estate, London and New York, 2004, certainly underlines this point, but also shows how some Iranians, contra to the country's literary traditions, stumble over the externals rather than appreciate the symbols.

[37] Translated by Revd Norman Sharp, quoted by Bishop Dehqani-Tafti in *Christ and Christianity in Persian Poetry*, p. 4.

[38] Translated by E. H. Whinfield and quoted by Bishop Dehqani-Tafti in *Christ and Christianity in Persian Poetry*, p. 6.

[39] See Bishop Dehqani-Tafti in *Christ and Christianity in Persian Poetry*, p. 7.

[40] Translated by A. J. Arberry, quoted by Bishop Dehqani-Tafti in *Christ and Christianity in Persian Poetry*.

[41] Bishop Dehqani-Tafti quoting Revd Sharp's translation, see *Christ and Christianity in Persian Poetry*, p. 8.

[42] See Bishop Dehqani-Tafti, *Christ and Christianity in Persian Poetry*, p. 11.

[43] Translated by Professor Soroudi, quoted by Bishop Dehqani-Tafti in *Christ and Christianity in Persian Poetry*, p. 12.

[44] The last verse of the poem, Border Walls, translated by Layli Shirani see www.forughfarrokhzad.org/selectedworks/selectedworks3.asp [last accessed 6 June 2008].

[45] See http://news.bbc.co.uk/1/hi/world/middle_east/707442.stm [last accessed 6 June 2008].

[46] While it is likely that most of these torchings were the work of Islamic extremists, the case of the Rex Cinema in Abadan where nearly 400 people were killed was almost certainly the work of SAVAK. See Chapter 4 for more details.

[47] The government produces about 30 per cent of all films made in Iran, subsidizes studios, cuts the duty on imported equipment and gives low-interest loans to independent production companies.

[48] Here are all the restrictions. No film shall: (1) Weaken the principle of monotheism and other Islamic principles or insult them in any manner. (2) Insult directly or indirectly the prophets, imans, the Velayat-e Faqih (supreme jurisprudent), the ruling council or the mojtaheds (jurisprudents). (3) Blaspheme the values and

personalities held sacred by Islam and other religions mentioned in the constitution. (4) Encourage wickedness, corruption and prostitution. (5) Encourage or teach dangerous addictions and earning a living from unsavoury means such as smuggling. (6) Negate equality of all people regardless of colour, race, language, ethnicity and belief. (7) Encourage foreign cultural, economic and political influence contrary to the 'neither West nor East' policy of the government. (8) Express or disclose anything that is against the interests and policies of the country which might be exploited by foreigners. (9) Show details of scenes of violence and torture in such a way as to disturb or mislead the viewer. (10) Misrepresent historical and geographic facts. (11) Lower the taste of the audience through low production and artistic values. (12) Negate the values of self-sufficiency and economic and social independence.

[49] For a very good survey see *Life and Art: The New Iranian Cinema* edited by Rose Issa and Sheila Whitaker, National Film Festival, 1999.

[50] See *Close Up Iranian Cinema* by Hamid Dabashi, Verso, London, New York, 2001, p. 252.

[51] So, for example, Hamid Dabashi argues that the National Geographic magazine is 'devoted to turning the rest of the world into a zoo so that the white American may look civilized' and then goes on to say that film festivals like Cannes where new wave films are very popular are 'cinematic versions of the National Geographic'. See *Close Up Iranian Cinema* by Dabashi, pp. 258–259. Or at the end of the film *Under the Skin of the City* an old lady turns to the camera and says 'Stop making these silly films! Make a film to show what I feel here' and points to her heart. One critic says this is directed towards the likes of Kiarostami, 'who have lately given up making real films'. See www.newrozfilms.com/under_theskin_ofthe_city.htm [last accessed 6 June 2008].

[52] 'Ayatollah Khomeini deemed that Norouz was an un-Islamic practice. Thus for a short period *Norouz* was halted, but soon re-emerged, due to protests by many Iranian citizens.' www.anthro.uci.edu/faculty_bios/maurer/AnthroMoney/iranian.html [last accessed 6 June 2008].

Chapter 3

Iran's Political Identity

If the ruins of Darius' magnificent spring palace at Persepolis in the south of Iran were located in the West it would be seething with tourists. Instead the site is often eerily empty, and badly looked after. It would seem the present Islamic government wants to forget about Iran's royalist past: but 2,500 years of history cannot disappear; it is a constant presence. It is there in the names of the ancient kings that people still choose for their children – Cyrus, Cambyses, Darius, Bahram, Ardeshir, Shahpur, Khosrow, Nader; it is there in palaces, streets, mosques and town squares built by the Shahs; it is there in all the history and literature, especially Ferdowsi's epic *Shahnameh*; and, above all, it still impacts how Iranians think about their political identity today. Their royalist past gives Iranians a great sense of pride in Iran and in being Iranian: this does not mean they support the dictatorial system of their kings, but they are proud of what they achieved. As well as pride, the royalist past also creates expectation. For all the successful Iranian kings rule under the 'charisma' of a special divine force, and a code of justice. These themes of greatness, religion and justice can easily be seen in the reigns of Iran's most famous kings.

The foundation

Most revered of all is Cyrus (580–529 BC) who united the two original Aryan tribes, the Medes and the Persians that had invaded the Iranian plateau in the sixteenth century. Cyrus established the largest empire the world had ever seen which stretched from India to Greece; freed the Jews from the Babylonian captivity in 539 BC;[1] and issued the world's first statement of human rights. This not only guaranteed his subjects freedom of religion, security of property, labour rights and impartial justice, but also laid down the two essential alliances that would form the foundation of Iran's political identity. First there is an alliance with Mazda, the main Zoroastrian god – 'Now that I put the crown of kingdom of Iran, Babylon/ and the nations of the four directions on the head with the help of (Ahura) Mazda . . .' And secondly there is an alliance with his subjects, that he will respect their rights. 'I announce that I will respect the traditions, customs and religions of the nations of my empire and never let any of my governors and subordinates look down on or insult them until I am alive . . .'[2] From this foundation the concepts of God's Representative on Earth, and a Just Ruler came to dominate the Iranian political identity.

Cyrus was not the only pre-Islamic king to be a high achiever. Darius (522–486 BC) was able to expand the empire into the Punjab and he won submission from both the Greeks of Thrace on the Aegean coast, and the king of Macedonia. He organized an administrative system where the empire was divided into 20 areas or satrapies and put under strong central control. It was later copied by the Romans. He developed a communications system that was the fastest in the world using post stations positioned at equal distances along the roads that connected the empire. The ancient historian Herodotus noted the determination of the royal riders – 'They will not be hindered from accomplishing at their best speed the distance which they have to go, either by snow, or rain, or heat or by the darkness of night'.[3] Darius celebrated the greatness of the Persian Empire at the spring palace he built at Persepolis. With steps wide enough for horses to ride up, and a hall for 10,000 people, this was the palace where Darius welcomed in the New Year, No Ruz, on 21 March, which like his throne, would banish winter darkness for his peoples, seen on the engravings on the walls of the palace as coming to pay him tribute. Darius had a short history of his reign inscribed in a rock at Behistun in Kermanshah and near Persepolis where he has his own epitaph written. He makes it clear that he ruled according to the principles set out in Cyrus' charter. There is much reference in his epitaph to Mazda, so 'A great god is Ahuramazda who created this earth . . . and who made Darius King'[4] and at Behistun he sets himself up as the protector of the weak – 'Darius the king thus says – What is right I love, The man who decideds for the lie I hate . . . and whoever injures, according to what he has injured I punish.'[5] These Achamenian kings, are the great heroes in Iran's political story. Cyrus founded an empire, Darius consolidated it, and their line lasted another 130 years, giving Iran two centuries of stability.

The altar and throne are inseparable

After Darius, the new king Xerxes nearly defeated Iran's long-standing rival Greece. He attacked and burnt the Acropolis, but then his army was beaten by the Greeks at the battle of Plataea in 479. After this the Achamenian line never regained its confidence, and in 332 Alexander of Macedonia (not the Great for the Iranians) successfully invaded Iran and burnt Persepolis in revenge for Xerxes' assault on the Acropolis. After this Iran was ruled by the Greeks and then the Parthians, but when the latter plunged into civil war Ardeshir managed to take the throne of Fars in AD 208. He was challenged by the Parthian king Ardavan and they decided to spare their armies and engage in hand to hand combat. Ardeshir believed that 'This throne and this crown were given me by God'[6] and so all agreed when he stood over the corpse of his rival. He proclaimed himself, 'King of Kings'[7] and claimed he was a direct descendent of the Achamenians. He certainly reminded Iranians of Cyrus and Darius. He again secured the entire Iranian plateau, driving even the Romans out of northern Mesopotamia. His son, Shahpur I outdid his father's victory over the Romans by capturing the Roman Emperor Valerian in front of the walls of Edessa in AD 260. Valerian spent the rest of his days as a prisoner of the Persians. Shahpur I's great grandson, Sharput II, humiliated another Roman emperor, Julian, and won back all of Armenia, and other lands and fortresses on their northern border.

The last two great Sasanian kings were Khosrow I (531–579) and Khosrow Parviz (590–628). Khosrow I, also known as Khosrow of the Immortal Soul, drove back nomadic invaders in the East and North into Central Asia and like the Shahpurs before him won a decisive victory over the Romans, sacking Antioch in Syria in 562. To celebrate Iran's new security, Khosrow issued a coin with the inscription on it, 'Iran Free from Fear' and by reviving the economy and law and order ensured his country enjoyed a peace dividend. So the eleventh-century-poet Ferdowsi writes – 'the Shah covered the face of the earth with his justice . . . Any man, small or great, would lie down to sleep in the open.'[8] Agricultural land was surveyed and the tax system adjusted accordingly so the royal court enjoyed better revenues. This enabled Khosrow to sponsor a large building programme, which included a magnificent palace in Ctesiphon. Here Khosrow sat on a solid gold throne and as his jewel encrusted crown was so heavy, it hung suspended over his head. As we will see in Chapter 8, Khosrow I was also a friend of the great church leader Mar Aba. The last great Sasanian king, Khosrow Parviz, crowned the military exploits of his dynasty by taking Alexandria, Jerusalem and Ephesus, and then pushing on to knock at the very doors of Constantinople. Khosrow Parviz's ambitions were thwarted by the superior naval power of the Byzantine rulers who were able to land an army behind the Persian lines and march on Ctesiphon.

Emerging out of the humiliation of the defeat by the Greeks, and the internal divisions that weakened the Parthians, it is not surprising the Sasanians were obsessed with maintaining power. And to augment this power Ardeshir, the founder of the dynasty, introduced a key principle of government. He told his successor Shahpur – 'consider the altar and the throne as inseparable'.[9] So Zoroastrianism developed from being a popular religion honoured by the Achamenians, to becoming the state religion under the Sasanians. And in a brilliant public relations coup, the sacred flame of the temple also became the king's flame – the Shah and Ahura Mazda were one. All the magnificence of the royal palaces underlined divine royalty, so that many visiting ambassadors would instinctively prostate themselves when they finally entered the royal presence. Zoroastrianism gave authority to the king, and so he rewarded the priests by making them first in the rigid Sasanian social order. After them came the military, the scribes, and finally the tradesmen, craftsmen and farmers. Long before Ayatollah Khomeini, Iran had a theocracy. The crucial role of Zoroastrianism established a contract whereby as long as the ruler shows he has 'charisma', looks after the poor and gives justice to all, then he deserves obedience. If he breaks this contract, then he can be challenged.

Religious protest

So when the Sasanian/Zoroastrian theocracy seemed to be more concerned with power than justice, this is what happened. From a village near Ctesiphon appeared Mani in the 230s preaching a more radical version of Zoroastrian dualism whereby all material wealth was evil, a clear challenge to the rich ruling order. Shahpur heard him and wisely sent him off to India on missionary journeys, but the Zoroastrian priests felt threatened and when Mani tried to settle again in Iran they persuaded Shahpur's successor, Bahram, to have him executed. This never happened as Mani died in prison in 276/277, probably murdered by his enemies.[10] At the end of the fourth century the Sasanian theocracy, suffering from drought, famine and military defeat, seemed to have lost divine support. Again the contract was being broken, and so another extreme prophet appeared, fiercely attacking the rigid social order and especially the Zoroastrian priests whom he believed had separated religion from morality and were oppressing the poor. Mazdak, whose religious beliefs sprang from Mani, has been called the world's first socialist as he called for property and women to be shared by all. Not surprisingly ordinary people supported him and raided palaces and harems. Probably fearing revolution the king, Kavadh, supported Mazdak. The nobles and priests promptly carried out a coup, imprisoned the king and installed his brother on the throne in 496. Kavadh's beautiful wife though seduced the governor of the prison, her husband escaped in her clothes, raised an army from an Eastern tribe known as the Ephthalites or White Huns, and regained his throne.[11] He had learned his lesson though regarding the Mazdakites and allowed his son to exterminate them in 524 or 528.[12]

The fact that Mani and Mazdak had both managed to gain the ear of the most powerful kings in the Middle East is remarkable. It underlines how the kings understood the contract with their people as started by Cyrus. They understood that they had to provide both charisma and social justice. So when a prophet appeared claiming to be God's messenger, preaching justice, and enjoying popular support, they took him seriously. And though both Mani and Mazdak are killed off by the threatened theocratic establishment, they are left in no doubt that they needed to rule justly, or face a clearer moral voice. As Mohammad Reza Shah discovered in the 1970s, this was not irrelevant history.

Worn down and weakened by constantly fighting each other for supremacy in the Levant, neither the Persian nor the Byzantine empires were able to withstand the Arabs onslaught in the early seventh century. Arabs had often raided beyond their borders, but now they were propelled by a fierce and fanatical belief that the whole world should bow to their new religion, Islam. Abu Bakr, Mohammad's successor, defeated the Byzantine army at Damascus in 635, and Umar, the Caliph after Abu Bakr, defeated the Persian army at Nahavand in 642. After the battle, the last Sasanian king, Yazdegerd III fled to Media, but was finally tracked down and murdered in 651.[13]

The Arab and Moguls invasions

The collapse of the Sasanian dynasty was a political earthquake for Asia, comparable to the fall of the Soviet Union in 1989. Certainly the Arabs proved to be a determined aggressor, and certainly the Persians were vulnerable due to their long wars with Byzantium – but also there was a fatal weakness at the heart of the Sasanian court. The kings and priests had neglected the contract with their people. While they suffered economic hardship, the court flaunted its wealth, and so violated their obligation to provide just rule. And rather than be the moral voice of the nation, the Zoroastrian priesthood remained indulgent at the head of a rigid class system. No wonder Iranians were attracted to the Muslim creed that insisted on the equality of all believers.

For the next 850 years there would be no Persian king like Cyrus or Shahpur, who were revered by their subjects and respected by the world. Instead Iran was ruled by foreigners, first the province of an Islamic empire, then a killing plateau for the Mongol hordes. Until the eleventh century the Muslim rulers were Arabs, first the Umayyads in Damascus, and then the Abbasids in Baghdad. For the eleventh and twelfth century the Muslim rulers were the Seljuq Turks, their leaders taking the title of Sultan. Iran was a colony, and Islam the new religion. Converting to Islam for the masses was not so onerous. Zoroastrianism had not only propped up an exploitive class system, but had also been abandoned by Ahura Mazda on the battlefield. Furthermore there were close links between the two faiths – both believed in angels, in a judgment day, and above all, in justice. So Allah replaced Ahura Mazda as the force of light, and Muhammad replaced Zoroaster as his spokesman. Changing their religion then for the people meant mainly changing their religious symbols.

However politically, the coming of Islam meant a radical change in the way authority was viewed. Till the seventh century the political identity of Iran had been very clear. A despotic king would be considered divine by his people, as long as he was 'charismatic' and just. And usually his son would succeed him. But in Islam in the seventh century there was no room for a king, let alone a divine king. All men were meant to be equal in the mosque, and in the new Muslim states, everyone's ultimate allegiance was to be with the *Ummah*, the community of believers, who were represented by a leader, or Caliph, elected by a council of elders, called the *Shura*.[14] Though this was a completely new way for Iranians to view political authority, after more than a thousand years, the Islamic view of power could not eliminate the monarchical view. It was too ingrained in the psyche of the people. Rather the two have constantly jostled to be the dominant influence in the Iranian political identity.

In the thirteenth and fourteenth century neither Islam nor the Persian monarchy held any influence in Iran: both were crushed by the Mongol hordes. In the thirteenth century Genghis Khan 'scourge of God' and devotee of the sky god Tengri, led his Mongol hordes through the northern Iranian plateau destroying all before him. Genghis Khan was followed by Hulagu who sacked Baghdad, and in the fourteenth century came the cruellest Mongol of all, Tamerlene. His parting gift to Isphahan illustrates his style. After ravaging the city, his soldiers built a pyramid of 70,000 skulls to commemorate their visit. The invasion of the Mongols is still a traumatic memory for Iran. Sandra Mackey, in her excellent book, *The Iranians* tells the story of when she was handed a red rose by a gardener in Mashad. He informs her in a sad voice that the intensity of the red comes from the blood in the Iranian soil. Sandra Mackey thought he was referring to modern times – SAVAK, the revolution, the Iran–Iraq war. 'No, no, madam, I am talking about the Mongols, that is why my roses are so red.'[15] The immediate impact of this memory on the Iranian political identity was to cause a resurgence of nationalism which would be fiercely protective of Iran's borders. The long-term impact, still in force today, is a deep mistrust of the foreigner.

The Safavids

Out of the horror of the Mongol invasions arose the Safavids, a new Iranian dynasty whose greatest king, Shah Abbas, stands on a par with the heroes of the Sasanian period. After his death in 1405, Tamerlene's empire soon unravelled. In Western Iran Turcoman tribes competed for power, and in the East, Tamerlene's successors tried to rule from Herat, and occasionally challenged the Turcomans. In 1506 the Uzbeks drove Tamerlene's successors out of Herat and it seemed Iran would again be invaded and become a province of a foreign conqueror. It was not to be. Ismail, the leader of a new movement called the Safavids, had won the allegiance of the Turkish tribes in the north-west of Iran and they defeated the Uzbeks at a battle near Merv in 1510. Ismail was now the undisputed ruler of Iran. Though his blood was technically Turkish, Ismail's family had lived in northern Iran for six generations. His ancestor, Sheikh Safi Al-Din (1252–1334) had been a renowned Sufi mystic and thousands flocked to him for prayer, first in Ardebil, and then in Gilan. The Safavid family were given much money and property, and Safi's descendants began to have territorial ambitions. They also changed their central religious allegiance from Sufism, to Shiism.[16] The Safavids gained unprecedented supremacy over the Turkish tribes when Ismail, aged just 13, became the new head of the order in 1500.

Claiming to be a descendant of Ali, Muhammad's son-in-law, and an incarnation of God and that Mahdi, the Twelfth Imam, would soon come to cleanse the world of sin, Ismail offered the down trodden peasants of northern Iran such an intoxicating mix of mysticism and hope that they separated from their tribal chiefs – and so from their Sunni Ottoman overlords – to join him. With an army of 7,000 he first conquered the east of Iran, making sure he gained the Shia holy sites of Karbala and Najaf, before turning to defeat the Uzbeks at Merv.

For the first time in over 850 years the Iranians had their own ruler – and they were forced to accept Shia Islam. One of Ismail's first orders was that the first three Sunni Caliphs be publicly cursed in all town squares and if any one protested, he told the Mullahs of Tabriz – 'God and the Imams are with me, and I fear no one; by God's help, if the people utter one word of protest, I will draw the sword and leave not one of them alive.'[17] Ismail was true to his word and many were slain if they refused to adopt Shiism. As seen in Chapter 1 his Shia faith was political as his rivals, the Ottomans in the West, and the Uzbeks in the East, were both Sunni. He was not ready to risk his men having divided loyalties. Internally too he wanted to reassert Ardeshir's principle of never letting the altar and throne be separate. And so he claimed to be 'God's mystery', the harbinger of Mahdi, to ensure his subjects looked to him as the provider of both physical and spiritual food. Iranians were more than ready to accept such a charismatic leader, for while being a colony of an Arabic/Turkish Islamic empire had been humiliating, though tolerable, to be left unprotected against the Mongols was unforgivable. They wanted the glory days of Cyrus and Darius again. So there is massive support for a mystical victorious Iranian military chief whose religion is focused on the leader, as it was under the Achamenians and Sasanians, and who claimed connections with the royalist past. The Safavids clearly understood the importance of this, so as well as claiming that Ismail was descended from Ali, they also claimed that Ali took Shahrbanou, the daughter of the last Sasanian king, Yazdegerd and gave her to his son, Hussein, to marry.[18] So the royal blood of Iran's ancient kings flows in the veins of the Shia Imams, whose descendant is their new king, Ismail.

Iran's adoption of Shiism was also a rejection of the alien feature Islam had brought into the country's political equation. Sunni Islam had shifted the country's ultimate allegiance to the external *Shura* – but this had failed Iran and left her raped and ruined. Now under Ismail, ultimate political allegiance returned to the victorious military chief who again became a divine king. But, as with the ancient monarchy, there is a contract. The king must have charisma and he must rule as a good Shia, which meant having a keen sense of justice as Ali had had. So Ismail is unashamedly reasserting the old contract that used to exist between Iranians and their ancient kings. He will be their charismatic all powerful king and priest, linked by blood to both the Shia and Persian heroes. But he will not just rule with brutal force. He will rule according to the principles of Shiite justice, as set out by Ali and Hussein.

While Ismail[19] laid the foundation for Safavid power which now ruled from the Oxus in the East to the Euphrates in the West, it was Shah Abbas (1587–1629) who truly restored Iran's greatness. Abbas inherited a kingdom threatened again by Turkish tribes, the Uzbeks, and the Turkish Sultan. Abbas reversed this by recruiting his own standing army, loyal only to him, made up of the victims of the Ottoman invasions. He made a humiliating peace with the Sultan while dealing with the Uzbeks, and then in 1605 he turned on the Sultan and regained not only Tabriz, but also Baghdad. By defeating the Sultan, Abbas sent a clear message to the world that Iran was no longer a pawn other powers could play with. And that included the European powers. In 1622 he ousted the Portuguese from the island of Hormuz in the Persian Gulf to make sure that Iran would benefit from the increase of trade now using sea lanes. Under Shah Abbas Iran prospered. Roads were built, new irrigation systems installed, and Isphahan became one of the most spectacular capital cities in the world. 'Palaces, mosques and colleges, avenues and gardens, public offices, bazaars, caravanserais, bridges, and forts rose at his command'.[20] Indeed Iranians say – *Isphahan, nesfe jahan* (Isphahan is half the world). To help with the building Shah Abbas transferred a whole town of Armenian Christians from Turkey to his new capital, where he housed them in their own area called Jolfa and let them build their own cathedral which still stands today. Going through the centre of the city is the Chahar Bagh which connected gardens and small palaces, and it ended in the magnificent 'maidan' with the vast Royal Mosque at one end, and the old bazaar at the other. At the eastern side of the maidan, began the royal palaces where Shah Abbas ruled as both 'the Shadow of God on Earth' and the 'Splendour of Darius'. Like Ismail before him, Abbas was unashamedly standing in the line of Iran's ancient kings who had been considered semi divine.

Decline of the monarchy

Shah Abbas and Iran shone on the political map in the early seventeenth century. The light then slowly dimmed, flickered and nearly went out till Reza Shah burst onto the political scene in the early 1920s. After Shah Abbas' death in 1629, his successors in the Safavid dynasty were weak. This is not surprising because to stop conspiracies Shah Abbas had his eldest son executed, two others blinded and the rest imprisoned in the harem. Wilfred Blunt records how the traveller, Pietro Della Vale spent an evening with Abbas, and then left him, 'leaning against a pillar listening attentively to the musicians. A deep melancholy had suddenly descended on him'. Blunt concludes that Abbas 'never forgave himself for the murder of his son'.[21] The surviving sons that followed copied Abbas' practice of killing off all possible contenders as that is the only art of kingship they had seen. They gave no time to the administration. Instead they indulged themselves in extravagant ceremonies, alcoholism, gluttony and the harem. The contract was being broken: Iran's enemies began to exploit the situation and by 1722 the Afghans were ransacking Isphahan. Then Nader Afshar, a camel driver turned soldier, took over Iran's armies, drove out the Afghans and founded a new dynasty. But Nader knew nothing of contracts. He ruled by brute force, imposing the death penalty on people who did not pay their taxes, and he used the country's wealth for war. When told that there would be no battles in heaven, he is said to have asked – 'How can there be any delights there.'[22] Militarily he was very successful; indeed he is called Iran's Napoleon, or the second Alexander. He pushed the Turks and Russians back from the west and north of Iran; he captured Kabul, and went on to take Delhi where he slaughtered 30,000 people after some disturbances. From the treasuries of the Moghals he brought the Peacock Throne and so much booty to Iran that he stopped taxation in Iran for 3 years. Though Nader's military exploits are recognized by Iranians, he is not revered like a Cyrus or Shahpur – because he made no attempt to underpin his rule with justice. In his later years he became so paranoid that his commanders concluded they had to assassinate him before he killed them. They murdered him in 1747. In contrast the next ruler of Iran, Karim Khan, tried to improve the lives of his subjects. He dealt with tax abuse, encouraged agriculture and trade, and greatly improved his capital, Shiraz. Unfortunately for Iranians his rule was very short and after his death in 1179 the country lapsed back into anarchy, till the Qajar dynasty emerged in 1794.

Though they ruled Iran for over 100 years, there was little greatness in the Qajars. Their founder Aqa Muhammad was an able administrator and military commander, but like Nader, he ruled by brute force. Taking Kerman from his rival Luft Ali Khan, he ordered that all the survivors have their eyes gouged out. His successors ruled oppressively, corruptly and decadently and lost land in the north to the Russians. In the mid-nineteenth century Nasir al din tried to modernize the country, but his administration could not handle the loans from Britain and Russia, who then, as creditors, gained more power inside Iran. Sensing his failure, Nasir al din retreated to his harem, where he had 1,600 women. He was eventually assassinated in 1896. His son did not even attempt modernization, but just used foreign loans for holidays in Europe. By the end of the nineteenth century, the Qajars have neither charisma nor a reputation for social justice. Out of the ruins of the traditional contract between the ruled and the rulers rose an alliance of Shiites and liberal politicians which brought about the constitutional revolution of 1906. This was ignored and then crushed by the Qajars who continued to rule reliant on the British and the Russians who effectively took over Iran during the First World War. After the war there was anarchy in Iran until the leader of the Persian Cossack Brigade,[23] Reza Khan Mirpanj organized a successful coup d'etat in 1921. After driving out the Bolsheviks from the north, and ruthlessly quelling rebellions in Gilan and among the Kurds, Reza Khan crowned himself Reza Shah Pahlavi in 1925.

Reza Shah's secular throne

Cyrus, Darius Aredeshir, Khosrow, Ismail, Shah Abbas – all had claimed support from either Azuhra Mazda or Allah via Ali: Reza Shah though had little time for religion. It was once reported to him that one Sayyid Ghazanfaar was claiming to be the Twelfth Imam. Reza Shah ordered the man's arrest saying, 'During my reign I will not permit any prophets to appear.'[24] With Kemal Ataturk's example in Turkey to inspire him, he wanted to turn Iran into a stridently nationalistic, modern, secular state. At first he toyed with the idea of becoming the president of a republic, but soon realized it would be better to use the power of Iran's pre-Islamic royalist past to strengthen his rule, and to help stamp out the power of religion. He attacked the Islamic culture by exploiting the tendency among Iranians to feel their culture is superior to the Arabic one and exalting Iran's pre-Islamic achievements. He banned men from wearing turbans and beards, and in 1935 he made it illegal for women to wear the veil. This was an offence punishable by a prison sentence and he sent his soldiers out to enforce the edict. At the same time he also attacked the actual power of the Shia clergy. The civil courts took over from the religious ones; he closed all religious schools, and opened compulsory state ones, and founded the University of Tehran; he expropriated all the wealth of the religious shrines; and he made every mullah liable for active military service. If any religious figure dared to challenge his power, Reza Shah's response was swift and sometimes violent. Once the Shah's wife went to the shrine of Fatimeh in Qom, Iran's religious capital, to pray and while there a mullah happened to see her face. He and his students told her off, as conservative Muslims do not believe a lady's face should be seen at holy shrines. The next day Reza Shah arrived at the tomb with 400 troops. 'He strode through the gate in his heavy military boots and across the graves of Shia holy men. Finding the offending mullah he knocked off his turban, grabbed him by the hair, and thrashed him with a riding crop.'[25] In 1936 there was a protest at Imam Reza's shrine in Mashad over the 'Pahlavi' cap, which the Shah had ordered all men to wear, as it stopped worshippers touching the ground with their foreheads when they prayed. The Shah's reply was to send troops into the shrine. They opened fire on the protesters and over a hundred people lost their lives. In the face of such ruthless hostility the senior clergy became passive and retreated from its traditional position at the heart of Iranian society. Some though of the junior clergy, such as Ruhollah Khomeini, looked to the day when the rights of Shiism could again be restored.

As well as eliminating Islam from the Iranian political identity, Reza Shah also sought to replace the traditional sense of justice represented by religion, with the popular new faith of the twentieth century: technological progress. Like both

Hitler, Stalin, and the Chinese today, Reza Shah believed that if he delivered a modern lifestyle to his people, then they should support his rule. His first aim was to make Iran's transport system suitable for the twentieth century. He built inter-city roads and in Tehran and elsewhere bulldozed down houses to make way for wide avenues. He also criss-crossed the country with its first railway network, famously making the German engineers and their families stand under the bridges when the trains first went over them. With a transport infrastructure in place, industrial manufacturing developed and during Reza Shah's reign over 300 large plants were built.[26]

Reza Shah was a man of Spartan tastes. He slept on the floor throughout his life and always wore his uniform. Such a man had little time for the sophisticated political classes whom he blamed for betraying Iran in the early twentieth century. Outside one of his palaces in Tehran is just the statue of his boot – the present regime wants the tourist to know that Reza Shah was a dictator, as indeed he was. Under him there was hardly any political life in terms of opposition. The press was muzzled; parliament rubber-stamped the king's decisions; and some of his political rivals and confidantes were imprisoned, some eliminated.[27] As we have seen, religious protests were put down robustly, and Reza Shah was ruthless with tribal rebellions. And certainly his style was very brusque. One day he arrived unexpectedly to inspect the regimental barracks where Lt-Colonel Hassan Arfa was in charge – 'He stopped in front of the windows of one of the armouries and said angrily: '"These sons of burned fathers can't even keep their windows clean!" And with his cane he broke all the window panes.'[28]

As a dictator Reza Shah created intense resentment, especially when he began amassing vast tracts of land in the 1930s; and among the peasants there was a lot of dissatisfaction as the agricultural sector was generally neglected. But, there was no serious opposition to his rule, and the numbers of political opponents who met harsh treatment is very small.[29] Given that Iran was in a state of anarchy when he came to power, it is clear that a strong hand was needed. This Reza Shah provided – and much more. Before his reign Iran was a medieval country; by the end of his reign in 1941 it was a modern state. In less than 20 years Reza Shah had established a centralized army and civil service, an air and naval force, a compulsory universal educational system, a judiciary, a transport infrastructure, an electricity network, a tax and banking system that kept the country out of foreign debt and a manufacturing industry. This is a remarkable achievement. With so many visible improvements affecting everyone's life, most Iranians concluded, as he thought they would, that it was better to support Reza Shah, rather than oppose him, for in a very real sense, he was delivering his side of the ancient contract Iranians have always had with their rulers. He was most definitely dynamic and charismatic. This is what Vita Sackville-West wrote about him in 1926 – 'An alarming man, six foot three in height, with a sullen manner, a huge nose, grizzled hair, and a brutal jowl – but there was no denying that he had a kingly presence.'[30] And as his many social and economic reforms impacted people's lives, so he was seen by the majority to be a just king. His memory lives on,[31] perhaps more than that of his son, as a constant reminder of what a real king can do.

Reza Shah was undone, not because of his domestic policies, but because of a fatal mistake in his foreign policy. As a fierce nationalist, who believed in strong government, he was a natural admirer of Adolf Hitler. He also wanted to use Germany to counter the influence of England, who had consistently used Iran for its own purposes and had infuriated Reza Shah in their dealings over oil. By the end of the 1930s Germany was Iran's largest trading partner, Hitler had pronounced Iran a pure Aryan nation, and German agents were very active inside Iran. At the outbreak of war in 1939 Reza Shah declared Iran to be neutral, but it was quite clear where his sympathies lay. After the 1941 German invasion of the Soviet Union, Iran became a front-line state and the Allied powers asked Reza Shah to expel all German agents. Here he made his fatal mistake: he delayed answering the request. In the raging battle for the soul of Europe, Reza Shah, a man with immense political acumen, should have seen that the Allies could never allow Iran, with her supply routes to the Soviet Union, her oil, and her access to the Gulf, to become an active ally of the fascist powers. The Soviet and British troops invaded and the Iranian army was helpless before their advance. Reza Shah could not bear ruling over an Iran under foreign control and on 16 September 1941 he went into exile to South Africa – another racist state – where he died in 1944. His son, Mohammad Reza, became Iran's last king.

Mohammad Reza's last throne

From the start of Mohammad Reza's reign the foundation of the traditional contract of the ruler and the ruled in Iran was crumbling. Used to the dynamic, experienced and charismatic Reza Shah, a man who had won power fighting Iran's enemies at the head of an 8,000 strong regiment, the country now faced Mohammad Shah, a 21-year-old fresh from an expensive boarding school in Switzerland where his closest friend was an openly homosexual boy[32]. That sense of the divine right to rule did not seem to hover over him. Eileen Humphreys writes he was – 'A more sensitive, less decisive character than his father, intelligent, hardworking but aloof and a little vain.'[33] Another Iranian writer is harsher – 'In his youth, as in much of his life, he was gaunt in countenance, vulnerable in physique, haunted by the spectre of his imposing father.'[34] Reza Shah obviously gave the same sort of treatment to his children in private as he gave to some of his subjects in public. Mohammad Reza Shah himself said this, 'He was a very great character, but we were all frightened of him. He only needed to fix his piercing eyes upon us and we went rigid with fear and respect.'[35]

There was little fear and respect for this new king. When he acceded to the throne his country was occupied, and his country's finances were being controlled by an American, Arthur Millspaugh who was not very successful. There was rampant inflation and in 1942 bad harvests exacerbated by speculators and hoarders caused famine in parts of the country. While the peasantry suffered most, the rich indulged in political in-fighting, producing 11 prime ministers between 1941–1946. Meanwhile the Soviet backed Tudeh (Communist) Party challenged the central government, especially in the north and around the textile factories of Isphahan. And both Azerbaijan and Kurdistan launched autonomy movements. In the midst of all this the new Shah seemed like a mere observer, hopelessly out of depth, devoid of divine charisma.

In the early 1950s the divine charisma was with an older man, Dr Mohammad Mossadeq. He was the son of a Qajar princess and had been the governor general of Fars and then the national finance minister in his early twenties before Reza Shah came to power. As an implacable opponent of Reza Shah, Mossadeq suffered house arrest in the 1930s, but with the abdication in 1941, he returned to parliament and was soon Iran's most popular politician. In 1949 he became the leader of a new nationalist party, The National Front, a coalition of diverse groups who all united around Mossadeq's passionate hostility to Britain's exploitation of Iranian oil and the Shah who allowed it. He had a strong case – the British had invested £22 million in 1908, and the return had been £800 million, with Iran only gaining £102 million.[36] Most Iranians did not know the exact figures, but they all sensed they were not getting a fair deal and so Mossadeq enjoyed a lot of popular support.

On 7 March 1951 the Shah's prime minister, Ali Razmara was shot by Islamic terrorists. Mossadeq stepped into the vacuum as the chairman of the commission looking into Iran's agreement with the Ango-Iranian Oil Company and with the support of parliament boldly nationalized Iranian oil on 15 March. On 29 April Mossadeq was elected prime minister, adored by the vast majority of Iranians. It seemed he was now the power in the country, rather than the Shah. He had many qualities of the true Iranian ruler. Like Ali he spoke up for the oppressed poor, and indeed on his own estates he had distributed all the land to his tenants; and in the tradition of all the great Iranian kings he had challenged the greedy foreigner, unlike the Shah who worked with them. Mossadeq was also a very charismatic personality. With his tall ageing frame, drooping shoulders, long nose and soft, sad eyes he stood out from the crowd as the country's natural father figure. And his oratory enthralled and enchanted Iranians. Sometimes in the parliament he would speak constantly for 2 days, and then collapse in a faint. He would then be taken home on a stretcher where he would hold court resting on piles of pillows, lying on his simple iron bed and dressed in pyjamas. Foreigners who had to visit him in his bedroom were completely confused: Iranians loved the drama.

Iranians might have loved the drama but the British were incensed as the Iranian oil fields were now supplying a quarter of the world's markets. Britain demanded a boycott on Iranian oil that most Western nations kept while production in Iran fell as there were no trained technicians to keep the black gold flowing. So oil income dropped dramatically, Iran was unable to borrow money internationally, and the government could no longer pay the bills. Believing all the anti-colonial rhetoric propagated by successive US governments, Mossadeq wrote to the American president Dwight Eisenhower for help. Unfortunately the British had already gained the president's ear, alerting him to the strength of the Tudeh (Communist) party in Iran and its close ties to the Soviets. They argued that Mossadeq, with his socialist sympathies and unpredictable behaviour, would never be able to protect Iran from Communism. In the black and white world of cold war politics, Eisenhower was easily convinced and Britain was able to introduce the Central Intelligence Agency (CIA) to its formidable network of royalist contacts in Iran. So Operation Ajax was born which led to the coup in August 1953. The head of the CIA Allen W. Dulles approved $1 million for Kermit Roosevelt, grandson of President Theodore Roosevelt to use in anyway to secure the downfall of Mossadeq. Roosevelt worked closely with General Fazollah Zahedi, a fanatical supporter of the Pahlavis, who had hundreds of pro-Shah contacts in the military and police. He first separated the communists from Mossadeq by hiring crowds to chant communist slogans and tear down statues of the Shah. On cue the American government demanded that the Mossadeq government quell the 'Tudeh' crowds and Mossadeq, sweetly walking into the trap, ordered the army out to crush the communists. The army, influenced by Zahedi, quickly obeyed. Having removed the threat of the communists rising up to support Mossadeq, Roosevelt and Zahedi now set out to capture the old prime minister. Roosevelt hired another crowd from the south of Tehran for $10,000 and on 19 August they marched chanting for the Shah. They arrived at Mossadeq's house demanding his arrest. They were joined by Zahedi whose tanks encircled the house. Mossadeq, dramatic to the end, tried to escape and jumped over the garden wall. He was soon arrested and later he was tried and sentenced to life imprisonment.

Throughout all this the Shah had been a minor actor. When eventually the conspirators called on him to act, he proved to be anything but heroic. On the orders of Roosevelt and Zahedi the Shah sent Colonel Nassiri on 13 August to dismiss Mossadeq. However when Mossadeq refused, and crowds poured into the street, the Shah ran away. He first flew himself to Baghdad, and then to Rome, where he was not even allowed to stay in his own embassy. It was as a guest of the Excelsior Hotel he received a telegram on 20 August saying 'Mossadeq overthrown; imperial troops control Tehran'. Apparently he went pale and whispered – 'I knew that they loved me.'[37]

This was sentimentalism. The Shah knew very well that he had been restored to power not by the love of the people, but by the ingenuity and bribes of the

American secret service. His job now was to collaborate with his protectors and until his overthrow in 1979 Mohammad Shah was one of America's most faithful friends. In 1954 his government signed a new deal with the Western oil cartels. This gave them effective control of oil production and distribution – and 50 per cent of the profits. And then every year the Shah spent billions of dollars purchasing military hardware from the Americans.[38] The Shah also knew that he could not rely on the love of his people to keep internal order. After 1953 he decided to use brute force. Using those same oil profits he vastly expanded the army and the police and purchased all he needed in terms of equipment and training to set up one of the Middle East's most effective secret services, SAVAK, which by the 1960s according to Amnesty International had 'the worst human rights record on the planet'.

Fortunately for the Shah the economy in the 1960s and early 1970s was growing so fast that most people were happy to exchange political freedom for a rise in their standard of living. But many were not. Not only were there the thousands of graduates from Reza Shah's universities, who had imbibed Western ideas of democracy, there was also this much deeper concept of the just and charismatic ruler which ran deep in the Iranian mind. As well as the cruelty of SAVAK, it was obvious that a small minority were getting fabulously wealthy, while for the vast majority of Iranians, both in the villages and the new slums in south Tehran, life was still 'nasty, brutish, and short'. Worse, it seemed the Shah, like his father, had little time for religion, and was more than ready to let Western fashions pour into the country. To his opponents in the mosque and the bazaar the Shah was betraying Iran's Islamic identity. Though aloof, unpopular, and surrounded by a fawning greedy court, the Shah nevertheless controlled the most powerful military machine in the Middle East. It seemed inconceivable that his opponents would ever be able to dislodge him. However that is exactly what happened in 1979 when Ayatollah Khomeini managed to bring about the last great revolution of the twentieth century.[39]

Iran's political identity and Christianity

The idea that a political identity which justifies a dictatorship can provide any bridges to Christianity is not immediately apparent. This is because in the West Christianity has become so entwined with democracy that the two systems are interchangeable. The assumption is that a 'Christian' country is a democratic one. In fact there is neither a historical nor an ideological link between Christianity and democracy. Historically the writers of the New Testament never questioned the legitimacy of political dictatorship and for most of its history Christianity has flourished in non-democratic countries. Ideologically the church has never looked to a majority of men for authority, but always to Scripture, tradition and inspired leaders.

While the Bible does not propagate democracy, it does however stress the importance of covenant and a just ruler which honours God. The central theme of both the Old and New Testaments is that God enters into a covenant, a contract, with people. And within this covenant, there is the figure of a just ruler who, under God, will provide both physical and spiritual blessings for his people. David in the Old Testament prefigured Jesus Christ in the New Testament who is both the just ruler, and the mediator of God's covenant with man. These Biblical concepts are much closer to the Iranian political identity than the concept of democracy. For while the Iranian political identity with Christianity affirms the need for a just ruler within the context of a covenant with God, democracy demands that the voice of the human majority must dominate, whatever the voice of justice or revealed religion might say. This concept is wholly alien to both Christianity and the Iranian political identity.

Christianity packaged with Western democracy then runs against the grain of Iran's political history: however Christianity freed from Western externals, with its emphasis on covenant and the just rule of charismatic King is very much a part of the Iranian political mind-set. The significance of this is not in any way to suggest that Iranians are yearning for a literal Christian political state, but rather to argue that the way Iranians think about politics means they have already built into their minds an intellectual structure that foreshadows central Christian beliefs. The royalist past has instilled into people's mind an expectation for a king who will enter into a contract with his people, and this is exactly what Christianity offers. In this way Iran's political identity is a bridge.

In recent years this bridge has become stronger for as political Islam has failed to deliver, so, similarly to what happened in Europe in the Middle Ages, people resent religion having political power. But this does not mean they will reject Christianity, because in stark contrast to Islam, Christ's kingdom 'is not of this world'. It is in the future. In 1979 when millions of Iranians swept into the streets to welcome Ayatollah Khomeini one can see how this was an expression of all the historical yearning they have for a just king. Now, as we will see, all that hope has turned to deep disillusionment, and it is extremely unlikely such crowds would ever gather for another human messiah. However because of the deep seated political mind-set of Iranians there might well be a readiness to transfer this hope of a charismatic covenant keeping King to another Messiah.

Iran's long royalist past clearly reveals that charismatic kingship and covenant lie at the heart of the country's political identity and though it is hostile to a Christianity wrapped up in Western democracy, it is not at all hostile to Biblical Christianity, rather it is a bridge, and this bridge is likely to grow stronger as disillusionment with the country's Islamic revolutionary government increases. It is the story of the revolution that brought this government to power that we now turn.

Notes

[1] See Ezra 1.1–8.

[2] The charter was written in cuneiform on a baked clay cylinder. It was discovered in 1878 during an excavation of archaeological sites in Babylon. See www.iran-chamber.com/history/cyrus/cyrus_charter.php for more about the charter [last accessed 6 June 2008].

[3] Quoted by Sandra Mackey in *The Iranians*, Plume, New York, 1998, p. 26.

[4] Eileen Humphreys in *The Royal Road*, Scorpion Publishing, London, 1991, p. 36.

[5] Quoted by Humphreys in *The Royal Road* from A. T. Olmstead, 'History of the Persian Empire', p. 33.

[6] Mackay, *The Iranians*, p. 33.

[7] Mackay, *The Iranians*, p. 33.

[8] Quoted in *The Royal Road*, p. 109.

[9] Quoted in *The Royal Road*, p. 98.

[10] There are claims that the corpse was stuffed with straw as a warning against other heretics. After his death his teachings continued to spread, his most famous convert being the young Augustine who became bishop of Hippo.

[11] The full story is told by Procopius – see Humphreys in *The Royal Road*, p. 108.

[12] The Mazdakites were eventually absorbed by Buddhism.

[13] His daughter Shahr Banu married Husayn ibn Ali, Muhammad's grandson, and gave birth to the Fourth Shia Imam, Ali Zayn al Abidin. His son Peroz fled to China.

[14] The Shi'as challenged the Shora's right to decide the succession, claiming that it should be by blood inheritance. For them this meant Ali should be the first Caliph as he was Muhammad's son-in-law. However the Shi'as never controlled the Caliphate.

[15] Mackay, *The Iranians*, p. 71.

[16] See Chapter 1 for a full discussion of the Shia faith.

[17] Quoted by Humphreys in *The Royal Road* citing E. G. Browne, p. 194.

[18] This claim was made popular by the Safavids who liked to link the Shia faith with Iranian nationalism. See Humphreys' *The Royal Road*, p. 194.

[19] Alarmed at the rise of a Shiite Persian, the Sunni Turkish Sultan turned from attacking Christian Europe to deal with Ismail. The Iranians suffered a terrible defeat at Chaldiran which left Ismail a broken man. He became an alcoholic and died aged 37 in 1524.

[20] Wilfrid Blunt, *Pietro's Pilgrimage*, James Barrie, London, 1953, p. 122.

[21] Blunt, *Pietro's Pilgrimage*, pp. 150, 154.

[22] Quoted in an article on Nader Shah from Iran Chamber website. See www.iran-chamber.com/history/afsharids/afsharids.php [last accessed 6 June 2008].

[23] The 8,000 Persian Cossack brigade was originally led by Russians. But after the 1917 Bolshevik revolution leadership passed to Reza Khan.

[24] Humphreys, *The Royal Road*, p. 237.

[25] Mackey, *The Iranians*, p. 181.

[26] In 1925 only about twenty modern plants existed, of which five were relatively large, employing about fifty workers each. By 1941 the number of modern plants

had risen to 346, of which 146 were large installations. www.irvl.net/Strats-Iran. htm [last accessed 6 June 2008].

27 Killed in prison: Modarres, a religious leader in 1938; Abdol Hosain Taimurtash in 1933, probably on the Shah's orders who suspected him of double dealing over oil negotiations; Sardar As'ad Bakhtiari, a keen supporter but who was arrested. Kept under house arrest: Mohammad Mossadeq, liberal opponent. See *Modern Iran* by Nikki R. Keddie, Yale University Press, 2003, Chapter Five.

28 Quoted by Humphreys in *The Royal Road*, p. 235.

29 See footnote 27.

30 Quoted by Humphreys, *The Royal Road*, p. 234.

31 In 2000 Reza Shah was voted the third most important Iranian of the twentieth century and most voted for him for being the father of modern Iran. Some comments are: Reza Shah is the father of modern Iran. After many years under the rule of the Qajar dynasty, Iran was in total ruin. He is greatly overlooked, mainly due to his son; yet he ignited the flame of nationalism and rekindled Persian dignity. Shervin Ansari; He delivered Iran to a position in which her move toward a modern civilization and ultimately controlling her own journey in the realm of history was inevitable. The good, the bad and everything in between tomorrow's Iran has Reza Khan's finger prints all over it. Aryaii@aol.com First and second place in the survey were taken by Mossadeq and Khomeini respectively. See www. iranian.com/Opinion/2000/January/Century/index [last accessed 6 June 2008].

32 His name was Ernest Perron, he was ten years older than the Shah, and was the son of the school's gardener. So strong was the friendship that Perron came back with the Shah where he remained a close friend till 1954. According to Abbas Milani of Stanford University Perron was 'openly gay.' See http://www.stanford. edu/~amilani/downloads/characterasdestiny.pdf page 3 (accessed 25 July, 2008)

33 Humphreys, *The Royal Road*, p. 240.

34 Abbas Milani, research fellow at Hoover Institute, essay on Mohammad Reza Shah, www.iranheritage.org/privatelives/abstracts_full.htm [last accessed 6 June 2008].

35 Soorya, 'The Autobiography of Her Imperial Highness', quoted by Mackey, *The Iranians*, p. 190.

36 See the *Wrath of Allah* by Ramy Nima, Pluto Press, London, 1983, pp. 5–6.

37 Mackey, *The Iranians*, p. 207.

38 By 1975 the Shah was spending $5 billion a year.

39 The story of the revolution is told in Chapter 4.

Conclusion to Part One

Religiously Iran is officially Shia, but soaked in Sufism; culturally the country accepts it lives in an Islamic culture, but her poetry, cinema and No Ruz festival speak of a much wider, more universal, more enigmatic world; and politically the nation has always looked to having a heroic, charismatic, king who enters into a just contract with his people.

There is nothing remotely Christian in the overall identity of Iran as a nation. Indeed it might seem that the whole notion that there can be any relationship between the Iranian identity and Christianity is simple, shallow and wishful thinking. Religiously Iran has been Islamic since the mid-seventh century, the only Shia Muslim nation since 1501 and the only Shia theocracy since 1979. Culturally nearly all its great artists have been faithful Shia Muslims and there has never been a cultural movement aimed at undermining Shia Islam's dominance. Politically no Iranian king, not even the Pahlavis, have tried to completely uproot Shia Islam, and now all political power in Iran flows from the Shia clerics. Generally speaking it would appear that there is little to say about the Iranian identity and Christianity; the two have little in common.

However our brief survey of Iran's religious and cultural identity shows that under the surface there are a number of factors that draw the Iranian identity closer to Christianity. Regarding religion we saw the main focus of the Shia faith was on the Imams, Ali, Hussein and Mahdi, who symbolize: commitment to the poor; a willingness to die for justice; and a determination to return to the world to restore righteousness. The Imams are at the heart of the Shia faith: Jesus Christ is at the heart of the Christian faith, and He was committed to the poor, died for justice and promised to return to restore righteousness. We also saw the wide and deep influence of Sufism on the Iranian identity which teaches that mankind is cut off from his origins and needs to submit to a shepherd who will teach him or her to repent and begin a spiritual journey which involves rejecting empty religious rituals and increasing self-denial till the seeker becomes one with God. As seen the philosophical context of Sufism and Christianity are very different, but the initial motivation and the practical steps the seeker needs to take are almost exactly the same. Furthermore, both in Sufism and Christianity, there is this expectation of supernatural revelation.

Culturally we have seen that while there is rarely anything maliciously hostile to Islam in the country's poetry and cinema; however there is no passionate love expressed for the religion. This ambivalence is partly due to the fact that the literature the Iranians love is in Persian, not Arabic; partly due to the inevitable theme of religious hypocrisy that is bound to occur in any country's literature, but most of all because the literature and the cinema opens up a grander and more enigmatic intellectual landscape than the mosque does. Many have this wider awareness due to the exceptional popularity of poetry in Iran, but even for the very few who are not familiar with the country's great literature, there is No Ruz, a festival all celebrate. Pre-dating Islam and so reminding Iranians of the great civilization established by their non Muslim ancestors, No Ruz clearly shows to all that Iran has a non-Islamic identity. They are Shia Muslims – but they can also join the world and dance for Spring using universal symbols that probably date back to the Sumerians.

This strong universal aspect to Iran's identity does not automatically bring the culture any closer to Christianity, but it does mean that Iranians tend to be open-minded, for the country's literature and cinema are constantly asking them to consider the great questions of life. It is because Iran has inherited this long-established culture of dealing with universal issues that many comment on the high level of intellectual activity there is in the country. Professor Vali Nasr points out that after English and Mandarin, Persian is the most popular language on the internet. It has more than 80,000 blogs. In Mathematics and Physics Iran is a leading player, and the fact that there have been more translations of Immanuel Kant into Persian in the past decade than into any other language shows there is no lack of interest in philosophy. With some justification Nasr writes – 'No other country in the Muslim world is so rife with intellectual fervour and cultural experimentation at all levels of society.'[1] It is this intellectual vibrancy in Iran's cultural identity that is relevant to Christianity: for Christianity is a universal religion with answers to universal questions. As such, in the cultural context of Iran, it virtually has a right to be heard.

Since 1501 the Shia faith has never had its status as the nation's state religion questioned. And when both the Qajars and then the Pahlavis became too dictatorial, the influence of the Shia faith grew as it allowed itself to be used as a vehicle for political opposition. Then in 1979 all power went to the Shia clerics. They literally ruled the country. Such a dominant influence seals the country off from having a meaningful relationship with any other religion, including Christianity.

However the question needs to be asked as to what would happen if the dominant influence of the Shia faith in Iran lost popular support. When considering the political identity of Iran we saw that the fate of rulers depended on whether they were able to be both charismatic and fulfil a social contract with their people. As in their religion, so too in their politics, Iranians look for a hero and in 1979 Ayatollah Khomeini brilliantly fused the two and became simply 'Imam'. For Khomeini this was the fulfilment of a lifetime's work and in his mind he was going to secure the future of the Shia faith in Iran and beyond for many years to come. Ironically he might well have undermined the future of the Shia faith in Iran. For until 1979 the Shia faith was generally quietist, uninvolved in politics. All the problems that people faced in their lives were blamed on the government, not the Shia faith. And so, as in most monarchical systems, dynasties came and went depending on their success: but the Shia faith remained. However since 1979 all the policies of both the initial revolution and the resulting government have been implemented in the name of the Shia faith. If the Islamic government was to prove unpopular, then it is not just the influence of the religious leaders who will suffer, but, as happened in Europe when the Catholic Church and the monarchy operated as one, the whole influence of the Shia faith will be undermined. And if the Shia faith is severely undermined, then the relationship of the Iranian identity with Christianity becomes a more intriguing question. For the culture gives Christianity a right to be heard, and when heard there is a hero and a spiritual journey that is not alien to the Shia familiar with Sufism.

First though it is necessary to look at the impact of the Islamic government in Iran to see whether it has impacted the popularity of the Shia faith. It is this we turn to in Part Two.

Note

[1] Vali Nasr, 'The Shia Revival, W. W. Norton, 2006. p. 213.

Part Two

Impact of Revolution

Chapter 4

The Revolution

The Iranian Revolution was all about identity. Reza Mohammad Shah did not leave Iran on 16 January 1979 because his people were hungry; he left because what he stood for had become anathema to millions. His hostility to Shiite Islam, the encouragement of Western culture and his political reliance on the West, especially the USA – all this was abhorrent to most Iranians. While the Shah had failed to identify himself with Iran, his rival Ayatollah Khomeini had and in his first major speech to the nation on Iranian soil he appealed to the armed forces 'to come back to the warm bosom of the nation . . .'.[1] The millions celebrating his return and who later voted for his Islamic government did not disagree: Ayatollah Khomeini was 'the bosom of the nation.' Given that Iran had always had a king, this was truly remarkable.

Khomeini's radical vision

As a brilliant Qom student, teacher and then a respected jurist, 'Mujtahid', Khomeini developed his political ideas as Reza Shah was humiliating the clergy.[2] However like the rest of his colleagues he had kept his head low as the Shah did not tolerate opposition. Using a policy of 'dissimulation'[3] Khomeini could legitimately pretend to be indifferent to the policies of the Shah, while in fact he was biding his time for an opportune time to respond. That came in 1941 when Reza Shah was forced to abdicate by the Allies and his son Mohammad Reza Shah was installed on the throne. The next year Khomeini anonymously published a book called *Secrets Exposed*, a stirring defence of the Ulama against secularism, with a stinging attack on the Pahlavis. As well as referring to Reza Shah as 'that illiterate soldier' who had plans 'to destroy the clergy in order to serve his masters (the British)',[4] Khomeini wrote this about the monarchy:

Apart from the royalty of God, all royalty is against the interests of the people and oppressive; apart from the law of God, all laws are null and absurd. A government of Islamic law, controlled by religious jurists (faqihs) will be superior to all the iniquitous governments of the world.[5]

For Iran this was an extraordinary and revolutionary vision: the concept of Iran without a monarchy was unheard of and as Shiites Iranians believed all government was imperfect till the return of Mahdi. To assert that a non-Mahdi human government was from God was almost blasphemy. Over the next 20 years Khomeini continued to develop his political ideas and in 1971 he delivered a series of lectures in Najaf which outlined his blueprint for an Islamic state. Titled 'Islamic Government' Khomeini radically rejected the whole system of monarchy, 'Islam knows neither monarchy nor dynastic succession'[6] and dealt head on with the Shia notion that there can be no religious rule before Mahdi. He argued that since God gave mankind the law, the Shari'a, therefore he must have wanted it to be obeyed, otherwise he would not have given it. So an Islamic state must obey the law, and the only way for them to know exactly how the law applies to their lives is for the society to be ruled by senior clerics – the *Velayat-e Faqih*, the guardianship of the jurists. In 1971 Khomeini's views on the monarchy and his doctrine of *Velayat-e Faqih* were irrelevant. Economic good times had come for many people; most Iranians were still instinctively royalist and certainly did not want a religious dictatorship; the Shah also had the largest army and most effective internal security apparatus in the Middle East; finally other senior Shia Iranian clerics, such as Ayatollah Kho'i and Shariatmadari, did not support Khomeini's theory of *Velayat-e Faqih*.

Khomeini and Iran's soul

Yet just 8 years later, on 16 February 1979, millions came out to welcome the 77-year-old Khomeini. Mohammad Reza Shah, like his father before him, was now in exile, the owner of just a small box of Iranian earth he had taken with him: Khomeini had the whole country at his feet. Khomeini had won the battle for Iran's soul and he had done this not by espousing populist economic or democratic slogans, but by consistently focusing on the issue of Iran's identity. Like all great leaders, he could see above the detail to concentrate on this central question. As seen in Chapter 3, Reza Shah's answer to the decline of Muslim countries was to marginalize religion and create a secular industrial society allied to the West where the new religion would be technology. Khomeini and many others totally rejected this answer and this identity. Despite the decline of Muslim countries since the advent of the industrial revolution, Khomeini still believed that the plan of God was to advance Shia Islam as the most perfect religion all over the world. Religion had to stay at the heart of the nation and there should be no alliances with foreigners, especially Westerners. For in Khomeini's mind the reason why Muslim nations were suffering a temporary setback was not because of religion, but because of Western imperialism and Zionism. These were the enemies of all Muslims. The former exploited Muslim nations for base economic gain, while the latter was an international conspiracy bent on advancing the interests of capitalist Jews, and so weakening Muslims.

After his anonymous publication in 1942, Khomeini limited himself to political references in learned religious journals out of respect for Ayatollah Borujerdi, Iran's most senior cleric, who had ruled that the clergy should keep out of political disputes.[7] But when Borujerdi died in 1961 and no one leader emerged from the remaining senior ayatollahs, Khomeini felt free to attack the government openly and challenge the Pahlavi vision for Iran. He chose issues that would separate the Pahlavi regime from Iran's Shia identity and national pride, always asserting in his speeches that the Shah wanted to destroy Islam and make Iran a slave of foreign powers. In 1962 the Shah's government introduced a bill whereby women would be able to vote in local council elections, and all could vote on any 'Holy Book', not just the Koran. Khomeini decided this signalled the 'destruction of Islam in Iran'[8] and launched a campaign against the bill which drew enthusiastic support from both the clergy and the merchants. The campaign was a success and the Shah's Prime Minister Alam withdrew the bill. While others celebrated, Khomeini warned that the 'regime's plan is to destroy Islam . . . They are readying themselves for a new assault on Islam.'[9]

For Khomeini the 'new assault' came when in January 1963 the Shah announced his 'White Revolution', a modernizing programme of land reform and education which again included votes for women. It was also widely seen as being a ploy by the Shah to keep in with President Kennedy whose foreign policy was committed to seeing 'liberal' progress in America's allies. In 1962 in a speech at the White House Kennedy had said, 'Those who make peaceful revolution impossible will make violent revolution inevitable.'[10] Always nervous the Americans might turn against him the Shah had taken Kennedy literally and launched a peaceful revolution. So for Khomeini and many others, the 'White Revolution' was inspired by a 'Jewish, Baha'i, and American conspiracy'[11] There were street demonstrations and strikes, and as the New Year in March 1963 approached, Khomeini issued a public statement that 'The Clergy Do Not Celebrate This Year' because the tyrannical regime was 'violating the sanctity of Islamic laws' and was about to draft 18-year-old girls into the army and force Muslims into the 'abyss of prostitution'.[12] This of course was nonsense, but never afraid to use Middle Eastern exaggeration Khomeini was simply underlining the central point of his campaign: that the Shah was betraying the identity of Iran. The Shah responded by threatening to deal with his enemies with 'the thunderous fist of justice'. Worshippers in Qom soon felt that fist when secret service intruders broke up a meeting in the courtyard of the Law College which ended with fatalities on both sides. Khomeini's movement had their first martyrs, and his language became harsher. Now the Shah was not only an enemy of Islam and an ally of the hated West, but was 'the successor of Genghis Khan', the loathed Mongol invader. As Muharram approached, the Shah's regime tried to ban all clerics from making political speeches, but Khomeini refused and used the occasion of Ahsura on 3 June to play on the religious and xenophobic passions of his listeners, identifying himself and his followers with the plight of Hussein at Karbala, and the Shah with Islam's enemies – America and Israel. His insults against the King reached new levels –

> You wretched, miserable man, forty five years of your life have passed. Isn't it time for you to think and reflect a little. You don't know . . . whether those who surround you will remain your friends. They are the friends of the dollar. They have no religion, no loyalty. O miserable man![13]

Not surprisingly Khomeini was arrested 2 days later. The hard-liners in the regime demanded his trial and execution, but the Shah held back. Massive demonstrations against the arrest swept across the country. At Veramin near Tehran 600 protesters were told to disperse by troops, but seeing themselves as modern-day followers of Hussein acting out Karbala they started to throw stones at the soldiers. The troops opened fire with machine guns, scores died and thousands then came out to mourn the victims. At a shrine in the south of Tehran, as many as 100,000 visited Ayatollah Shariatmadari as he sat weeping under a tree in the courtyard. In the face of such emotion the government backed down, Khomeini was released from prison, and even visited by Javad Sadr the Minister of the Interior. Khomeini had won a great victory, and it is interesting to note how the original cause for his protest had long been forgotten. Centre stage in 1963 was not female suffrage, but the fate of Iran's religious identity which according to Khomeini was another Hussein being betrayed and murdered by a new Yazid, the Shah.

Widening Khomeini's support

Till now most of Khomeini's support had come from fellow clerics and the traditional bazaaris, but he knew this was not enough to bring about an Islamic government, especially when his fellow Ayatollahs, Shariatmadari and Golpaygani, were much less zealous. He needed wider support and using the policy of dissimulation (taqiyya) he sought the backing of the secular opposition to the Shah – the nationalists, the liberals and Marxists – who had no clear leader. He would draw them into his camp, but keep quiet about his plans to establish a religious dictatorship. The Shah soon gave him an opportunity. In 1964 the government passed a bill giving all Americans diplomatic immunity for any civil or criminal act – and so handed Khomeini the perfect issue to unite secular and religious opposition under his leadership. As he said to a confident on hearing the news – 'All the world's freedom fighters will support us on this issue.'[14] On the occasion of the birthday of Fatimah, the prophet's daughter, Khomeini made a brilliant speech, accusing the Shah of selling out to the

Americans and reducing Iran to a colony. As usual he made sure his illustrations were extreme and vivid –

> They (the Shah's government) have reduced the Iranian people to a level lower than that of an American dog. If someone runs over a dog belonging to an American he will be prosecuted. Even if the Shah himself were to run over a dog belonging to an American he would be prosecuted. But if an American cook runs over the Shah, the head of State, no one will have the right to interfere with him.

Khomeini went on to identify himself as the true guardian of Iranian nationalism –

> If the religious leaders have influence they will not permit this nation to be the slaves of Britain one day, and America the next . . . they will not permit Israel to take over the Iranian economy.

And he ended by calling for God to overthrow the government –

> O God, destroy those individuals who are traitors to this land, . . . to Islam . . . to the Qoran.[15]

With this speech Khomeini now became a national political leader, speaking out for all Iranians wounded by Iran's relationship with America. A week afterwards he was arrested and sent into exile to Turkey instead of facing death. Fearing the wrath of his people, possibly Allah, and certainly loathe to have the blood of a martyred Ayatollah on his head Mohammad Reza Shah could not bring himself to sign Khomeini's death sentence. With Khomeini in exile, oil revenues rising, Lyndon Johnson a firm friend, the Shah though in the late 1960s and early 1970s seemed secure. Certainly he faced opposition both from the clergy and especially from the left, but supported by his security force SAVAK with reportedly 60,000 agents,[16] who had no qualms about using torture,[17] his enemies were soon silenced. As well as killing, arresting, torturing and exiling at least 600 clerics just in the 1970s,[18] the Shah also struck at their economic power by taking over the Endowments Organization which administered religious donations, and their intellectual influence by closing down their publishing houses. In 1976 he even created a new calendar based on the founding of the Persian Empire by Cyrus the Great, to replace the Islamic one which started from Mohammad's flight to Medina in AD 622. When he first came to power, the Shah was more moderate towards the clergy than his father had been; now he was just as determined to irrevocably modernize Iran's identity.

Ayatollah Khomeini was even more determined that Iran's identity would remain thoroughly Shia. Responding to constant petitions from clerics, human rights organizations and the United Nations, the Shah had allowed Khomeini to move to the holy city of Najaf in Iraq in 1965. Though he made little impact on Najaf itself, dominated by senior clerics such as Ayatollah Hakim, Khoi and Shahrudi, Khomeini was able to keep in close contact with his constituency in Iran. Hundreds of his former students and supporters came to visit him, and in the 1970s he started to give them cassette-tape recordings of his fiery sermons denouncing the Shah which they smuggled back into Iran. Here also he had very able lieutenants such as Khamanei and Rafsanjani who organized a network of cells called the Coalition of Islamic Societies. One of the ablest lieutenants was Morteza Motahhari whom Khomeini appointed as his official representative with authority to collect donations. Motahhari had great skill in public speaking both to the educated and others. He applied the Shia stories to contemporary politics, and used Ali as the reason why Muslims should not accept unjust rule. Perhaps more than any other Motahhari kept alive the flame of revolutionary Islam while Khomeini was in exile. Khomeini was also greatly helped by two great literary figures: Jalal Al-e Ahmad and Ali Shariati. Al-e Ahmad denounced the cultural alienation Iran was facing due to 'Westoxication', and as seen, called the country back to its Shia roots. He died suddenly in 1969, but his mantle was more than taken up by Ali Shariati. He built on Ahmad's theme of alienation, but went on to sharply distinguish between the Shiism of Ali, and the Shiism of the Safavids, by which he meant the Pahlavis. The former was passionate and pure, willing to work to create a just society; the latter was cowardly and corrupt, irresponsibly submitting to unjust rule.[19] The thousands of new students who ironically owed their education to the Pahlavis were electrified by Shariati, for here was a language of protest rooted in Iran's history, seemingly free from the secular notions of the European enlightenment or its illegitimate godless child, Marxism.

Though Khomeini loathed all forms of deviancies from Shia Islam,[20] and refused to call Shariati a martyr when he too suddenly died in 1979, he still benefited from the intellectual bridge Shariati had built between his vision of Islam and more left leaning students. Knowing he would need the support of the youth he used his time in Najaf to establish links with student bodies, especially the 40,000 who were studying abroad and would come back as the country's leaders. Khomeini made sure the religious students kept his name alive, not of course as the cleric who wanted to set up a religious dictatorship, but as the ageing hero in exile who constantly challenged the autocratic Shah. In 1974 the Shah gave up all pretence of progressivism and created a one-party state, telling Iranians to either join his party, 'Resurgence' or leave the country. A prosperous economy might have held back the protest Khomeini longed to lead, but in the late 1970s there was a recession and thousands of villagers who had arrived in the cities as a result of the Shah's land reform policies found their incomes dropping, or, as was the case for 400,000[21] construction workers in 1978, losing their jobs all together. This made the Shah more vulnerable.

The Shah: An easy target

If the Shah had been a charismatic patriotic monarch, seen to be serving his people, in touch with their pain, delighting in their culture, then much would be tolerated. However the Shah was an aloof, distant figure. Never a confident public speaker he was unable to rouse a crowd in the way Khomeini could, and after an assassination attempt in 1949 he was rarely seen in public. Rather than serving his people and sharing their pain, it seemed the Shah and his court were wasting inordinate amounts of money on self-indulgent living, epitomized in the extravagant celebrations he hosted in 1971 at Persepolis to commemorate 2,500 years of Persian monarchy. For 5 days foreign guests lived in tents with marble bathrooms and feasted on food and wine flown in from Maxim's of Paris. While Reza Shah lavishly entertained his guests, ordinary Iranians, who were not allowed near the celebrations, complained about its $200 million estimated cost, especially when there were food shortages in Sistan and Baluchistan provinces. A part of the Shah's aim was to re-identify Iran as a pre-Islamic civilization, but Cyrus and Darius understood there was a contract with the people whereby the ruler should provide justice for the ruled. The Persepolis celebrations and the constant pictures of the Shah and his family jet setting around the world suggested he was not keeping the contract. Their suspicions were more than confirmed later on in September 1978, when the Central Bank revealed that the Shah's most 13 senior military officers had sent more than $253 million out of the country. Conscripts were getting $1 a day.[22] Educated in Switzerland, put into power by the Americans, and now at ease sipping French wine with Europeans in the shadow of Persepolis, the Shah neither gave the impression of being patriotic, nor of delighting in traditional Iranian culture. Even more shocking for most ordinary Iranians was the way Western culture was being tolerated by his government. With the 20,000 Americans who arrived in the mid-1970's to support the Shah's military machine, came also mini skirts, rock music and pornographic films. In 1978 the whole country was stunned when a Brazilian dance troupe performed sex on stage at the Shiraz Arts Festival. One of the key supporters of this festival was Empress Fara, the Shah's wife.[23] To many Iranians it seemed the Shah was allowing the great and ancient Persian culture to be raped again.[24]

With this smell of greed, corruption and lust lingering over the uncharismatic 'American' monarch, he became an easier and easier target for his rival to attack, especially as Khomeini had all the qualities the Shah lacked. Khomeini was overwhelmingly charismatic, even more so because he was in exile; there was nothing remotely luxurious about his lifestyle and not a murmur of irregularity about his financial affairs, though millions of tomans came to him in donations; and he was born and bred in a traditional Iranian provincial town, enjoyed its culture, and had won respect from his own people through courage and hard work. By the mid-1970s there was no question as to which leader more closely represented the identity of Iran. With his lieutenants able to call on a massive network of mosques, and having used dissimulation to draw in much of the secular opposition which was especially active in universities, Khomeini was now in a position to bring people into the streets. It was the Shah who again virtually gift-wrapped the opportunity for him, helped by his ally the American president.

The Revolution begins

President Carter's public pronouncements in 1977 on the importance of human rights in US alliances scared the Shah into relaxing his government's iron grip on the country. In fact, concerned to keep oil prices down and maintain security for its intelligence collection sites on the Iran–Soviet border, President Carter had no intention of making life difficult for the Iranian monarch. This was made clear when the Shah visited Washington in November 1977. Relieved, the Shah set about dealing with his opponents in the usual manner so from Najaf, Khomeini castigated President Carter for hypocritically espousing a human rights policy that was only implemented when it suited America. With such a highly volatile situation the Shah's regime now lit a fuse that started the revolution. On 7 January, 1978 an anonymous editorial appeared in the government newspaper *Ettala'at* implying that Khomeini was 'a foreigner, an agent of the British, a drunkard, and a closet homo-sexual'.[25] This set off large demonstrations in Qom, and fatefully for the Shah's regime, his soldiers killed both students and mullahs. Isolated in his palaces, surrounded by a fawning court, the Shah had more firmly than ever identified himself with Yezid, the cruel killer of Ali for the Shiites, and stretching further back to Iran's Zoroastrian era, he was the king, who had lost the *farr*, the sign of divine favour. So even Iranians who did not naturally support Khomeini, this vicious insulting of an old religious teacher and the reckless killing of his followers now drew them to him as the most legitimate symbol of opposition to the Shah. With this article and the killings at Qom the Shah sealed his defeat in the battle for Iran's soul.

Khomeini and his allies now used the Shia mourning cycles, especially the *arba'een*, the 40-day anniversary, for the victims at Qom to bring out thousands of demonstrators onto the streets across the country, both in the major cities, and the small towns and villages.[26] At each major demonstration there were more fatalities, for example, in Tabriz troops killed at least 19 (opponents claim 432) and injured 100 (opponents claim 1,500), and this set of another cycle of 40-day anniversaries. On 29 March there were demonstrations in 55 cities, and on 10 May in 24. Then on 19 August arsonists locked all the doors of the crowded Cinema Rex in Abadan and set the building alight: 377 were killed. Despite the fact that Islamists had burnt down other cinemas, most Iranians, with a penchant for conspiracy theories, believed the Abadan attack was the work of SAVAK because all news like this took time to be reported as it had to pass through so many censors. However this news was immediately printed across the country, so proving in many people's minds it was ordered by the government. So rotten was its reputation it was easily assumed they would burn people alive to turn the nation against Khomeini. Crowds of nearly half a million now gathered in Tehran demanding 'Death to the Pahlavis' and 'Khomeini is our leader'.

As in a game of chess when final defeat depends on making terrible moves till your opponent says check mate, so the Shah continued to make dreadful political mistakes. With Tehran awash with demonstrators the Shah still thought he could solve the problem with the bullet. On 7 September he imposed martial law, but many did not hear the order and on the 8th around 20 – 25,000 demonstrators took to the streets. Under orders to break up all demonstrations, Major General Oveisi's troops used live ammunition. Blood flowed, hundreds died and the Shias had yet another Karbala. Reportedly crying at a cabinet meeting after the massacre and then sacking the prime minister, the Shah looked more pathetic and vacillating than ever and opposition to his rule now spread further throughout the country. Thinking that Khomeini was able to influence events in Iran too closely by being in Najaf, the Shah got Saddam Hussein to expel him,[27] and allowed him to go to Paris. This was another terrible mistake. From Paris Khomeini could actually control events more. He had better telephone contact with his disciples, and greater access to the world's media who made pilgrimages to his house in Neauphle-le Chateau to interview him.[28] Sometimes there were as many as 400 journalists on 1 day.[29] While the Shah made mistakes, Khomeini continued to make brilliant moves. After the September 8th massacre he immediately exploited the ever widening support for the opposition and ordered a national strike. By mid-October the country was at a standstill, with even the Shah's palaces lacking fuel. By early November the government was losing $74 millions a day in oil revenue. In response to the Shah's belated offer of becoming a constitutional monarch, an idea countenanced by other religious leaders such as Ayatollahs Shariatmadari, Golpaygani and Najafi-Mar'ashi, Khomeini was single-mindedly dismissive. The only future Khomeini sanctioned for the Shah was abdication followed by an Islamic trial. In the war for Iran's identity, compromise was never on Khomeini's agenda.

The end and the beginning

Fittingly the final end for the Shah came during Muharram, the month when all Shias mourn the death of Hussein at Karbala. As it started on 2 December, a curfew descended on all Iran's cities: but they could not be enforced. Rather than stay inside, young men preferred to die for the Iranian identity they believed in, and that was Hussein. So they donned white burial shrouds and dared the army to act. Instead of shooting though, up to a thousand conscripts a day were deserting, and despite calls in his inner circle for ruthless repression, the Shah, dying of cancer, was unwilling to bequeath to his son a blood-bath. So the crowds grew again and by the time Ashura came on 10 and 11 December about nine million were demonstrating across the country, two million in Tehran alone.[30] All were shouting 'Allah Akbar, Khomeini Rahbar' (Allah is Great, Khomeini is our leader). Unwilling to order a crackdown, all that was left for the Shah to do was to arrange his departure. He sacked the military government, and appointed Shapoor Bakhtiar, a veteran liberal democrat politician, to form a new government while he prepared for a 'vacation'. The Shah left the country he had ruled since he was 21 years old on 16 January 1979. Just before he boarded

> his silver and blue Boeing 707, a colonel of the Imperial Guard threw himself at his monarch's feet, kissed his shoes, and pleaded with him to stay. The Shah bent down and spoke a few words. When he rose, the face of the Kings of Kings held the agony of the moment.[31]

The Shah had lost the battle for Iran's identity. Apart from his elite and some of the rich living in the fashionable boulevards of the north of Tehran, the country had rejected his vision of a modern, secular Iran which came with the price of a military dictatorship and dependence on the West. Instead they preferred Iran's historic religious identity which was now going to be used in a radically new way.

As the Shah flew towards Cairo, so a line from Hafiz was passed around – 'When the demon departs, the angel shall arrive.' Nobody knows how many came to welcome Khomeini on 1 February, estimates vary from 1 to 3 million. The size of the crowd though did not go to Khomeini's head, instead he focused on what the revolution was all about – Iran's identity as a Shia nation. So after a very short statement at Tehran airport he went straight to the city's main cemetery to say prayers and give a speech by the gravesides of the martyrs to the revolution. Unlike the Shah who was always seen sitting in his palatial surroundings, Khomeini, well understanding the power of pictures, knelt on the bare earth and identified himself immediately with the heart of the Shia faith: a 'shahid', a martyr. And from here he made his appeal to the army to come back 'to the bosom of the nation'. It did not take them long. On 9 February the technicians at the Doshan Tappeh Air Force base known as the *homafars* gave their formal salute to the Imam. Furious the Shah's Imperial Guards attacked airbases around Tehran and there was a full-scale battle, with the *homafars* receiving considerable support from both the Mojahadin-e Khalq and the People's Fed'iyan. Elsewhere police stations and army barracks were attacked and weapons stolen. The army imposed a curfew which Khomeini ordered the people to ignore, and then he made his final move to secure power. He threatened all out 'jihad' with any army unit that did not surrender. The next day

General Gharebaghi announced the army would be neutral in 'political disputes' and ordered his troops back into their barracks. The revolution was over.

In 1979 there was no competition between the Shah and Khomeini in terms of who appealed to an identity that most Iranians preferred. At the end of his reign the Shah had ruled so harshly he had managed to destroy the identity for Iran that he epitomized. Nearly 30 years on some might argue that the impact of Khomeini and his successor Khamanei has also damaged the Iranian religious identity they represent. It is to this question we now must turn.

Notes

[1] Baqer Moin, *Khomeini: Life of the Ayatollah*, Thomas Dunne Books, 1999, p. 202.

[2] See Chapter 1, p. 21. Khomeini obviously felt the climate created by Reza Shah personally. He complained in 'Secrets Exposed' that nobody was now even willing to give a cleric a lift in their car, and if they were, any fault that occurred in the car was blamed on the mullah.

[3] 'Dissimulation is my path and the path of my forefathers' is what he once told a friend when challenged about this.

[4] Moin, *Khomeini: Life of the Ayatollah*, p. 60.

[5] Nikki R. Keddie, *Modern Iran*, Yale University Press, 2003, p. 192.

[6] Keddie, *Modern Iran*, p. 193.

[7] In October 2006 Ayatollah Borujderdi's son, Hossain, who is also an Ayatollah, was arrested by the Iranian government and detained in Evin prison for arguing against Khomeini's doctrine of Velayat-e Faqih.

[8] Moin, *Khomeini: Life of the Ayatollah*, p. 75.

[9] Moin, *Khomeini: Life of the Ayatollah*, p. 80.

[10] Kenneth M. Pollack, *The Persian Puzzle*, Random House, 2004, p. 81.

[11] Pollack, *The Persian Puzzle*, p. 88. The Bahai's were a nineteenth-century offshoot of Islam, loathed by the Shia devout.

[12] Moin, *Khomeini: Life of the Ayatollah*, p. 90.

[13] Moin, *Khomeini: Life of the Ayatollah*, p. 104.

[14] Moin, *Khomeini: Life of the Ayatollah*, p. 122.

[15] Moin, *Khomeini: Life of the Ayatollah*. Much of the speech is quoted on pp. 122–127.

[16] Robert Fisk, *The Great War for Civilisation*, Harper Perennial, London, New York, 2006, p. 201.

[17] Torture methods included attaching electrical wires to the genitals, beatings on the soles of the feet, nail extraction, 'cooking' strapped down suspects on electrified beds, burning the nipples of females with cigarettes, rape and placing snakes on prisoners bodies. See Fisk, *The Great War for Civilisation*, p. 121.

[18] Pollack, *The Persian Puzzle*, p. 119.

[19] For a more detailed contrast between Ali and Safavid Shiism see Keddie, *Modern Iran*, pp. 203–204.

[20] 'I despise these treacherous groups, whether communist or Marxist, or deviant from the Shia faith under whatever name or title and I consider them traitors to the country, to Islam, and Shiism.' Moin, *Khomeini: Life Of The Ayatollah*.

[21] Pollack, *The Persian Puzzle*, p. 120.

[22] See Dilip Hiro, *Iran Today*, Politicos, London, 2006, pp. 125–126.

[23] Mackey, *The Iranians*, p. 261.

[24] One of Azar Nafisi's students said America, 'was the Great Satan because of its sinister assault on the very roots of our culture'. Azar Nafisi, *Reading Lolita in Tehran*, Fourth Estate, New York, 2004, p. 126.

[25] Pollack, *The Persian Puzzle*, p. 127.

[26] 'While left wing and Mosaddeqish groups had more influence in the industrial and urban areas . . . the countryside was totally Khomeini's'. Moin, *Khomeini: Life of the Ayatollah*, p. 194.

[27] Saddam was happy to let Khomeini go, as there was always the danger Khomeini would stir up Iraq's Shias. Later Saddam always said that one of the greatest mistakes of his life was not executing the radical cleric.

[28] For a wonderful description of the atmosphere in the house and one such interview see Elaine Sciolino's *Persian Mirrors*, Free Press, New York, 2005, pp. 48–52.

[29] Moin, *Khomeini: Life of the Ayatollah*, p. 192.

[30] Nearly every book about this day has a different estimate, so Baqer Moin has 17 million across the country and 2 to 3 million in Tehran. Nobody knows – but it was enough people to convince the Shah he had to go or order a bloody crackdown.

[31] Mackay, *The Iranians*, p. 283.

Chapter 5

War

Under Ayatollah Khomeini Iran experienced a lot of war and many people died before their 3 score years and 10. Inside Iran all opposition to the Islamic Republic was eliminated, most of it by terror; outside there was military action in the Gulf and Lebanon; and with Iraq, Iran waged the longest war of the twentieth century. The dominance of conflict entrenched the Islamic Revolution in power: it also raised questions about the religion in whose name it happened.

War with the Royalists and Liberals

Very few Iranians who supported Khomeini when he arrived back in 1979 had read his theory of *Velayat-e Faqih*: for them he was the only hero who could oust the hated Shah. In Paris he had shrewdly kept quiet about the *Velayat-e Faqih* and talked more about a 'progressive Islam' promising the new Islamic Republic 'would ensure freedom, independence, and justice.'[1] Also in Paris the press saw him with people like Bani-Sadr, Ebrahim Yazdi or Sadegh Ghotbzadeh, western educated, suit wearing Islamists called 'neckties' by journalists. So it was assumed that Khomeini would be a guide and real power would rest with these 'neckties'. Once back in Iran this assumption continued as Khomeini chose Mehdi Bazargan, a French educated engineer and former Mossadeq aide, as his first prime minister. However the words Khomeini used when appointing[2] Bazargan should have made careful listeners wary about this assumption that others would rule. He said – 'I hereby pronounce Bazargan as the Ruler, and since I have appointed him, he must be obeyed. Opposing this government means opposing the Shari'a of Islam . . . Revolt against God is blasphemy.'[3] Bazargan 'must be obeyed' because Ayatollah Khomeini, acting as the *Velayat-e Faqih* had appointed him. Khomeini, not Bazargan, is the new king, the ruler in touch with God, or for the more sceptical, a religious dictator: 'the short, balding, and bespectacled'.[4] Bazargan was just a temporary tool of convenience. This reality became clear as the revolution clamoured for revenge against the royalists. Bazargan was determined the rule of law should prevail. He wanted proper courts with juries, defence lawyers and trained judges. However in Khomeini's mind a man was not tried by a group of 12 peers, a Western tradition, but by the law of Islam and the only people who could interpret Islam correctly were the clergy. Khomeini was also a pragmatic politician. He knew his own constituency wanted violent punishment for the royalists and he did not want to be swept aside by this rage: he wanted to lead it. Also many feared that Washington would try and reinstall the monarchy, as they had done in 1953. So royalists were not just defeated foes: they were potentially dangerous collaborators.

The royalists then were not for the likes of Bazargan to deal with and Ayatollah Khomeini turned to one of his trusted students, Sheikh Sadeq Khalkhali[5] and appointed him the head of the Revolutionary Courts. Khalkhali turned a classroom at the Rafeh School where Khomeini's entourage had based themselves into an improvised courtroom and on 15 February four generals, including an ex SAVAK chief General Nassiri, were 'tried' and found guilty. They were then taken to the roof of the school and shot. In the next few months at least two hundred other royalists were executed, including the Shah's longest serving Prime Minister, Amir Abbas Hoveida.[6] Bazargan was appalled, and speaking for all liberal democrats, appeared on TV to condemn these kangaroo courts. But Khomeini's version of justice, as led by Khalkhali, was spreading throughout Iran. After dealing with the royalists, Khalkhali moved on to treat Kurdish rebels and drug dealers with Islamic justice before he was removed from office in December 1980 due to irregularities in his official accounts. Still, in less than 2 years it is estimated he had ordered the execution of nearly 8,000 people.[7] One of these 8,000 was a 14-year-old boy from Baluchistan. As Khalkhali was leaving at the end of his day's work, he was told that the boy had been completely innocent, to which Khalkhali responded, 'Well if he was innocent he had gone to heaven; and if he was guilty he deserved to die.'[8] Khalkhali was clearly disturbed: it was rumoured one of his favourite past-times was killing cats – hence one of his nicknames was 'Gorbeh', cat, and once when asked how he felt about the decrease in the number of executions by journalists, Khalkhali had chuckled and replied 'I feel hungry'.[9] Khalkhali never felt any remorse for his role in this reign of terror. He believed that as a Hojatoislam, one rank below an Ayatollah in the Shia ranks, he had the right to exercise judgment, once saying – 'The most important thing in Islamic justice is the wisdom of the judge . . . Even if a man decides against him, it means nothing if the judge decides otherwise.'[10] Regarding the royalists and those involved in SAVAK he also believed, probably rightly, that he was representing the will of the millions who had demonstrated against the Shah: 'I issued judgment and acted as the conscience of 35 million people' he once said.[11] And for every death sentence he handed out, he believed he was supported by Ayatollah Khomeini under whose picture the Revolutionary Courts sat. In an interview with a French magazine *Le Figaro* he stated this clearly. Asked if he should be charged with crimes against humanity, his reply was – 'No. It is not possible. If I had acted wrongly, Imam Khomeini would have told [me]. I only did what he asked me to do.'[12]

Those who had longed for the rule of law looked to Bazargan to intervene, but, in his own words, he was a 'knife without a blade'.[13] For Khomeini made sure that real power rested with revolutionary institutions that reported to him, and left the more normal, but powerless ones, to Bazargan. So the Revolutionary Courts emerged to operate alongside the normal courts; alongside local government and the police, there were the Komitehs and Hezbollah, the Party of God. The Komitehs operated out of local mosques and were – and still are – essentially vigilante groups, while the Hezbollah are really organized armed gangs, more than able to enforce the will of the Komiteh. The military had declared its neutrality, but as the Shah had personally appointed all its senior members from the rank of major upwards, Khomeini was wary about their loyalty. As well as executing 85 senior officers between February and September 1979, and purging another 12,000 by September 1980,[14] Khomeini's regime also established the Revolutionary Guards to be a parallel military force. It was started in May 1979, and drew 6,000 recruits: by the end of the year it had over 100,000. At the start of the revolution much of the activity of these groups was spontaneous, but soon they were brought under the authoritarian political control of the Islamic Republic Party (IRP) established with Khomeini's blessing by one of his most trusted students, Mohammad Hosseini Beheshti, who had already proved himself a very skilled organizer as a leading light in the Coalition of Islamic Societies in the 1960s.

While these powerful groups, wholly loyal to the revolution, swiftly gained strength, Khomeini made moves to legitimize his doctrine of *Velayat-e Faqih*. He knew there would be much reservation about this, so he proceeded in two stages. First he pushed for a referendum solely on the question of whether the people wanted an Islamic Government. Bazargan, opposed to a clerical dictatorship, argued for a choice between a religious and a secular government. Khomeini refused as he only wanted to use the referendum to give the appearance of popular support. For Khomeini it was all theatre and one of its most ironical aspects was that Khomeini himself, who had accused the Shah of betraying Islam for giving women the vote, now encouraged them to go to the polling booth. It was their Islamic duty. Once in the booth the people just had to say 'yes' or 'no' to the question – 'Do you want an Islamic Republic?' They had no idea what the constitution of this Islamic Republic would be, and many naively hoped it would be democratic, especially as this was the impression the IRP had given.[15] Not surprisingly 97 per cent voted 'Yes'. Khomeini was now ready to move on to the second stage of his plan, defining the Islamic Republic so that the *Velayat-e Faqih* was the dominant figure. While in Paris the modernists had drawn up a draft constitution which made no mention of the *Velayat-e Faqih*, and this was duly published, with Khomeini's blessing, in June 1979. Bazargan then made plans for there to be elections to a 300 strong Constituent Assembly which would take the final decision on its details. The naïve hope of democracy was still in the air. Without any consultation with Bazargan, the Revolutionary Council, made up of 16 Khomeini loyalists, now declared that the constitution would not be decided by the Constituent Assembly, but by a much smaller group of 72 (the number of the slain at Karbala), to be known as the Assembly of Experts. Elections were set for 3 August, and the Khomeinists worked hard to ensure it was dominated by clerics, which it was. Some say the elections were rigged.[16] More confident that he could finally end his forced and deceitful marriage of convenience with the liberal democrats Khomeini's language became threatening, and in the street Hezhbollah were let loose on their supporters. Regarding those who were against the Assembly of Experts, Khomeini called them, 'misguided people' and even more ominously as 'enemies of Islam'. Realizing the Assembly of Experts would officially give Iran a religious dictatorship the National Democratic Front organized a massive demonstration on 12 August, the anniversary of the CIA coup against Mossadeq. It was violently attacked by Hezbollah thugs, as were its offices. That same month over 40 newspapers were also closed by order of Tehran's Revolutionary prosecutor. The Prague Spring was truly over, war with the liberals had begun, and Khomeini's comment to his detractors was, 'When we want, we can throw you into the dustbin of death.'[17]

The Assembly of Experts completely revised the modernists' draft constitution and while the legislative and executive wings of the government were similar to what one would find in the West, the Assembly of Experts had made sure that all real power rested with clerics. There was an elected president, and members of parliament, but all candidates and all legislation could be vetoed by an unelected 12-man Council of Guardians which was appointed by the *Velayat-e Faqih*, to whom every area of government – the legislature, the judiciary, the military – had to submit.[18] As a foregone conclusion, Ayatollah Khomeini was declared the *Velayat-e Faqih* on 14 October 1979. Now to completely rout the liberal democrats, Khomeini needed Bazargan to resign, and for the people to vote for this new constitution. The resignation came after Bazargan found his government completely powerless when radical students invaded the American embassy and took the staff hostage in early November in response to the US government allowing the dying Shah to enter their country for medical treatment. Bazargan's demands for their release met an overwhelming silence from Khomeini so he had no choice but to resign. Then, as Sandra Mackay colourfully puts it, Khomeini 'whipped the fifty-two American hostages to win his definition of the Iranian state'.[19] For with the US Embassy constantly in the news, the heart of the revolution – fighting the wicked Shah and his American backers – was kept at the forefront of people's minds. Just after Ashura, on 1 and 2 December, the constitution was approved by a 99.5 per cent margin. Sixteen million had voted for an Islamic theocracy.

War with the Mojahedin

In the war for control of Iran after the revolution, the royalists had either fled or been executed, while the liberals had first been duped and then outmanoeuvred.

Khomeini though had other opponents, most notably the Mojahedin, who were not shy to shed blood. From their founding in the mid-1960s as an opposition group to the Shah advocating a mix of Islam and Marxism, the Mojahedin Khalq (People's Combatants) had advocated violence. In the 1960s and 1970s they murdered a number of royalist officials, as well as seven American technicians. Active supporters of Khomeini as the man to oust the Shah, they had played a crucial military role on 8 February fighting against the Imperial Guard. They were also involved in the seizure of the American embassy, again showing their penchant for violence by demanding the execution of all the hostages. They themselves occupied the American consulates in Isphahan and Tabriz. Having given such support, they expected at least a seat for their leader Massoud Rajavi, at the ruling table. There was no such seat. Instead Khomeini let it be known that he considered them as being 'monahfaghin' (hypocrites), 'contaminated with the Western plague . . . trying to mix Islam and Marxism',[20] his lieutenants were ordered to make sure all Mojahedin influences were kept out of the Revolutionary Guards, and in January 1980 Massoud Rajavi was barred from being a candidate in the presidential elections stipulated by the new constitution. At this point the Mojahedin went underground and into official opposition against Khomeini. With active groups throughout the country, they enjoyed considerable support, especially among students, and with a charismatic and determined leader who inspired total loyalty among his followers, they had everything to fight for. The battle began in earnest when Khomeini thwarted the presidency of Bani Sadr who had won 75 per cent of the vote under the new constitution by supporting the IRP party. Bani Sadr called this tantamount to 'committing suicide'[21] and in reply parliament impeached him. While Bani Sadr, and Massoud Rajavi went into hiding, eventually escaping to Paris, the Mojahedin foot soldiers came out onto the street. As with the rallies against the Shah there is no agreement on the actual numbers. The Mojahedin say that on 20 June 1 million demonstrated against the dictatorship across the country, with 500,000 in Tehran;[22] the government said 100,000. It was met with ruthless violence. The Revolutionary Guards opened fire on the crowds, at least 20 died, and a thousand were arrested. The Mojahedin responded with a devastating bombing and assassination campaign. During his Friday sermon 27 June 1981, Iran's present Supreme Leader, Ali Khamanei lost the use of his right arm when a small explosive planted in a tape recorder went off. Then next day a massive bomb hidden in a rubbish bin during a routine morning meeting exploded at the IRP main offices. Of the 93, 70 were killed, including the party's leader and effectively the second most powerful man in the country, Ayatollah Beheshti. The government immediately made the official number murdered as 72 to correspond with the number who died with Hussein at Karbala. At their grave-side, Ayatollah Khomeini blamed the Mojahedin. Having no theology of forgiveness, he publicly damned them – 'You are breathing your last breath – you are going to hell.'[23] The Mojahedin responded by saying they could put a bomb under the Imam's bed, but would not as they wanted to make him face a trial.[24] That autumn they

assassinated about a thousand radical clerics and government officials throughout the country, including the newly elected President Raja'i, his prime minister
and three other officials. The constant cry of the huge crowd who accompanied
their coffins to join Beheshti and others was 'Revenge, Revenge, Revenge'.[25]

It was ferocious. Khomeini's regime gave the Revolutionary Guards and Courts
complete freedom to do whatever was necessary to eliminate the Mojahedin.[26]
To round up as many suspects as possible the regime encouraged neighbours
and families to spy on each other. Once arrested suspects faced the same
cavalier approach to justice as pioneered by Khalkhali. So for just possessing a
piece of Mojahedin literature, young students could be sentenced to 20 years
imprisonment. Many others were sentenced to death: some went before the
firing squad, but many others were hung in groups on scaffolding, cranes, and
even in one case on the cross bar of a set of children's swings – a macabre photo
opportunity for the media. Nobody knows exactly how many were arrested
or executed in this reign of terror. Amnesty International say 2,500 were executed by the end of 1981;[27] others say 5,000;[28] the Mojahedin claim a total of
7,746 were killed if one includes violence at demonstrations and extra-judicial
killings.[29] By the end of 1982 the war in Iran was over. Nearly all Mojahedin
activists were either dead, or in prison – or in exile where they were very active.
From Paris they immediately began making contacts with Saddam Hussein who
had invaded Iran in September 1980, and in 1986 they moved their headquar-
ters to Iraq, and their military wing fought with the Iraqis against their fellow
Iranians. Just days after Iran ended the war with Iraq in July 1988, Rajavi ordered
several thousand of his soldiers in Iraq to invade Iran for operation 'Eternal
Light', fancifully telling them that all the people would rise up in welcome
and travel with them to Tehran.[30] This was nonsense as Iranians loathed the
Mojahedin for siding with Saddam Hussein, but Rajavi's followers believed
it and invaded with equipment most of them did not know how to use.[31] They
were either slain or beaten back. The Iranian government said it killed 4,800
combatants, while the Mojahedin said the number of their dead was 1,304.[32]
This fiasco had terrible repercussions inside Iran, not least because Rajavi in his
far-fetched talks had referred to Mojahedin prisoners in Iran playing a liberating role. The regime, already vulnerable due to the public disquiet about
the Iraq war, sent a three-man committee, armed with a letter from Ayatollah
Khomeini, to tour Iran's prisons and decide on the fate of all the Mojahedin
sympathizers who had been arrested in 1981 and 1982. Much of the details
of their *modus operandi* became known due to the public protests of Ayatollah
Khomeini's designated successor, Ayatollah Montazeri. According to him this
committee were not easily persuaded that a suspect had had a change of heart.
According to one report one young man was asked –

'Are you willing to go to the war front and fight the Iraqis?' He answered yes.
Subsequently, the prisoner was asked: 'Are you willing to walk over a mine field?'

The prisoner answered, 'Not everyone is willing to walk over a mine field.' Following this exchange, it was determined that the prisoner is still a believer in his cause.[33]

Again the exact number of those executed is not known. Ayatollah Montazeri put the figure between 2,800 and 3,800; opposition activists said they had the names of over 4,000; and Rajavi claimed it was over 12,000.[34] Even after their absurd invasion, the Mojahedin still dreamed of power. They stayed allied to Saddam Hussein and took part in his murderous campaign against the Shiites in the south of Iraq after the second Gulf War. They also carried out a few bomb attacks in Iran, including one on Khomeini's mausoleum near Tehran which risked the lives of civilians. However after the debacle of the failed invasion in 1988 support really began to ebb away. The movement turned more in on itself and took on the characteristics of a religious cult. Indeed the Iranian journalist Amir Taheri calls them the 'most ruthless sects seen in the last century' and detailed how a Mojahed could not go to the cinema, watch TV, listen to the radio, or even read a book or the Koran without their leader's permission.[35] Masoud Bani-Sadi, a cousin of the ousted president, and for many years a very senior member of the Mojahedin, gives the same impression in his book *Memoirs of an Iranian Rebel*.[36] So intense was their control of its members that people were asked to confess their private sexual urges, and senior leaders were even ordered to divorce their spouses to be freer to love the movement.[37]

Due to its sheer public brutality, this war against the Mojahedin has had a major impact on the Iranian psyche as nearly everyone in the 1980s either had a friend, or acquaintance, or had at least heard of someone in their neighbourhood who was executed. There were many macabre stories – of Revolutionary Guards raping virgins to stop them going to heaven, their supposed reward in the Islamic tradition; or bodies being drained of blood for the war effort. The age of these 'enemies' adds painful poignancy: they were mostly in their early twenties, or teenagers, and at least one who was just 10 years old.[38] Many of them were simply swept up in the very revolutionary fervour that Khomeini himself had created, and in their youthful idealism had been attracted to a more socialist interpretation of Islam. Many were imprisoned for just having Mojahedin literature, and then later in 1988 executed unless they said they wanted to walk across mine fields. A tragic and typical example was Fuad, the young brother-in-law of the Nobel Prize winner Shirin Ebadi. In 1982 he was a 'sweet seventeen year old, enchanted with the revolution's idealism . . .'. Then, 'for the crime of selling newspapers Fuad was sentenced to twenty years imprisonment'. In 1988 the family received a phone call to report to Evin Prison. Shirin Ebadi's husband, Javad, went the next day with an uncle – 'It wasn't hard to find the right office: they just followed the path of ashen and sobbing relatives. "Here" said the prison marshal, handing Javed a bag. "These are your brother's possessions. He has been executed."'[39] Unlike Khomeini's war against the royalists, all this brutality had nothing to do with securing Iran's Islamic identity, as the Mojahedin were just as strictly Islamic as the Khomeinists. It was solely about the power to interpret Islam and this civil war made clear that to establish a particular view of Islam, violence had the last word.

War with the communists

The final internal enemy to be destroyed were the communists, who were mainly associated with the Tudeh (Masses) party. After the 1953 anti-communist coup, the Shah used SAVAK to demolish the party, and about 2,000 were arrested.[10] In the 1960s a group of students left the Tudeh Party and formed the Marxist-Leninist People's Fadaiyan Guerrilla Organization who believed that acts of terror against the Pahlavi regime would awake the revolutionary desires of the working classes. As poor people crowded into appalling slums, and the number of factory strikes increased in the 1970s, it might seem that these parties, some still supported by the Soviets, posed a greater threat to Khomeini than the Mojahedin. But Khomeini knew their creed had never taken root in Iran; that the Soviets were hated as much as the British for occupying the country; and that with over 80 different groups[11] emerging after the revolution they had no effective unity. Khomeini borrowed the anti-imperialistic language of communism when it suited him, and with this he duped the left into thinking that he deserved their support,[12] but his main appeal was always to people's religious nationalism. Compared to the Mojahedin who drew on Shia roots, Khomeini did not view the communists as such a serious threat.

Nevertheless he dealt with them with shrewdness. Inspired by a fanciful view of history where the rule of the proletariat was inevitable, communists gave themselves wholeheartedly to Khomeini's revolution, assuming that once the working classes had risen up, so their superstitious Ayatollahs would be swept aside.[13] Khomeini, ever pragmatic, was ready to have their support at the beginning of the revolution, and was then very skilful when he turned against socialism. To the dismay of radical communists he persuaded the Tudeh Party to act as collaborators and give contact details to the regime about both the Fadaiyan and Mojahedin cells.[14] They claimed that Khomeini had to be supported for his defiant rejection of Western imperialism, but behind this rhetoric lay the grubby issue of power and dominating the left. Blinded by ambition, they never saw that Khomeini would dispense with them once they had served their purpose. This came with the defeat of the Mojahedin at the end of 1982. The Tudeh Party dared to criticize Khomeini's policy of taking the war into Iraq. They were easily crushed. The senior leaders fled into exile, while up to 5,000 foot soldiers went before Islamic firing squads.[15]

When Khomeini died in 1988 only his eyes gazed out at Iranians from thousands of murals and posters. He had no rivals. His victory in the war for domestic control was total. However it had come at a price: for behind those eyes were at least 20,000 Iranians who had been executed in the name of his revolution. Every Iranian knows that the message of Khomeini was ultimately: 'Agree with my Islam, or die.' Furthermore his method of victory was marked by constant deception. For a politician this was perhaps normal: but Khomeini never saw himself as a mere politician. He was the Imam, the Spiritual Leader, the only man who could interpret God's law. And yet this Imam steeped in Islamic law, deceived the liberal democrats, the Mojahedin, the Tudeh Party and every Iranian in 1979 who dreamed of creating a society where the rule of law would be above the word of a dictator. This is now history, but it is not forgotten and might well impact the Iranian identity's relationship with Shia Islam.

War in the Gulf and Lebanon

Even before Khomeini had fully established his own power in Iran, he declared war on the whole non-Muslim world. He said in March 1980 that, 'We shall export our revolution to the whole world. Until the cry "There is no God but God resounds over the whole world there will be struggle."'[46] This was not idle talk and his regime immediately started to spread their revolution in its own region – to Saudi Arabia, the Gulf States, Lebanon, and of course Iraq.

With excessively wealthy Sunni monarchs, propped up by the West, and ruling over often impoverished Shias, Saudi Arabia and the Gulf States were the immediate targets for the revolution. A training camp for small arms and explosive use was set up in Tehran for Gulf Shia extremists and in 1979 and 1980 Iran supported Shia uprisings in Saudi Arabia; in 1981 150 Shias with links to Tehran attempted to overthrow the government in Bahrain; in 1983 there was a similar coup attempt in Qatar and there was a bombing campaign in Kuwait; and also that year Khomeini called for an Islamic uprising during the Haj in Mecca. His designated deputy, Ayatollah Montazeri publicly called the house of Saud a 'bunch of pleasure seekers' and Satanic, asking, 'How long must Satan rule in the house of God?'[47] The Iranians started annually agitating in Mecca and in 1987 their demonstration resulted in over 400 deaths and many were hurt, including Khomeini's wife Batoul. The Iranians blamed the Saudis and next day their embassies were attacked.

Iran's activities in the Gulf were unsettling, but ultimately unsuccessful in changing the status quo. This was not the case in the Lebanon where the arrival of 1,000 Revolutionary Guards in Baalbeck in the summer of 1982 radically changed the unjust situation for the Shia population. Though the majority, they were accorded less power in the constitution than the Sunnis and the Christians, but their secular politicians had achieved little. Khomeini's soldiers were determined to change this. They also relished the chance of confronting both Israeli and American influence in the country. With many of the Shias feeling oppressed and looking for more extremist causes, and with a number of mullahs having studied under Khomeini in Najaf, the Iranians were welcomed, especially as they also set up social services nobody else was providing. Soon they had doubled their number through local recruitment as well as drawing in other radical groups under the overall leadership of a party called 'Hizballah'. The character of Baalbeck changed – posters of Khomeini appeared everywhere, bars were closed down, women wore veils and the mosque buzzed with extremist preaching. Locals called it 'Little Tehran'.

By 1983 the grievances of the Shias had grown much worse. Maronite Christians had massacred thousands of Palestinians in the Sabra and Satilla refugee camps in retaliation for the assassination of their leader Bashir Gemayel, but America still recognized Gemayel's brother as the head of the Lebanese government, and then asked him to sign a peace treaty with Israel which was completely unacceptable to most Muslims in the region, including Hizballah. Their violence made the Americans retreat. On 18 April, before the signing of the treaty, a truck bomb killed 63 people outside the American Embassy in West Beirut, including 17 Americans. The treaty was still forced through, but on 23 October, in response to the US shelling of Muslim positions, a suicide bomber drove a massive truck bomb into the US Marine complex in Beirut, killing 241 Marines. Another bomb exploded near the French compound where 57 died. Ten days later another truck attacked a building in Tyre housing Israeli soldiers, killing 29. It took the FBI 3 years to confirm that the axle of the Mercedes Benz truck used in the attack against the Marines had come from an assembly plant in Iran, but long before everyone knew that Tehran was behind the bombings.[48] The Americans now withdrew, first underground, then to ships, and then finally they left Lebanon as Hizballah and the Syrians drove the Maronites out of West Beirut. This was a victory for Khomeini's revolution. His soldiers had radicalized the Shia of Lebanon, and humiliated the Great Satan (USA), and the Little Satan (Israel). Though some Iranians grumbled at the funds going to the Lebanon when they themselves were hard pressed, nevertheless Khomeini's policy was generally considered a success.

War with Iraq

There was no sense of success at the end of Khomeini's most ambitious project to export the revolution. Instead Iran was left traumatized with 300–400,000 dead, and at least half a million wounded.[49] It is easily assumed that Saddam Hussein started the Iran–Iraq war. Tempted by the disarray the revolution had inflicted on Iran's armed forces, the lucrative prize of oil fields in the neighbouring Iranian province of Khuzestan, and the opportunity to establish himself as the undisputed leader of the Arab world, Saddam made an unprovoked attack. Saddam though was neither the aggressor nor the perpetuator of this 8-year-long war: it was Ayatollah Khomeini. Saddam Hussein stood for everything Khomeini loathed; indeed he was a reincarnation of his worst enemy, Reza

Shah. Like the first Pahlavi king, Saddam was an upstart soldier who had won political power by violence; he was avowedly secular; he courted both the USA and Soviet Union; and he oppressed not just the majority Shias in Iraq, but all Shias everywhere by his control of their holy sites, Najaf and Karbala. In Khomeini's mind, Saddam Hussein had no right to exist.[50]

As soon as Khomeini appointed Bazargan's government, Saddam assured Tehran of Iraq's friendliness and invited the new prime minister to Baghdad. The invitation was rejected and Tehran recalled its ambassador, consistently insulted Saddam Hussein, calling him a 'puppet of Satan' and 'mentally ill',[51] condemned the government as no more than a military clique, and openly called on its people to overthrow the regime. On 19 April 1980 in a newspaper article Khomeini wrote, 'The Iraqi people must not fall into the hands of its aggressors. Its duty as well as that of the army is to overthrow the Ba'ath, that non-Islamic party'.[52] The Iranians also supported Iraqi Shia terrorist groups who launched a campaign of assassinations, nearly killing Saddam's deputy, Tariq Aziz on 1 April 1980.[53] At the same time Tehran let it be known they did not feel obliged to abide by the terms of the Algiers agreements, with Khomeini ominously saying, 'in traditional Islam there are no borders dividing the faithful'.[54]

If Saddam had been the ambitious aggressor wanting to seize more oil fields, he would have attacked Iran in February when the country was literally without a leader. Instead he waited as there was no need for such aggression. In 1979–1980 the Iraqi economy was enjoying outstanding prosperity with oil revenues of around $33 billion per annum. Saddam's agenda was ambitious development programmes, not attacking Iran which would risk economic progress. However in Khomeini's world there was no place for Saddam Hussein, so Saddam's choice was to either face constant calls for his overthrow from Tehran, or to use his own army to wage a limited war and send a clear message to Tehran to back off. Staying in power was Saddam Hussein's oxygen so he chose the latter.[55] He claimed that Iran had shelled Iraq on 7 September 1980, and then on 22 September Iraq invaded at three points along a 400-mile front. This was the blitzkrieg that framed Iraq as the aggressor: but the root cause was in Khomeini's mind.

Saddam's invasion was hesitant, some called it 'most pathetic',[56] because his main aim was to warn Iran. And so just after 1 week he ordered his troops to stop advancing and announced he wanted to negotiate a settlement. Tehran was in no mood to talk, especially as the invasion had released a surge of nationalistic and religious support for Khomeini. There were at least 8 more attempts by Baghdad or their allies to sue for peace over the next 8 years to end the conflict, but Khomeini always wanted more war. In December 1980 Saddam announced there would be no further advances into Iran. Tehran responded by a ferocious counter attack and began to drive Iraqis from its territory. Again Iraq wanted to talk: in February 1982 Taha Yasin Ramadan,

Iraq's first deputy prime minister, said his country would retreat from Iran, once negotiations had begun. Then in April Saddam himself announced that Iraq would withdraw – he only needed assurances that negotiations would begin. Iran's reply was three more offensives that by May 1982 had forced the Iraqis to begin withdrawal from all Iranian territory. Desperate to halt an Iranian invasion of Iraq, Saddam now ordered the assassination of the Israeli ambassador to London calculating correctly this would spur Israel to attack the Palestine Liberation Organization (PLO) in Lebanon. Once the Israeli invasion began in June, he told Tehran that the war must stop and Iranians and Iraqis together must go together to liberate the Palestinians. Iran's reply reveals where the source of hostility in this conflict had always been. Iran was certainly going to liberate the Palestinians, but they would go via Baghdad. So on 21 June 1982, one day after Saddam's peace offer, Khomeini wilfully committed his country to a full scale invasion of Iraq to overthrow Saddam Hussein's infidel regime. His chief of staff declared Iran would 'continue the war until Saddam Hussein is overthrown so that we can pray at Karbala and Jerusalem'.[57]

The price Iran paid in human life for this strategy was tragic. In ousting the Iraqis from Iran, 'human wave' attacks had proved successful. This was when thousands of young inexperienced volunteers, with no other weapon except a copy of the Koran were urged on by mullahs to be mine sweepers and ammunition fodder to prepare the way for the professional soldiers.[58] Inside Iraq the Iranians used the same tactic, but here the Iraqi lines of defence were much stronger than they had been inside Iran – and the Iraqis also used chemical weapons. Throughout 1982 and 1983 hundreds of thousands of Iranians hurled themselves against the Iraqi defences hoping for a breakthrough, or a coup in Baghdad. There was neither, just the constant arrival of corpses in Iran and the cry of wailing mourners. When on some days up to 6,000 were killed,[59] many others were bulldozed into mass graves. By the end of 1983 it is estimated that 120,000[60] Iranians had been killed trying to 'liberate' Iraq. Despite this appalling waste of life Khomeini rejected two more offers for negotiations. In September 1982 Saudi Arabia offered a peace deal which included $70 billion in reparations to Iran. Saddam immediately accepted the plan, and many pragmatists in Iran were keen. But Khomeini dismissed the offer. In early 1984 Saddam made further calls for a cease-fire. The reply was Operation Dawn and Khaibar, attacks which used up to 500,000 men along a 150-mile front. The only gain from this was Majnun Island in the middle of marshland. Finally realizing the futility of 'human wave' attacks, the Iranians switched to more conventional tactics and after intense preparation achieved their one major victory inside Iraq in February 1986 when they captured the Fao Peninsula. This severely dented Saddam's prestige and so yet again he made a plea for peace on 3 August. Now his only condition was the root cause of the war, his right to exist, which of course Khomeini rejected.

This was the final appeal Saddam made to bring about a ceasefire and he now played two cards that Khomeini had no answer to. He forced other powers to get involved in the war, and he made life so unpleasant for Khomeini's constituents that many asked for peace. To widen the war Saddam Hussein started a tanker war which by the end of 1987 had brought in a multinational armada of 50 warships to protect oil supplies, including the Soviets and 22 US vessels with 15,000 men.[61] To intimidate Khomeini's constituents Saddam ordered that bombs and new Scud missiles rain down on all Iran's cities. Over 200 missiles hit Tehran and Qom from February to April 1988; sometimes there would be 17 in 1 day. The impact on morale was devastating, especially when the government started handing out gas masks in case the missiles started to carry chemical weapons. Not surprisingly there was a mass exodus to the countryside and, exactly as Saddam had hoped, public support for the war slumped. Though the disquiet about the war unnerved Iran's leadership, it was ultimately the American presence in the Gulf that finally convinced them it had to end. Since their arrival in the summer of 1987 the Americans had swiftly shown the Iranians their supremacy. In September they had captured the vessel 'Iran Ajr' that was laying mines; in April 1988 they destroyed three offshore oil platforms and three Iranian naval ships; then fatefully on 3 July Iranian boats fired at a US helicopter investigating distress calls sent out by two tankers. In response American ships, including the USS Vincennes, set off to engage the Iranians. At the same time the regular civilian Iran Air flight 655 to Dubai took off from Banda Abbas and its trajectory meant it flew straight at the Vincennes which somehow mistook the rising air bus for a descending Iranian F-14 fighter plane. The Vincennes shot it down: 290 passengers and its crew perished.[62]

The Americans claimed the incident was an accident but most Iranians believed their government who said it was a deliberate attack. All that night on Iranian TV there were pictures of trigger happy Americans[63] firing missiles, followed by footage of corpses floating in the sea. The message to the Iranian public was clear: we are now fighting the Great Satan who stoops to slaughtering civilians to crush the Islamic regime. Later that month Hashemi Rafsanjani, the commander-in-chief, held a meeting with all the leaders of the army and the Revolutionary Guards. The conclusion was unanimous. Iran did not have the resources to win a war against both Iraq and the USA and there had to be a cease-fire. The stark choice then put to Ayatollah Khomeini by President Rafsanjani was either the survival of his revolution or risking everything in a suicidal show down with the USA. On 20 July Khomeini signalled he would accept the UN resolution calling for a cease-fire and issued a written statement – 'Taking this decision was more deadly than drinking hemlock. To me, it would have been more bearable to accept death and martyrdom . . . Today's decision is based only on the interest of the Islamic Republic.'[64] Khomeini drank his hemlock and kept on living. At least 300,000 others had believed his poisonous fantasy of liberating Jerusalem and were no more. And the question Iranians still ask as they visit the countries' vast cemeteries and stare at the fading photographs of Islam's dead soldiers is – what was this war for? History's answer is obvious: absolutely nothing. After the cease-fire the boundaries were exactly the same, and Saddam Hussein was still in power.

Khomeini not only wilfully sent hundreds of thousands of Iranian men to an early death. He also sent children. On 20 March 1982 'Khomeni announced "as a special favour" schoolboys between the ages of 12–18 years would be allowed to join the Basij and to fight for their country.'[65] Thousands responded, driven by a mixture of patriotism, peer pressure, adventure and the manipulative pleas of mullahs who toured the schools extolling the virtues of martyrdom. Once they joined up the boys were given a white cloth as a sign of Hussein's shroud and a plastic key 'issued personally by Khomeini'[66] to reassure them of their entrance to heaven once martyred. Then they were sent to their deaths, either to blow up mines, or waste enemy ammunition. Here is how one Iraqi officer describes their attacks –

> They come on in their hundreds, often walking straight across the minefields, triggering them with their feet as they are supposed to do. They chant 'Allahu Akbar' and they keep coming, and we keep shooting, sweeping our 50 millimetre machine guns round like sickles . . . Once we had Iranian kids on bikes cycling towards us and my men all started laughing, and then these kids started lobbing their hand grenades and we stopped laughing and started shooting.[67]

Some were captured and kept in horrific conditions in Iraqi prisoner of war camps. At Salaheddin camp in Tekrit Mehdi Shamlou was crammed into a cell with 50 others, whipped 3 times a day, and witnessed these volunteer boy soldiers, some as young as 10, being given to Iraqi wardens for their pleasure.[68] Many died of sickness, and a few survived till eventually Iran and Iraq arranged prisoner of war swaps, sometimes years after the war had ended.

Conclusion

Ayatollah Khomeini never regretted this appalling suffering he was causing. Indeed he said he was only ending the war because of the advice of his military leaders. He himself was still ready to see more bloodshed. Cynics might explain Khomeini's love of war as a way of maintaining his own power. Certainly it helped unite the country behind his authority: but his determination to invade Iran in 1982, when all his most dangerous foes had been defeated and willingness then to see hundreds of thousands slaughtered in suicidal attacks needs another explanation. It is found in the answer Khomeini gave to his old student Mehdi Haeri Yazdi who visited him to ask him about the countless thousands dying in the war.

He found Khomeini alone, sitting on a rug in his garden before a small pool. He (Haeri) opened up his heavy heart to Khomeini and asked his mentor if he could not find a way to stop the awful slaughter . . . Khomeini made no sound until Haeri stopped talking. Then, without turning his head and in even but reproachful tones, he asked, 'Do you criticize God when he sends an earthquake.'[69]

Like the ancient kings of Persia, Khomeini believed he was God's Shadow on Earth, or, in the mystic Mulla Sadra's spiritual journeys, in which Khomeini was an expert, he thought he had journeyed to heaven, and had now returned to the world united with God.[70] He never saw himself as just a mere politician, rather he was the 'Imam', the Perfect Man, the one 'to bring about the unfolding of the divine scheme'.[71] However in 1988 the Imam did not seem very perfect, nor his scheme very divine, to most Iranians. For from his arrival in Tehran in 1979 their days had been marked by violence that had gained nothing. The angel had come, but he was not an angel of peace: he was an angel of war, constantly asking for more young blood to be shed for his religion. And that religion was Shia Islam. So in people's mind it was not just Khomeini who had executed their teenagers for possessing some Mojahedin literature and sent their children to be blown up by Iraqi mines: it was Shia Islam. Some would argue that this was not true Islam, many others now are not so sure, and so as the credibility of Christianity suffered after two European wars between 'Christian' countries, so the overwhelming impact of Khomeini's wars has been to dislocate Iran's relationship with her national religion.

The war ended 20 years ago, but this impact is still widely felt. Those who fought in the Khomeini's battles are now middle aged and in positions of responsibility, while their children have grown up surrounded by the appalling legacy of war. Furthermore both young and old have had to contend with the economic consequences of Khomeini's conflicts. These cannot be compared with the trauma of violence, nevertheless for the past 25 years Iranians have grappled with financial insecurity and slowly but surely this undermined the credibility the government and the religions it represents. It is to this we now turn.

Notes

1. Baqer Moin, *Khomeini: Life of the Ayatollah*, Thomas Dunne Books, 1999, p. 197.
2. This happened on 5 February before the Shah's last prime minister, Shapoor Bakhtiar had fled Iran. He escaped to France dressed as a woman where he was assassinated in 1991.
3. Moin, *Khomeini: Life of the Ayatollah*, p. 204
4. Sandra Mackay, *The Iranians*, Plume, New York, 1996, p. 288.
5. When being interviewed by the author V. S. Naipaul in 1981, shortly after leaving the government, Khalkhali boasted of his closeness to Khomeini – 'I was taught by

Ayatollah Khomeini, you know. And I was the teacher of the son of Ayatollah Khomeini.' He thumped me on the shoulder and added archly, to the amusement of
the Iranians, 'So I cannot say I am very close to Ayatollah Khomeini.'
V. S. Naipaul, *Among the Believers: An Islamic Journey*, – Alfred Knopf, New York,
1981, 'Khalkhali on the Execution of Hoveyda', pp. 53–56, www.hoveyda.org/
naipaul.html [last accessed 6 June 2008].

6 On 7 April Khalkhali went to Qasr jail where Hoveida was being kept, ordered
all the prison doors to be kept shut and personally locked up all the phones in
a fridge to make sure no news leaked out. Hoveida was called and accused by
Khalkhali of 'friendship with Israel, subservience to the United States, undermining Islam . . .' After listening to Hoveida for 2 hours, Khalkhali told him to write
his will, and then sentenced him to death as 'a doer of mischief on earth'. He was
executed by firing squad that same afternoon.

7 See Robert Fisk's *The Great War for Civilisation*, Harper Perennial, London, 2006,
p. 161.

8 Adel Darwish, 'Obituary: Ayatollah Sadeq Khalkhali Hardline cleric known as the
"hanging judge" of Iran', *The Independent*, 29 Nov. 2003.

9 See Fisk's *The Great War for Civilisation*, p. 159. Khalkhali also appears as slightly
unbalanced in V. S. Naipaul's description of his encounter with him in 1981 . . .
at one point the wise interpreter of Islam seemed to lose control of himself. Naipaul writes, 'His mouth opened wide, stayed open, and soon he appeared to be
choking with laughter, showing me his gums, his tongue, his gullet'.

10 See Fisk's *The Great War for Civilisation*, p. 160.

11 See 'Ayatollah Sadeq Khalkhali', www.telegraph.co.uk November 2003 [last
accessed 6 June 2008].

12 Darwish, 'Obituary: Ayatollah Sadeq Khalkhali', 29 Nov. 2003.

13 Moin, *Khomeini: Life of the Ayatollah*, p. 215.

14 Efraim Karsh, *The Iran–Iraq War 1980–1988*, Osprey Publishing, Oxford, 2002,
p. 19.

15 See Nikki Keddie's *Modern Iran*, Yale University Press, 2003, p. 247.

16 See Keddie's *Modern Iran*, p. 247.

17 Mackay, *The Iranians*, p. 296.

18 For an excellent overview of the Iranian Constitution see http://news.bbc.co.uk/
1/shared/spl/hi/middle_east/03/iran_power/html/default.stm [last accessed
6 June 2008].

19 Mackay, *The Iranians*, p. 295.

20 Moin, *Khomeini: Life of the Ayatollah*, p. 239.

21 Robin Wright, *In the Name of God*, Bloomsbury, London, 1990, p. 96.

22 See Masoud Banisadr, *Masoud*, Saqi Books, London, 2004, p. 158.

23 Mackay, *The Iranians*, p. 305.

24 See Banisadr, *Masoud*, p. 159.

25 Mackay, *The Iranians*, p. 306.

26 Ramy Nima, *The Wrath of Allah*, Pluto Press, London, 1983, p. 114.

27 Moin, *Khomeini: Life of the Ayatollah*, p. 242.

28 Karsh, *The Iran–Iraq War 1980–1988*, p. 73.

29 Kenneth Pollack, *The Persian Puzzle*, Random House, 2005, p. 190.

[30] Masoud Bani-Sadr, 'Memoirs of an Iranian Rebel', Saqi Books, London, 2004, p. 283. The author was at the meeting discussing this and writes as follows – 'Rajavi called for silence and replied, "We will not be fighting alone" we will have the people on our side . . . Wherever we go there will be masses of citizens joining us . . . We will be like fish swimming in a sea of people. They will give you whatever you need.'

[31] Bani-Sadr, *Memoirs of an Iranian Rebel*, p. 285. 'Thanks to the Iraqis we received new equipment daily. We had no clue how any of it worked.'

[32] Bani-Sadr, *Memoirs of an Iranian Rebel*, p. 292.

[33] Human Rights Watch http://64.233.183.104/search?q=cache:GgCJjHkKNgIJ: hrw.org/backgrounder/mena/iran1205/iran1205.pdf+Iran%27s+interior+mini ster+1988+executions&hl=en&ct=clnk&cd=5&gl=uk [last accessed 6 June 2008]. Ayatollah Montazeri lost his position as Khomeini's designated successor due to this protest, and was put under house arrest.

[34] Bani-Sadr, *Memoirs of an Iranian Rebel*, p. 301.

[35] www.benadorassociates.com/article/6169 [last accessed 6 June 2008].

[36] Bani-Sadr, *Memoirs of an Iranian Rebel*.

[37] Bani-Sadr, *Memoirs of an Iranian Rebel*, p. 311, 341. Ironically the Mojahadeen mirrored the regime in its authoritarianism, so while Ayatollah Khomeini's word was final as the only true interpreter of Islamic law, Rajavi's was the only ideologue able to interpret how a Mojahed should live. The only difference is that Rajavi later had a high priestess to connect his followers with him, his wife Maryam.

[38] See Fisk's *The Great War for Civilisation*, p. 338.

[39] Shirin Ebadi, *Iran Awakening*, Random House, New York, 2006, p. 87.

[40] Pollack, *The Persian Puzzle*, p. 73. Ramy Nima in *The Wrath of Allah*, Pluto Press, London, 1983, p. 36 puts the figure arrested at 5,000.

[41] Andreas Malm and Shora Esmailian, *Iran on the Brink*, Pluto Press, London, 2007, p. 18. The authors also present a fascinating chart detailing the doctrinal leanings of all these different groups.

[42] 'The fundamental reason for the Left's loyalty was Khomeini's anti-imperialist stance; in that regard, he was seen as a hero'. Malm and Esmailian, *Iran on the Brink*, p. 37.

[43] See 'The Failure of the Left', Workers' Liberty – www.workersliberty.org/ node/6516 [last accessed 6 June 2008]. The communists believed in a two-stage revolution whereby the working classes first joined forces with a democratic anti-imperialistic movement (Khomeini's revolution), and then brought about the dictatorship of the proletariat.

[44] See 'The Failure of The Left' –. The Tudeh party told its supporters in August 1981: 'Uncovering the policies of the counter-revolution in the workplace, in the family and in any place where the masses are present is one of most important duties.' Also see Malm and Esmailian, *Iran on the Brink*, p. 37. Also see 'Rebels with a Cause' by Maziar Behrooz, I. B. Tauris, 2000, p. 126.

[45] See Moin's *Khomeini, Life of the Ayatollah*, p. 255, also Wright's *In the Name of God*, p. 124. The crackdown on the Tudeh party had the immediate effect of Moscow resuming arms sales to Iraq.

[46] Wright, *In the Name of God*, p. 108.

47 Pollack, *The Persian Puzzle*, p. 199.

48 Further evidence of their involvement is the fact that the Iranian ambassador to Syria, Ali Akbar Mohtashami, knew the name of the Tyre bomber – it was Ahmad Ghaser. Wright, *In the Name of God*, p. 121.

49 Dilip Hiro (*Iran Today*, Politicos, London, 2006, p. 223) puts the number of war dead at nearly 300,000, while Pollack in *The Persian Puzzle*, p. 238 has 400,000. Pollack then reckons that Iran 'suffered more than one million casualties', while Mackay writes it was 750,000 (*The Iranians*, p. 332).

50 'For Tehran three factors made Iraq the prime target for the engineering of Islamic revolution: the secular nature of the Baathist regime; the oppression of the Shia majority; and the existence of six Shia holy sites in Iran'. Dilip Hiro, *The Longest War*, Paladin, 1990, p. 28.

51 Pollack, *The Persian Puzzle*, p. 183.

52 See www.al-moharer.net/moh255/i_ebeid255b.htm [last accessed 6 June 2008].

53 For a full account of this attack see *The Iran–Iraq War*, Chapter One, 'Towards War the University Bombing', www.al-moharer.net/moh255/i_ebeid255b.htm [last accessed 6 June 2008].

54 Pollack, *The Persian Puzzle*, p. 183.

55 Karsh in his *The Iran–Iraq War 1980–1988*, states this argument clearly – 'War was not his (Saddam's) first choice, but rather an act of last resort . . . . It was a preemptive move designed to exploit a temporary window of opportunity in order to forestall the Iranian threat to his regime' p. 27.

56 Pollack, *The Persian Puzzle*, p. 184.

57 Karsh, *The Iran–Iraq War 1980–1988*, p. 35.

58 'These massed human-wave assaults were horribly wasteful of manpower but frequently swamped the defences or panicked the Iraqi soldiers into abandoning their positions. Once the Pasdars and Basijis had punched through the Iraqi lines, mobile Army detachments would exploit the breakthrough.' Pollack, *The Persian Puzzle*, p. 191.

59 'History of Iran: Iran–Iraq War 1980–1988', Iran Chamber Society, www.iran-chamber.com/history/iran_iraq_war/iran_iraq_war2.php [last accessed 6 June 2008].

60 'History of Iran: Iran–Iraq War 1980–1988', Iran Chamber Society.

61 Malm and Esmailian, *Iran on the Brink*, p. 195.

62 For an account that shows the raw suffering of this tragedy and gives the clearest explanation see Fisk's *The Great War for Civilisation*, pp. 318–334.

63 According to Robert Fisk, The Vincennes had already been nicknamed 'Robocruiser' before this incident, and the Captain of another ship, the Sides, called the destruction of the aircraft, 'the horrifying climax to Captain Rogers' aggressiveness.' See *The Great War for Civilisation*, pp. 324–325.

64 Karsh, *The Iran–Iraq War 1980–1988*, p. 79.

65 Karsh, *The Iran–Iraq War 1980–1988*, p. 39.

66 Karsh, *The Iran–Iraq War 1980–1988*, p. 62.

67 Karsh, *The Iran–Iraq War 1980–1988*, p. 62.

68 See 'Our Boy: Their Prisoner of War', www.iranian.com/Nov95/POW.html#Abuse [last accessed 6 June 2008].

[69] Vali Nasr, *The Shia Revival,* W. W. Norton, New York, 2006, p. 120. After hearing this Haeri got up and left without a word. He never spoke to Khomeini again.

[70] This might be another reason why he replied 'Nothing' to the journalists who asked him how he felt about his return to Iran after years of exile. For if you have been to heaven and back to earth, what is it to return to a mere country?

[71] See Moin's *Khomeini, Life of the Ayatollah,* p. 297.

Chapter 6

Economic Hardship

There is a joke about a martyr, a 'Shahid', of the Iran–Iraq war who asks Khomeini about heaven.

> 'Oh, imam, tell me about paradise' the martyr asked. 'Well', said the ayatollah, 'There is no war, and the electricity works.' 'Oh, tell me more' begged the martyr. 'All the foods are available, the finest meat and abundant fruits' replied the imam. 'More', beseeched the martyr. 'There is plenty of time to play, and everyone is happy.' Khomeini responded. 'And more!' said the Shahid on his knees. 'Well, to summarize' the imam said, 'it is like the good old days of the shah.'[1]

Under both the Pahlavi monarchs the financial situation of many Iranians, especially the middle classes, improved dramatically. Then Ayatollah Khomeini arrived, declared the revolution was not about lowering the price of melons, and living standards plummeted. Though the government denied it, inflation soared to 30 per cent and higher;[2] often one salary per household was not enough; the proud Iranian rial that had yielded so many dollars was now scorned; and unemployment rose. It seemed that Khomeini's regime had inherited a potentially prosperous economy and ruined it.

For the revolution brought US sanctions; the departure of foreign investors; the nationalization of major industries and banks; the birth of the 'bonyads', huge informal charitable groups; special treatment for the bazaaris and unaffordable subsidies. The impact of all this on the economy was wholly negative. US sanctions slashed Iran's access to a massive foreign market and put huge pressure on the country's military and infrastructure which relied heavily on spare parts from the USA. The sanctions also caused a capital drain from Iran, as did the regime when it declared that all business had to be Islamic. International investors had no idea what this meant and went elsewhere. Investors were also wary about nationalization. Given Khomeini's own antipathy to excessive wealth, his use of anti-imperialist jargon which demonized international capital and the support he had received from left wing groups, it is not surprising there was wholesale nationalization at the start of the revolution. All the debilitating characteristics of state control soon began to appear as the government and its allies came to control up to 70 per cent[3] of the economy. There is inefficiency as managers are shielded from the reality of the market place, so many state businesses operate at a loss. This is especially true of the main utility industries – oil, gas, water and transport.[4] At the same time, keen to create jobs, the government has allowed its state businesses to be often grossly overmanned, so causing more loss-making inefficiency. And there is excessive red tape for private business, so for example to obtain one letter of credit from a bank three separate ministries must be contacted, and five different departments of the Central Bank.[5]

While private industries operate in a suffocating world of regulations, the bonyads have huge economic power and operate beyond the reach of the law. Set up to administer the assets of the Shah and the incomes from the holy sites with a brief to help the poor, they became the personal fiefdoms of senior clerics and enjoyed favours. They did not have to submit audited accounts, were able to ignore tax, currency and tariff laws, and were allowed to borrow from the state at half the normal interest rate. Bonyads soon became massive economic empires, able to muscle out all other competitors. The Foundation for the Oppressed and War Veterans controls an estimated $12 billion in assets. As well as owning thousands of factories with nearly half a million workers, they own shipping lines, Iran's largest soft drink company, chemical plants and a lot of property. The foundation that administers all the wealth that pours into the shrine of Imam Reza in Mashad has an annual budget of over $2 billion and controls most of the economy in Kurasan.[6]

The bazaaris (merchants) have also enjoyed special treatment. As traditionalists who had suffered financially under the Shah's rule, they were Khomeini's second most important allies after the mullahs. The Shah had started to police their closed world to punish hoarders and in 1975 alone his courts had issued 250,000 fines and sentenced 8,000 bazaaris to prison sentences.[7] All of this ended in 1979. The rich bazaaris found themselves in the corridors of power, and returned to their usual practice of hiding information to avoid tax. As prices soared and basic commodities became scarce during the war years the public complained about bazaar hoarding, so much so that some politicians were critical. Rather than tolerate any anti-bazaar legislation Khomeini used his personal influence to appeal to the merchants to exercise restraint, and told the politicians not to 'prevent the bazaar from doing the things it can do'.[8]

As well as depriving the government of tax income, this policy of protecting the bazaaris means their monopolies keep out the benefits of competition. As Elaine Sciolino so aptly puts it, 'The bazaari aren't investors looking to build the country for the long haul. They are cash and carry merchants looking for quick deals.'[9]

Another group the government was committed to were the 'mostazafin', or the 'deprived', who had flocked to Khomeini's banner. Throughout the 1980s electricity and other services were brought to poor areas, and massive subsidies were paid out to keep the price of very basic necessities such as petrol, gas, water and electricity extremely cheap, not just for the poor, but for everyone. Initially these subsidies, which have come to account for 25 per cent[10] of the country's GDP, played an important role in shoring up support for the regime, but for at least a decade now it has been clear that they must be drastically reduced for Iran to balance her books.

The revolution brought rough winds for the economy: the war with Iraq brought a storm. Saddam's attacks focused on Iran's oil producing areas and caused a dramatic decline in oil revenues. This, combined with a sharp increase in military spending, meant the regime had to dig deep into the nation's foreign exchange reserves. They dropped from $14.6 billion in 1979 to just $1 billion at the end of 1981.[11] The country was on the edge of bankruptcy and the people felt it. To save foreign exchange non-essential imports were cut to a minimum, so for much of the war there were shortages of basic commodities such as paper and soap. Even some food items were in short supply as agriculture production slumped when thousands of workers left for the war. This was when Iran started to become a 'nation of cab drivers' as bread winners took on second jobs to survive. It was this economic hardship that partly brought people onto the streets in 1988 demanding an end to the pointless war. Economic reconstruction was now the priority, but it was a monumental task.

Though many bereaved families were generously compensated by the government, still the outright loss of life had a devastating economic impact on many. Also another 2.5 million Iranians had been made homeless and over half a million had become physically or mentally disabled. Material damage, especially in Khuzestan and the other war zones was horrific. Four thousand villages were wiped out; six towns were virtually levelled, and the city of Khorramshahr, Iran's most important Gulf port, was totally ruined. Of the 52 towns that were damaged, for 15 of them between 30–80 per cent were destroyed. One estimate regarding the cost to housing exceeds $18 billion. The natural environment was also badly damaged. About 3 million date palms and at least 5,000 hectares of orchards were destroyed, while up to 130,000 hectares of natural forests and over 700,000 hectares of pasture land were ruined. Much of the farm land in the south became useless due to contamination coming from chemical weapons and unexploded mines. About 250 kilometres of the coast from Abadan to the Strait of Hormuz was polluted by tar and asphalt, while the sea was affected by oil leaks and sunken ships, crippling the fishing industry. The impact of the war on public services and manufacturing was worse. Damage to roads and railways, electricity, gas and water supplies were all intense in the war zones, while across the country manufacturing fell to 20–30 per cent of its capacity. Worst hit of all was the oil industry whose revenues make Iran economically viable. Kharg Island, Iran's main loading terminal was so badly attacked in 1982 that the country's exports were halved, and the massive oil refinery at Abadan was destroyed, along with at least half the actual city. The lack of refineries in Iran is still causing problems. After surveying all this damage, Iran issued the official economic cost of the war that had gained nothing: $300 billion.[12] Not only had Khomeini sent Iranians to be slaughtered at the front, his religious regime had emptied the nation's coffers.

In the immediate post-war era, Iran's leaders knew the economy had to be the priority for their political survival. As well as reconstruction, they were also faced with a huge surge in the numbers of people entering the labour market. There were thousands of soldiers returning from the front, and then there were the children of Khomeini's baby boom. He had urged people to have larger families to have more supporters of his revolution. So soon Iran had one of the youngest populations in the world, (about 65 per cent of the population is under 25).[13] However after 1988 there was no war for them to go to: but they all needed jobs.

To spur economic growth Khamanei, the new Supreme Leader after Khomeini's death in 1989, and Hashemi Rafsanjani, the President from 1989 to 1997, began a process of privatization, and allowed in some foreign investment. The Tehran stock exchange was reopened; the currency devalued; free trade zones, such as on Kish Island, were established; and in 1993 up to a thousand public enterprises were privatized. It seemed these polices worked. Immediately after the war the economy grew at about 8 per cent[14] a year, and in the past 3 years it has averaged at 5.8 per cent.[15] That is very healthy. The profits from manufacturing are even more impressive. They rose to 12 per cent in the 1990s and from 1995 to 2003 they were 16–19 per cent.[16] Regarding inflation and unemployment the figures are not so pleasant, but neither are they dire. Due to the amount of state money poured into the economy, inflation has remained at about 15 per cent, which is a cause for concern. However it is certainly not critical and indeed if Iran is compared with 'emerging' economies, rather than developed ones, then this rate is acceptable. With between 700,000 to 1 million people entering the labour market every year, the challenge of creating jobs has been formidable. The government has not provided for all, but till now it has managed to create between 300,000 to 500,000 jobs per year[17] which has kept the official unemployment rate at between 11 to 15 per cent. This is on a par with Bahrain and Oman, and much lower than South Africa (25 per cent), Libya (30 per cent) and Djibouti (50 per cent).[18]

From these figures it would seem Iran's government had brought the economy out of the storms of the 1980s, easily blamed on what they called an 'imposed' war, and steered the country into calmer waters. There is some truth in this. Clearly many people began to enjoy better standards of living seen in the number of smarter cars on the streets, the house building boom, and the ever increasing crowds that shop – both in Iran and Dubai. This recovery though is primarily due to an increase in the oil prices in the early 1990s and since 2004. It is this huge increase in energy revenues that has allowed the government to invest in new businesses, and subsidize state industries, which are both protected from outside competition.

So though the framework Rafsanjani set up has benefited the economy, its health is completely dependent on the black gold. Furthermore many argue[19] that if the Iranian economy had been properly managed over the past 25 years there would have been massive growth because the country is so rich in natural resources, 10 per cent of the world's oil fields, and 15 per cent[20] of her gas. The reason why there has not been growth are all those negative features introduced with the revolution – the US sanctions and uncertainty for investors; excessive state control in league with the opaque but powerful bonyads and bazaars; and unaffordable subsidies. US sanctions have actually got worse since 1995 as the US has threatened to punish any company that deals with Iran – not just US ones. This has kept foreign investors away, as has the continued perception that even after Rafsanjani's overtures, Iran is a frustrating place to have dealings with. Indeed in the Wall Street Journal's *Index on Economic Freedom*, Iran came 156th out of 157 countries, beating only North Korea.[21] Still 65–80 per cent[22] of the economy is effectively controlled by the government, not least because of the overlap between the state industries and the bonyads, who often bought any assets sold by the government, so effectively keeping Rafsanjani's much publicized privatization within the ruling elite. Hence about 80 per cent of the Tehran Stock Market is owned either by the state or the bonyads[23] and this causes inefficiency and widespread corruption. For example '18.5% of the electricity produced in Iran is wasted before it reaches to consumers due to technical problems and mismanagement.'[24] As for corruption, Iran is ranked 105 out of 163 in the International Corruption Perception Index.[25] Insider trading is the norm, and as mentioned there is no regulatory control for the bonyads and little for the bazaars. Finally subsidies continue to be a huge drain on Iran's national purse, with the 18 per cent of the 25 per cent [26] of the GDP being spent on energy subsidies coming in for special criticism from experts. This subsidy till recently meant a litre of petrol was 3p, thus creating huge domestic demand which cannot be met as Iran does not have enough refineries. So the government must import more than 40 per cent of its petrol.[27]

Though these long-term problems mean Iran will never reach its economic potential, they do not signal an imminent collapse of the country's finances. The ever increasing demands for energy, especially from China and India will keep Iran's oil and gas revenues flowing and this will keep the flawed economy afloat. The crucial issue though is not the cold facts of an economic graph, but the emotional impression most Iranians have regarding their government's handling of the economy. It is not good. They believe that with the country's vast oil and gas reserves they should be enjoying a much better standard of living, at least comparable with the lifestyles of the Europeans and Americans they can see on their satellite TVs and computer screens. There should be jobs for young people, reasonable salaries so people can plan to marry, and they certainly should not have to read in the Iran Daily about 7.4 million Iranians living below the poverty line (which the paper defined as less than $178 per month for a family of 4.6 people).[28] This accusation that the government has failed to deliver prosperity is mixed with three more serious ones: workers' rights have been ignored; unemployment has driven people to heroin and prostitution; and, most damning of all, the senior clerics presiding over this human misery have grown obscenely rich.

All trade unions are illegal in Iran, and strikes are *haram*, so completely banned. The *Shora-ye Eslami*, an Islamic council, is meant to look after the interests of workers, but when these councils first made their presence felt in the early 1980s the then head of the judiciary Musavi Ardabili made it very clear whom they were working for – 'The management is the brain, the Islamic council the eyes, and the rest are the hands.'[29] As most industry is owned directly or indirectly by the government who are keen to see good profits, this inevitably meant that the management has put pressure on their staff to increase output. And these councils, true to Mr Ardabili's comment, have not been speaking up for the workers, but instead they have been on the look out for troublemakers. In recent years there have been quite a few as frustration at low salaries, often paid late, and especially temporary contracts, has driven workers to bypass these councils and take more direct action. This has revealed the government's antipathy for workers' rights.

Since 2004 there has been a lot of protest. In January construction workers building a copper smelting plant near Kerman demonstrated for permanent contracts; in March up to a third of all teachers joined a strike for better salaries; in September brick workers near Tabriz went on strike, also for higher wages, and won; throughout 2004 textile workers in Sanandajj, capital of Kudistan staged sit-ins against redundancies and poor working conditions. They fought on till November 2005 when the management gave in to all their demands. The year 2004 also saw disturbances at the massive Iran Khudro car factory just outside Tehran. The Middle East's largest car manufacturer, with profits of $405 million in 2004 and $573 million in 2005,[30] Iran Khudro is in many ways a success story for Rafsanjani's new economic policy. But the workers have suffered. Only a quarter of the company's 58,000 workers have permanent contracts, which means given the extent of unemployment managers can easily impose longer hours on workers with temporary contracts. If they complain, there are plenty more people to hire. Anger at this boiled over in January when two men suddenly died of strokes during night shifts. Other workers immediately blamed the conditions imposed on them by the management and downed their tools. Their main demand was for temporary contracts to end. The government response was to increase security. Tension continued throughout 2005. In May a 30-year-old man died in another night shift accident at Iran Khudro causing more stoppages and leaflets began to circulate referring to the management as 'killers' who do not care about 'the expendable lives of the workers'.[31] In the autumn of 2005 the Tehran bus drivers began a protest which gained international coverage. In September they all drove with their lights on

as a complaint against unpaid wages, and then on 17 October they refused
to collect fares from any passengers. The government insisted that only the
Islamic council could represent the workers and promptly arrested their leader
Mansour Ossanlou and 14 others. The drivers went on strike and the capital
ground to a halt. To bring them back to work the mayor met them, promised to
get their leaders released and told the bus company to consider their demands.
The drivers went back to work, but nothing changed, so they planned another
strike for 28 January 2006. This time the government moved in advance and
during the night before the strike arrested over 1,000 drivers and their families,
while soldiers kept the busses running. This level of intimidation had the
desired effect. The bus drivers went back to work, and all the detained, except
their leader, were released. Mansour Ossanlou was kept at Evin till August, often
in solitary confinement, and then released on the condition of paying over
£80,000 bail – the equivalent of 125 years' wages[32]. The bus strike received the
most publicity, but there were many others in 2005 – 140 strikes in October and
120 in November alone.[33]

As the number of protests has grown so more networking has developed
between labour groups. This has been greatly helped by email which cannot be
closely controlled.[34] So on 16 July 2005 strikes against the delay in the payment
of wages were held in Bushehr, Yazd, Sushahr; Ilam, Qom, Golestan – and the
Iran Khudro plant. And May Day has again become a special day for workers
to raise their voices. This certainly happened in 2005. To try and control the
situation the government allowed over 20,000 workers to assemble in the Azadi
football stadium. They thought they were going to hear about their rights, but
instead Rafsanjani wanted to get their votes for the forthcoming election. This
did not go down well – 'People started booing and shouting "the government
should leave us alone", "abolish slavery in Iran"'. When an official started telling people to vote for Rafsanjani: 'some activists then stormed the podium and
pulled down the microphone while the masses in the stadium simply walked
out.'[35] News of this even got into the national press with the Iran Daily putting
its finger on the heart of the problem – 'The labour force wants temporary
contracts to be revoked and real wages to be declared, but nobody is paying
attention.'[36]

Though it can be fairly argued that these conflicts are a normal, even healthy,
feature of growing economy and that eventually the Iranian government will
address the demands of the workers and allow proper trade unions, it is again
the general perception that matters, not the complicated business of how economic growth relates to the labour force. And the general feeling, especially
underlined by the bus drivers' strike, is that the government is ready to bully
and intimidate to increase profit, rather than support the workers. In short people believe the government, despite all its rhetoric, sides with the rich against
the poor, and this inevitably impacts the way they think about the government's
religion.

Again it is probably unfair, but the government is widely blamed for the tragic fact that Iran has a very high number of drug addicts. The United Nations World Drug report in 2006 that 2.8 per cent of the nation's 47 million 15–64-year olds are addicts: that is 1.3 million.[37] Other estimates put the figure at nearer 4 million.[38] The pain of this statistic in terms of shame, sickness, imprisonment, and, for some, death is then shared by every addict's relatives. This means many more than the official 1.3 million addicts are impacted. In the midst of the trauma the addiction causes people look for a root cause, and the one most frequently cited is unemployment: because the teenagers have no hope of finding a proper job and getting married, they turn to drugs. And unemployment is the government's fault. Of course the argument is flawed, but again it is the emotional impression that matters. The same argument is used against the government when people consider prostitution. It is impossible to give exact figures, but all the evidence points to a tragic rise in the number of women and young girls selling their bodies to make ends meet. Mohammad Ali Zam, the head of Tehran's cultural and artistic affairs said in 2000 there had been an increase in prostitution of 635 per cent.[39] Iranian officials in 2002[40] said there were up to 300,000 sex workers on the streets of Tehran alone. In 2003 there is documented evidence in Iranian newspapers of 23 legal cases involving prostitutes, their clients and the ring leaders. Typical is the story covered by the Iran Daily on the 7 April when 90 people were arrested in 20 brothels involved in sending girls to the Persian Gulf States. Another in Etemad Daily on the 14 July reports on girls aged between 13–30 being kidnapped and used by the sex gangs.[41] As seen here the age of the girls can be very young, indeed one report in 2004 has said the average age in Tehran was just 14 years old.[42]

The pain of this prostitution is made worse as the government's religion does not condemn it. For while Shia Islam demands that a woman does not show her hair in public, *Sigheh*, temporary marriage, is legal. And as the legal age of marriage in Iran is 9, even *Sigheh* with a very young girl is allowed. Ideally the couple should get a blessing from a mullah, but this is not compulsory, and they can betroth themselves for as little as an hour. It is also ironic that along with major cities, Iran's major religious shrines at Qom and Mashad are busy centres of prostitution. This is what the Canadian journalist, Iranian born Camelia Fard,[43] discovered when she visited Qom. At the graveyard surrounding the shrine of Masoumeh[44] she found women in chadors sitting 'silent and motionless on the dirt graves', then –

> ... clusters of young seminary students, clad in the traditional turbans, robes, and capes worn by mullahs, teemed into the courtyard, ... looking at the women to see who was new and who had been there many times before. A thin young boy, watering can in hand, washed the floor of the courtyard all day, looking for a customer who would want his services for an introduction to one of the women.[45]

She managed to talk to some. There was Mehri aged about 20, the widow of a truck driver who had seven children to feed. And there was Fatima, a 16-year-old who was being forced to marry a 60-year-old man. So she ran away from home and has ended up selling her young body to feed herself. These girls were given less than $5 when their 'marriage' was consummated.

All the anger Iranians feel about: inflation, unemployment, the trampling on workers' rights; the epidemic of heroin addiction; and the selling of young female flesh – becomes very bitter when people consider how the clerics who have presided over this human misery have fared. Some of them have grown very rich. Even in the early days of the revolution there were jokes about the size of mullahs' stomachs, and in the mid-1990s speculation about their wealth was rife. Then as the internet became more accessible so street gossip became more official. For example Paul Klebnikov,[46] amongst others, wrote an explosive article titled *Millionaire Mullahs* in 2003. Describing the relationship between the government and the bonyads as 'crony capitalism', Klebnikov focused especially on the family of Hashemi Rafsanjani, 'the father of privatization'. Just 30 years ago the Rafsanjanis were small-scale pistachio farmers, now they are the richest family in Iran, worth at least one billion dollars a year. Hashemi Rafsanjani is at the centre of this business empire, which as one Iranian says is like 'an octopus'. One brother has headed up Iran's largest copper mine; another led a state-owned TV network and now owns a large company Taha that imports printers; a cousin dominated the country's lucrative pistachio industry. The younger generation has also fared well. One of Rafsanjani's sons has a key role in the ever rich Ministry of Oil, while another heads up the construction of Tehran's underground system which has already spent $700 million. His youngest son Yaser owns a 30-acre horse farm in the north of Tehran[47]. In the opaque world of Iran's economy it is rumoured the Rafsanjani family also controls the plant assembling Daewoo cars in Kerman, and they practically own Kish Island, a free economic zone set up by Rafsanjani when he was president.

Rafsanjani is the richest, but there are at least seven others in the clerical elite who were worth more than $200 million in 2003, when before the revolution they would have had modest wealth. There is Ayatollah Vaez Tabasi, the head of Imam's Reza's shrine in Mashad worth well over $700 million; Mohsen Rezai, former leader of the Revolutionary Guards and close friend of Hashemi Rafsanjani, worth $660 million; the late Ayatollah Ali Meshkini who chaired the Assembly of Experts, was worth over $300 million; Ayatollah Mohammad-Ali Taskhiri, former head of the Islamics Culture and Communication Organization who is also worth over $300 million, as is Ayatollah Mohammad Yazdi, the former head of the judiciary; Ayatollah Abolghassem Khazali, member of the Council of Guardians whose interests in the paper and book industry have given him a fortune of over $200 million; and finally there is Ayatollah Ahmad Jannati, another member of the Council and close friend of the Supreme leader, who also has a personal fortune of over $200 million.[48]

Given the state control of the economy and the overlapping relationship between the government, the bonyads and the bazaaris, it was inevitable that the mullahs and the merchants who came to power together in 1979 were going to do well. Reacting to the way Iran had seemingly been 'sold' to America under the Pahlavis their instinct was to nationalize for Islam in the early years, but historically both groups were for private ownership, and so under Khamanei and Rafsanjani they started to sell off government assets – to each other and their friends. As seen they have grown extremely rich. This mullah money leaves a bitter taste seen when the students protesting in 1999 chanted, 'The mullahs have become God and the people have become poor'[49] and dramatically proved by Mahmoud Ahmadinejad's surprise victory against Rafsanjani in the 2005 presidential elections which he won by appealing to this sense of economic injustice. He nicknamed Rafsanjani *Akbar Shah*, painting him as an indulgent and corrupt Pahlavi; flaunted his own simple lifestyle; and promised to put oil money on the people's plates. President Ahmadinejad's plans to be Iran's Robin Hood though have run into difficulties. Rather than confronting the corruption and the economy's long-term problems, he has limited his government to noisy tinkering which has upset friends and enemies. He abruptly increased the minimum wage, an announcement that had to be changed when unemployment leapt; he told the banks to cut their interest rates to below 12 per cent while the rate of inflation is thought to be between 12–15 per cent which brought panic and a spree of selling at the Tehran Stock Market; and he caused havoc, especially for international businesses and travel, when in the spring of 2006 he ordered the clocks not to be moved forward. Probably his one success has been his 'love fund' whereby newly weds from poor backgrounds can get a government grant, but this has had no impact on the root problems of the economy. This tinkering, and the President's tendency to suddenly announce grand expensive populist projects while touring the provinces, alarmed Iran's establishment and in June 2006 they sent him an official warning. Fifty-seven senior economists wrote him an open letter highlighting the inflationary damage his policies were having on the economy.[50] He has also faced criticism from his own political party about inflation.[51] And he famously upset the general public in the summer of 2007 by raising the price of a litre from 3p to 5.5p in a bid to reduce the subsidy for petrol. Even this small increase caused violent protest with petrol stations being torched. It would seem that President Ahmadinejad is unable to restructure an economy that has been built for the interests of the clerical elite. And with its main architect, Hashemi Rafsanjani,[52] still a very powerful politician, it is unlikely this will change. The establishment is going to get richer, while most will struggle with inflation, unemployment, low wages and unfair working conditions. Others continue to sink in addiction and prostitution.

Stepping back it is fair to say there is an emotional sense of injustice brooding over the Islamic Republic's economic record. As seen in Chapter 3, there is a strong theme in Iranian history that the ruler enters into a contract with the people whereby they give their devoted allegiance, but he must provide justice. The Islamic Republic has certainly demanded and often received devoted allegiance, but most Iranians believe, and outside observers agree, that the rulers of Iran have set up an economy that favours the clerical/merchant establishment. And though there is no question of Iran sinking into extreme poverty, especially with the continuing rise of the price of oil, nevertheless this feeling that Shia Muslim rulers are acting unfairly instinctively leads people to question the authority of the religion that is sanctioning this injustice.

If an Iranian has not suffered due to war – either external or internal – or had to endure economic injustice, which is extremely unlikely, it might be they would have no reason to question either their government or its religion. However the Islamic regime has not just brought them a devastating war and a difficult economic situation: there has also been unprecedented intrusion into people's personal lives and a severe clampdown on all free speech in the political arena. This too has caused widespread resentment against a compulsory religion which gives its agents such power. It is to this cultural and political authoritarianism we now turn, before assessing the overall impact of the revolution and its consequences on the Iranian identity.

Notes

[1] Robin Wright, *In The Name of God*, Bloomsbury, London, 1990, p. 177.
[2] Nevertheless, a 30 per cent inflation rate persisted, a black market rate on the United States dollar flourished, and foreign exchange controls continued. Inflation was continually understated by the government. The government asserted that the inflation rate had fallen from 32.5 per cent in FY 1980 to 17 per cent in FY 1983 and to 5.5 per cent in FY 1985; independent analysts, however, claimed that a more accurate inflation rate for 1985 was 50 per cent. US Library of Congress http://countrystudies.us/iran/63.htm [last accessed 6 June 2008].
[3] Nikki Keddie's *Modern Iran*, Yale University Press, 2003, p. 256.
[4] Abbas Bakhtiar, 'Ahmadinejad's Achilles Heel', Iranian.com 25 January 2007.
[5] Elaine Sciolino's *Persian Mirrors: The Elusive Face of Iran*, Free Press, 2005, p. 325.
[6] For more on the 'bonyads' see Sciolino's *Persian Mirrors*, pp. 326–327; Bakhtiar, 'Ahmadinejad's Achilles Heel'; Nicholas Birch, 'In Iran, Clerics' Wealth Draws Ire' Foundations Under Clerical Control Have Grown in Influence since the 1979 Revolution, www.csmonitor.com/2003/0820/p06s01-wome.html [last accessed 6 June 2008].
[7] Dilip Hiro, *Iran Today*, Politicos, London, 2006, p. 12.
[8] Hiro, *Iran Today*, p. 18.
[9] Sciolino's *Persian Mirrors*, p. 330.
[10] 'The Big Squeeze', *The Economist*, A special report on Iran, 21 July 2007, p. 10, their source, the IMF.
[11] Efraim Karsh, *The Iran–Iraq War 1980–1988*, Osprey, Oxford, 2002, p. 74.

[12] For more detail regarding the economic cost of the war, including a sector by sector breakdown, see Hooshang Amirahmadi's 'Iranian Recovery from Industrial Devastation during War with Iraq', www.unu.edu/unupress/unupbooks/uu21le/uu21le0e.htm [last accessed 6 June 2008].

[13] Bakhtiar, 'Ahmadinejad's Achilles Heel'. For a detailed discussion also see 'Population Dynamics in Post-Revolutionary Iran: A Re-examination of Evidence' by Hassan Hakimian in *The Economy of Iran* edited by Parvin Alizadeh, I. B. Taurus, 2000.

[14] Amirahmadi's 'Iranian recovery from industrial devastation during war with Iraq'.

[15] Kelly Campbell, USIPeace Briefing.

[16] A. Malm and S. Esmailian, *Iran on the Brink*, Pluto Press, London, p. 53.

[17] Campbell, USIPeace Briefing.

[18] CIA World Fact Book.

[19] See, for example, 'The Big Squeeze', p. 9.

[20] www.nationsencyclopedia.com/Asia-and-Oceania/Iran.html [last accessed 6 June 2008].

[21] Malm and Esmailian, *Iran on the Brink*, p. 48.

[22] 'The Big Squeeze', p. 10.

[23] Malm and Esmailian, *Iran on the Brink*, p. 51.

[24] Bakhtiar, 'Ahmadinejad's Achilles Heel'. Here he is quoting Baztab.com.

[25] www.transparency.org/policy_research/surveys_indices/cpi [last accessed 6 June 2008].

[26] 'The Big Squeeze', p. 10.

[27] 'The Big Squeeze', p. 10.

[28] http://irandaily.ir/1385/2623/html/economy.htm#s162825 [last accessed 6 June 2008]. The report in the Iran Daily on 30 July 2006 said the poverty line was $178 per month for an average family of 4.6 people. In January 2005 a member of parliament claimed 90 per cent of Iran's population were living below the poverty line.

[29] Malm and Esmailian, *Iran on the Brink*, p. 70.

[30] See Iran Daily – http://irandaily.ir/1384/2518/html/economy.htm [last accessed 6 June 2008].

[31] Malm and Esmailian, *Iran on the Brink*, p. 74.

[32] www.labournet.net/world/0703/iran3.html [last accessed 6 June 2008].

[33] For further details regarding strikes since 2004 in Iran see Malm and Esmailian, *Iran on the Brink*, Chapter 6 'Outcry', pp. 71–90.

[34] Governments can block websites, but the sheer number of emails and the multiple ways of sending and receiving them makes it virtually impossible for the authorities to closely track them.

[35] Malm and Esmailian, *Iran on the Brink*, p. 85.

[36] Malm and Esmailian, *Iran on the Brink*, p. 85.

[37] www.unodc.org/pdf/WDR_2006/wdr2006_volume2.pdf [last accessed 6 June 2008].

[38] www.payvand.com/news/06/oct/1031.html [last accessed 6 June 2008].

[39] http://news.bbc.co.uk/1/hi/world/middle_east/822312.stm [last accessed 6 June 2008].

[40] www.payvand.com/news/02/dec/1032.html [last accessed 6 June 2008].

[41] For a complete breakdown on all the documented cases involving sex workers in Iran for 1995–2003 see the research by Donna Hughs from Rhodes University www.uri.edu/artsci/wms/hughes/documented_rings.doc [last accessed 6 June 2008].

[42] Malm and Esmailian, *Iran on the Brink*, p. 60.

[43] For her reporting Ms Fard spent 11 weeks in prison.

[44] Masoumeh was the sister of the Eighth Imam, Reza, who is buried in Mashad.

[45] 'She found prostitution among Iran's holy men' www.uri.edu/artsci/wms/hughes/prostitution_holy_men [last accessed 6 June 2008].

[46] Paul Klebinov was tragically murdered a year later in Moscow, probably by agents of Russian mafia godfathers he had exposed.

[47] See Paul Klebinov 'Millionaire Mullahs – Who Controls Iran Today?' www.iranian.com/Travelers/2003/July/Rich/ [last accessed 6 June 2008].

[48] See 'Iran's rulers amass fortunes through sleaze' – www.iranfocus.com/modules/news/article.php?storyid=5609 [last accessed 6 June 2008].

[49] See Sciolino's *Persian Mirrors*, p. 317.

[50] http://news.bbc.co.uk/1/hi/world/middle_east/6744841.stm [last accessed 6 June 2008].

[51] *The Guardian*, Thursday, 20 September 2007.

[52] In September 2007 Rafsanjani was elected head of the Council of Experts the powerful group that decides who the next supreme leader will be. He gained more votes than hard-liner Mesbah-Yazdi who is considered Ahmadinejad's mentor. So the election has been interpreted as a rebuff to Ahmadinejad.

Chapter 7

Cultural and Political Authoritarianism

In 1979 millions of Iranians rose up under the unifying banner of Shia Islam to oust a despised king and establish a new government. Most were proud that their traditional religion had protected their Iranian identity from 'cultural invasion'. But once the king had gone, this banner of Islam did not stay flying on the top of government buildings. It came down and covered every aspect of every Iranians' life. Given that one of Ayatollah Khomeini's most important scholarly works was *Tahrir al-Vasilah*,[1] a detailed and comprehensive manual on how all Muslims should live, it is not surprising he wanted Iranians to follow Islamic rules. However for the vast majority of people this was rather unsettling.

The revolution's control over culture was immediate, comprehensive and far reaching. The impact was immediate as nearly all the new dictates regarding culture were issued in 1979. They were comprehensive in that the main institutions of the country – the bureaucracy, the armed forces, the universities and schools, the judiciary, business – all were reformed to make sure they reflected Islamic values. Now ability alone was not enough to secure a place at university, or a government job: one's Islamic credentials had to be strong. It was far reaching in that the power of the new laws affected the smallest and most private of aspects of people's lives. By the end of 1979 Iranians were told how they should dress, socialize, court each other, celebrate weddings, choose names for their children, participate in sport and what music they could (usually not) listen to. The new Islamic rulers also wanted to control very carefully what Iranians watched and read. This cultural control was implemented seemingly in the name of Islam and the fervent anti-Westernism that Khomeini had infused into the religion. However if one steps back, this cultural agenda is actually dominated by two more universal factors: one is male honour as measured by female chastity, the other is political power.

Women and male honour

A highly visual part of the cultural invasion that came with the alliance with America was the impression that women should be objects of glamour and sexual gratification. This was anathema to Islam and not just traditional Iranian values, but also Asian ones. In the East it is seen as the responsibility of the men to make sure the women in their family are kept chaste. If their sister or daughter is seen to be too flirtatious, or begins a relationship without permission, this brings dishonour on the whole family, and their own manliness comes into question. Not only is their own honour measured by the chaste behaviour of their women, but the whole family line is affected in that if there is doubt over a woman's sexual discipline, then the legitimacy of the all important son who will carry on the family name is undermined.[2] This concern for manliness and reputation is strongly reflected in Islamic values (as they are in the Bible) and so the revolution totally rejected the liberal Western view of women, and radically promoted their role as chaste sisters and faithful wives. This impacted all of the legislation that reshaped Iranian culture post 1979.

Legal status

Shortly after the success of the revolution laws were introduced to underline how women were not equal free agents out in the world where, by implication, they could undermine morality. Their value regarding compensation and their testimony in court became half that of a man's; and while a man could divorce his wife orally by just repeating his wish three times, the wife had to ask her husband for permission. If divorce happened the children always went to the father. Some professions, such as being a judge, became off limits. And while a woman could be stoned to death for adultery, her husband could have up to three other wives, and as many temporary ones as he wanted. For millions of women these laws were deeply offensive. After the revolution the young judge Shirin Ebadi who had fervently supported Ayatollah Khomeini had to first face the trauma of being demoted to a clerk just because of her gender, and then deal with these new Islamic statutes. They filled her 'with a boundless rage'.[3] She was not the only woman to feel vulnerable and insulted by the new legislation and during the 1980s women campaigned for more equality with partial success. They were greatly helped by the war which sent more women to work; the great increase of girls in education by the end of the 1980s and most crucially by the fact they had the vote which Ayatollah Khomeini did not dare withdraw when he gave the people a referendum. In the 1990s they were also helped by the example of the daughters of revolutionary leaders who had active careers such as Ayatollah Khomeini's Zarah, or Hashem Rafsanjani's, Faezeh. By the mid 1990s this pressure had improved women's legal options – they were able to start divorce proceedings; the *mehr* (the money the man promises to give if the marriage ends) was linked to inflation; more favourable employment laws were introduced; and more professions were opened for them.

Compared to many other Muslim nations, Iran's overall record on women's issues since 1979 is very good. Over 95 per cent of girls attend elementary school and they then go on to take up 40 per cent of all university places; a third of all government employees are female, with some professions having a major female presence, such as teaching or publishing, where 140 leading ones are led by women. And not a few women have risen to positions of great power, such as Massoumeh Ebtekar who was the vice president of the environment under President Khatami, or Fatemeh Javadi who is vice president under Ahmadinejad. Despite the introduction of Islamic laws at the start of the revolution, it would be completely wrong to suggest that Iran is horrifically oppressive to women. Compared to Saudi Arabia where women cannot even drive, Iran is much more advanced. However compared to other non-Muslim countries, which all Iranians can find out about via the internet, the adherence to the Islamic principle that a women is worth half a man makes all women feel very vulnerable, and some scholars argue that economically women suffer.[1]

Dress

This vulnerability is painfully underlined every time they step out into public, for their dress is a matter of great interest to the revolutionary government. To be modest all females from the age of 9 have to wear head scarves and manteaus, loose fitting plain coats while excessive make-up and smoking in public were banned. The overall impact of these rulings was to ensure that in public a woman did not in anyway appear attractive or 'available' to other men. The glory of her hair, the redness of her lips and the colour of her clothes were delights only to be enjoyed by her family members. It would be completely wrong to suggest that in 1979 the majority of Iranian women resented having to wear a scarf. Millions before the revolution wore it out of choice, and when the secular Reza Shah made it illegal, many women stayed at home rather than appear in public without their head uncovered. And just prior to the 1979 revolution many girls, especially students, would wear a scarf as a way to protest against the Pahlavis. So being encouraged to wear a head scarf was not out of line with the Iranian culture, however the way bad 'hijab' (Islamic dress) could lead to arbitrary arrest, this was unnerving. While their mothers were at worse irritated or insulted,[5] their daughters, who had never seen the scarf as a symbol of protest, were angry and saw the dress code as oppressive. So during the 1990s teenage girls stretched the rules as far as possible, wearing shorter manteaus, pushing their colourful scarves back to show off their hair and wearing plenty of make-up. Their youthful beauty was soon caught in the crossfire of the battle between the conservatives and reformists that began in earnest in 1997 and is not yet over, though at present (2007) the conservatives have the upper hand. Unveiled women for conservatives constitute a part of 'a colossal tidal wave of immorality'[6] and since the 2005 election of President Ahmadinejad, there has been a noticeable increase in the number of 'morality' police patrolling the streets cautioning thousands and arresting hundreds of women for bad 'hijab'.[7] As has been emphasized, wearing the scarf is still very much a part of the

Iranian culture.[8] It is the way the dress code is enforced which is deeply unpopular. One blogger talks of 'the patrol cars that put fear into our youth', another of how 'everyone feared being arrested' and another of 'the hand on my shoulder that abruptly swallows my world'.[9]

Gender segregation

The protecting of women from strange men is also the raison d'être in the official gender segregation in public which affects everyone. In theory the sexes cannot be together unless they are family but these rules are irrelevant for most Iranians as their whole social life is focused on family gatherings anyway. As for young people who do want to meet separately from their families, they have found ways round these rules as it seems every visiting Western journalist to affluent north Tehran has discovered. However those rules are still there, and when challenged by the Revolutionary Guards the experience can be humiliating. For 'doctar baazi' (chasing girls), young men can be arbitrarily arrested, beaten up, brought before the Revolutionary Courts and fined. This creates fear – and cynicism. For sometimes a bribe has to be paid to these devout enforcers. As with the dress code for women, the spirit behind these rules of segregation are completely in line with Iranian culture where a girl seen to have been with other men loses her value as nobody wants a second-hand wife. Whatever liberal Western journalists might write in their excitement at seeing young people at a party, this aspect of Iranian culture is deeply rooted. The issue is not then the mentality behind the regulations, but again the way they can be enforced.

These segregation rules are particularly irksome for weddings. For Iranians a good wedding is not about speeches, but dancing. Mixed dancing though is taboo and there are no large hotels or halls that would allow it. The problem is that most families though need a hotel as weddings in Iran are never small. So what often happens is that everyone is invited to the hotel where the sexes eat in different salons. Then there is a private party later. This is where the dancing happens. Having to have a segregated hotel reception is frustrating enough, but this dancing stage for the hosts can be even more fraught. Tipped off by neighbours or just the amount of noise, the Revolutionary Guards might turn up. Their presence is of course threatening, for they can take guests to the Komiteh, and the Komiteh can take them to the Revolutionary Courts. But what it usually means is that the father of the groom, for it is they who fund the wedding in Iran, not the father of the bride, has yet another bill to pay.

Sport is also affected by the mentality that women must not be seen to be available to other men. So it is all segregated, and if women want to play a game like golf, skiing, bicycling or paragliding where they will be in the public eye, they must wear their manteau and scarf. In a hall or stadium in front of fellow females they can wear normal games clothes. This rule even extends to the

Caspian Sea where a tall canvas wall runs from the back of special beaches right out into the sea. Men will go to one side, women the other. At other beaches only men can swim. This is no doubt grating, but on the whole segregation has helped women in sport. Before the revolution traditional families would not allow their daughters to get involved as it was mixed; now they can. Women are active in at least 25 sports, including motor-racing; there are about 16,000 coaches and referees; they have over 56 who train at an international level;[10] and the daughter of ex-President Rafsanjani, Faezeh, is the founder of the Islamic Women's Games which are regularly held in Tehran and have nearly a thousand competitors from across the Muslim world.

The main problem for women in Iran is not the fact that men cannot watch them, but that they cannot watch men. And the men they want to watch are the footballers. However the senior clergy have pronounced that it is un-Islamic for women to be able to see the bare legs of strange men, so they are kept out of the stadiums. This has caused immense frustration among female fans, so much so that they have been known to ignore the rule. In December 1997 about five thousand of them broke into the Azadi Stadium to welcome home the team who had beaten Australia in the qualifying game for the 1998 World Cup. The authorities had told them to keep away to 'ensure the dignity of Islam', but these women were too determined. An instinctive populist who saw that Islam's dignity could easily survive women attending football games, President Ahmadinejad lifted the ban in April 2006. The senior clergy were not amused, and in early May the supreme leader Ayatollah Khamanei replaced it.

It is again the whole issue of female chastity that lies behind the government's rulings on music. While there is dispute among Muslim scholars as to whether music is 'haraam' (prohibited) or not,[11] there is a general consensus among the devout that all Western music, classical and certainly rock, belongs to the world of partying, alcohol and sexual temptation. Writing in 1910 the respected Muslim scholar Mustafa Sabri argued that music affected the mind, making the lonely more alone, the tired more wearisome, and worst of all it agitated 'feelings of love and romance'.[12] If this was his view of Mozart and Bach, one wonders what he would have written about the Rolling Stones or Madonna. As well as the fear of immorality, there was also cultural pride as Western music was a pleasure enjoyed by the European colonial elite who had humiliated the Muslim world. So in 1979 Ayatollah Khomeini, the arch Islamist and nationalist, condemned all Western music as 'intoxicating'. It was banned from the air waves, music cassettes and records became illegal, and Iran's most famous female singer, Googoosh and the rest of Iran's pop community headed for exile in Los Angeles. Though easily available on the black market with Western music banned there was increased interest in traditional classical Persian music. The Tehran based professor and singer Shajarian soon being able to pack out concert halls around the world. However again gender segregation meant that

women were not allowed to perform in front of mixed audiences and even with
traditional music there was a lingering suspicion over the whole enterprise. So
all new official recordings had to be vetted, especially for the lyrics, and on TV
only the face of the musician would be shown, not the actual instrument. Then
in late 1996 the Supreme Leader announced that music corrupts the minds of
young children and all instruction for the under 16s was banned in government
schools. With the election of Khatami in 1997 there was a general easing of
restrictions, but then in 2005 Ahmadinejad, seeking to revive the memory of
Khomeini, reinstated the total ban on Western pop music. This is just a gesture
as with the internet and satellite TV the ban is a lost cause. Nevertheless the fact
the government tries to intrude into such matters of personal taste is offensive
and for the young it is as if their government is almost opposed to life. This feeling is well summed up in this open letter to the Supreme Leader on a blog:

> Dear Leader of the Revolution, Your Holiness, Have you ever fallen in love?
> Have you ever danced? Have you ever worn jeans? How many times has
> the scent of springtime in Shiraz driven you wile? Have you ever listened to
> Persian classical music? Or what about rap? Did you ever whistle?[13]

The determination to keep women pure has dramatically impacted all cinema
and TV. So for dramas good 'hijab', even for scenes set inside a house, is an
absolute must; directors have to be very creative to explore romantic themes;
and often they have to suffer a ban for a while till the religious experts make up
their mind whether a particular image is acceptable.[14] Despite these frustra-
tions, as discussed in Chapter 2, they have risen to these challenges. The state
controls all the TV and radio stations in Iran[15] and the senior executive of Iran's
national broadcasting organization is appointed – and sacked – directly by the
Supreme Leader. So the staff must uphold Islamic values and there can be dire
consequences if they fail. Once a woman was asked on a radio interview who
her role model was and she said it was a Japanese TV soap opera star. Unfortunately for the producers Ayatollah Khomeini was either listening (his family
complained he was obsessed with the news and even took the radio to the bath-
room with him), or somehow heard about this. He was furious: the woman
should have said her role model was Fatimah, the daughter of the prophet
Mohammad. For this gross failure to uphold Islamic values the broadcast director at Tehran radio was sentenced to 5 years, three others involved to 4 years,
and all were to get 50 lashes.[16] Later Ayatollah Khomeini pardoned them, but
he had certainly sent a clear message to everyone in the media. Likewise with
the print media editors must be very careful in their portrayal of women, and if
a foreign language magazine has a woman showing too much flesh, the censor's
pen will get to work.

Politics

Film, TV and Radio

Presenting women as chaste is then the first factor behind much of the Islamic revolution's impact on culture. The second dominating factor is politics which also means the treatment of Islam. So the censor's eye has always been keen to mark for removal any artistic content that might either undermine Islam, or the Islamic Republic. So though Shajiran is easily Iran's most popular singer, he rarely gives concerts in Iran where he lives and works because he likes to use poems such as *Winter* by Mehdi Saless,[17] or *The Bird of Dawn* by the early twentieth-century scholar and champion of the 1906 constitution, Malek Bahar. These poems have clear political overtones and are frowned upon by the regime. With film the regime is as equally sensitive, so Masoud's Kimiaei's *Khateh Ghermez* (Red Line) made in 1980 was banned because it showed that the origin of the revolution was linked to secular intellectuals, and not just religious fundamentalists. And Bahram Beizai's *Margh Yazdegerd* (Death of Yazdegerd) made in 1981 was also banned as the censors believed it was implying that the glories of Iran's pre-Islamic past were spoilt by the invading Arab armies. Other films[18] have been banned for having too morbid endings that might spoil the people's revolutionary spirit. The regime's concern over its reputation even reaches into Turkey where it made sure the authorities there stopped the showing of the American comedy *Naked Gun* as it had comical allusions to Ayatollah Khomeini, and *Veiled Threat* where a CIA agent helps a family escape Iran after the revolution. As Mohsen Makmalabaf has made clear, films are often caught in the crossfire of the political conflict that has been raging in Iran since the mid 1990s between conservatives and reformists. So after being fiercely attacked by the conservative press for two films, *Time For Love* and *Nights of Zayandeh Round* which dealt with human love he retorted – 'The writer of these columns knows well that these arguments have nothing to do with him. The fight is over nothing other than the struggles between different factions who seek power.'[19]

As TV and radio is state controlled it poses no political threat to the regime: every station adheres faithfully to the government's line on every political issue. So Saddam was always an apostate; the Iran–Iraq war was imposed; Israel is a usurping Zionist state, and the country's nuclear programme is peaceful. The authorities have always been particularly sensitive about anything that would undermine the authority of the Supreme Leader, so for example in October 1991 a live broadcast from the Majlis was simply switched off because an argument about Ayatollah Khamanei had become too heated.[20] However for curious and questioning Iranians this sort of broadcasting is boring[21] so in the early years of the revolution they tuned into the BBC World Service or even

Radio Israel which maintains a high quality Persian programme. Then in the 1990s there was great demand for satellite TV as it became available. It is estimated that Iran now has 34 million dishes serving an audience of around 20 million.[22] Since 1994 it has been illegal to own or use a satellite, but the government has been wary of making itself too unpopular by meting out ferocious punishments and has limited itself to sporadic campaigns of confiscating the dishes and fining owners. These have increased under President Ahmadinejad, but nobody seriously believes that Iran will ever be satellite TV free, and it is likely that the government's unpredictable response to the spread of the satellite dishes will continue.

There are certain elements in the government who believe in taking action to especially block the broadcasts of opposition groups into the country. There was an attempt to do this in 2005 prior to the presidential elections, but the technology used was so strong it upset normal TV and mobile phone networks. There are also reports that the Revolutionary Guards are seeking to obtain more sophisticated equipment to be able to block more successfully. However there are almost certainly other people in the regime who realize for good reasons that satellite TV will never have a dramatic impact on the country's political landscape. First the average dish brings in over 600 programmes into people's homes and by far the most popular channels are the entertainment ones, not the political ones. Then secondly the majority of Iranians still do not have access to satellite TV, so even if there was a political voice that managed to compete with the dancing girls there would still not be the same focus as there was when everyone had radio and could listen to exactly the same reports on the BBC Persian service in the late 1970s. The regime is also helped by the fact that many of the opposition political programmes are less than impressive. They often feature well oiled looking elderly men in Los Angeles studios insisting they are going to liberate Iran. Every sane viewer knows their life is far too comfortable in America and they are going to get straight back into their cars and drive home. Perhaps the Revolutionary Guards will bring in much tougher controls, but to date enforcement has been lukewarm, which probably indicates that others in the regime are ready to tolerate the dishes for the reasons above. Perhaps they have read the Roman satirist Juvenal who said people only really want cheap bread and the circus. So if they are happy with this satellite circus and as it poses no serious threat to the government, they might as well keep it, especially as it is free.

Newspapers and the reform movement

There is no such laxness when it comes to the printed press. The constitution guarantees freedom of the press, and unlike broadcasters, newspapers are not officially owned by the state. However all their material must be in accordance with Islamic principles which are ultimately defined by the Supreme Leader. Immediately after the revolution, relishing their new found freedom from dictatorship, Iranians soon found they could read over 250 different newspapers representing a whole spectrum of political opinion. As the regime began to feel threatened by other Islamic groups, especially the Mojahadeen, so this season of freedom came to an abrupt end in November 1980 when Khomeini asked the faithful – 'Why do you not stop these newspapers? Why do you not shut their mouths? Why do you not stop their pens?'[23] His servants moved into action, opposition newspapers were closed down, and soon the only ones left were those funded by the governing elite. So both of Iran's two leading nationals, *Kayhan* and *Ettela'at* are owned by the massive Bonyad-e Mostazafin, and both its editors are appointed by the Supreme Leader. Controls for the publication of new newspapers and magazines are stringent: would-be publishers must first receive confirmation from the government that they are 'morally fit'; their journalists must all be accredited with the Ministry of Culture and Islamic Guidance; and then two copies of every issue published must be sent to this ministry. If officials then deem that any of the material 'that denies or weakens the principles of Islam' the staff can face arrest and trial, the publishing house closure and the owners financial ruin. Given the extreme sensitivity of the regime it is not surprising that most publications have been very cautious. This sensitivity is well illustrated by the case of the cartoonist Manouchehr Karimzadeh who wanted to depict the poor state of Iranian football with a picture of a bearded player with an amputated leg and foot in the science magazine *Farad* in April 1992. Unfortunately for Karimzadeh some officials thought his footballer looked like Ayatollah Khomeini. Mobs gathered outside the magazine's office demanding the death sentence, and the cartoonist had to appear before a Revolutionary Court where he was sentenced to a year's imprisonment, a fine and 50 lashes.[24]

Such a climate in the 1980s and early 1990s did not encourage any political questioning in the press of the fundamentals of the Iranian Revolution. The only debate seen was the one going on within the elite, first of all between Hashem Rafsanjani's pro-economy pragmatic stance reflected in *Ettela'at*, and the Supreme Leader's more isolationist view, supported in *Kayhan*. However in May 1997 when the reformist Mohammad Khatami unexpectedly won over 70 per cent of the popular vote in the presidential elections a major political battle opened up between the reformists and the conservatives[25] and one of the bloodiest battlefields was the press. In two previous administrations Khatami had served as head of the Ministry of Culture and Islamic Guidance (1982–1986; 1989–1992) where he had established a reputation for encouraging artistic creativity and supporting a freer press. Indeed in 1992 he resigned over the then government's punitive stance against the press. Though Khatami wanted to give Iranians more cultural freedom within Islamic boundaries, his overall aim was much more political. He wanted the country to be governed by clear laws which while protecting Iran's religious traditions, could not be changed overnight in the name of Islam. This was a call for democratic accountability at the heart of government, instead of dictates from the country's unelected institutions always ready to demonize opposition policies as hostile to Islam.

Khatami understood very clearly that a free press was crucial to such democratic accountability, and so with his arrival as president there was a surge in new independent publications appearing. It was the *Tehran Spring*, when the news-stands became exciting places to visit. 'The newspapers enhanced our morning routines delightfully', wrote Shirin Ebadi, 'I picked up five or six regularly and sat down with a steaming cup of tea, savoring the new ritual. It was so civilizing to finally have a national conversation about where the country was headed.'[26] In the mind-set of the conservatives there was no room for democratic accountability at the heart of the government of God. Here only the Supreme Leader could correctly interpret Islamic rules. So though the hard-liners were initially unnerved by the popularity of the reformists, with these dogmatic beliefs and the judiciary, Revolutionary Guards and numerous vigilante groups under their control, they soon found the confidence to resist the reformist tide. Much of their efforts were concentrated on intimidating the new reformist press. In January 1998 the head of the judiciary Mohammad Yazdi bluntly told the public that it was none of their business whom his courts arrested – 'Why would we tell you what is going on? Do we have to tell you the reason for an arrest?'[27] In April, reacting to criticism over the imprisonment of President Khatami's ally, the Tehran Mayor Karbashi and reports that his municipal officials had been tortured in detention, the judiciary ordered police raids on the offices of three reformist papers – *Hamshari* (Fellow Citizen), *Iran* and *Jame'eh* (Society). The latter had made many powerful enemies since its launch in February. It had accused the director of the massive Bonyad for the dispossessed, Rafiq Dost, of corruption; claimed that the commander of the Revolutionary Guards General Safavi had said that his men had to 'root out counter revolutionaries wherever they are. We have to cut the throats of some and cut the tongues of others'; and even questioned the legitimacy of the unelected Supreme Leader when President Khatami had won over 20 million votes. The judiciary closed down *Jame'eh* on 11 June, but a few days later the reformist Minister of Culture issued the editor a license to open another newspaper, and *Tous* appeared. Mohammad Yazdi responded by attacking journalists who 'use their pen to attack the strong roots of Islam' and on cue the *Tous* offices were ransacked and its editor Mashallah Shamsolvaezin beaten up. The Supreme Leader sealed the paper's fate. On 1 September before a group of the Basiji in Mashad he accused the 'pen holders' of being more dangerous than 'bandits' and warned that 'Those who oppose the ghesas (stories in the Koran) are mortad (apostates). There is no question about the punishment of a mortad in Islam.'[28] On 15 September he again referred to 'a dangerous, creeping, cultural movement writing against Islam' and invited the judiciary to take action saying, 'I am now waiting to see what the officials will do.'[29] They were not hesitant.

The next day *Tous* was closed down and four of the paper's staff were arrested. In September another five reformist publications were stopped, and a letter from the conservative Majlis demanded erring journalists be tried before the Revolutionary Courts. The staff of *Tous* were released on bail in October having spent time in solitary confinement. They had also appeared before those courts and been charged with 'enmity with God', an offence that carries the death sentence.[30]

President Khatami kept on speaking out for a free press, arguing that to push public opinion underground would only cause 'a later explosion'.[31] With this support *Tous* re-emerged under the title *Neshat*, with Mashallah Shamsolvaezin again the editor, and other reformist titles, such as *Sobh-e Emrooz* published by Khatami's political advisor Saeed Hajjarian, *Zan*, a paper for women controlled by Rafsanjani's daughter Faezeh, and *Salam*, which was especially popular with students. So despite all the intimidation in September there was still a Reformist press to report on the brutal murders of dissidents and intellectuals that began in November 1998. On 22 November the 70-year-old leader of Mossadeq's National Front party, Daryush Foruhar, and his wife Parvaneh were ruthlessly stabbed in their home.[32] Later that month the dissident poet Mohammad Mokhtari went missing. His strangled body eventually turned up in a morgue on 9 December. Two days later the body of the translator Mohammad Pouyandeh was found under a Tehran bridge. He too had been strangled. Others who were killed or went missing were Majid Sharif (found dead 24 November), who advocated a more modern interpretation of Islam; Pirouz Davani (went missing 28 August, reportedly executed 22 November), an advocate for democracy; Rostami Hamedani (went missing mid December), a colleague to Davani; Fatemeh Eslami (strangled 13 January 1999); Javad Emami, a judicial expert and his wife (killed 17 January); and Mahmoud Ghafouri (reported missing 20 January 1999).

Whoever organized these murders did not realize it would turn into a major political crisis[33] because of the press. The papers reported every detail, publicly aired the widespread suspicion that intelligence officers had been involved, and demanded a thorough investigation to bring those responsible for the violence to court. Particularly vocal in this campaign was Akbar Ganji who argued that these murders were a normal part of business in the Islamic Republic whereby at least 50 dissidents had been killed in the past 10 years.[34] He was particularly critical of ex-President Rafsanjani's role in these matters. Week after week he characterized the conservatives as 'the rotten core of a corrupt and disreputable system, and the Iranian public, who had never seen quite the like of this before, lapped it all up'.[35] People were furious and President Khatami pressed ahead with an investigation which ended up with the government making this unprecedented announcement on 4 January 1999 –

Unfortunately a small number of irresponsible, misguided, headstrong and obstinate staff within the Ministry of Information who are no doubt under the influence of undercover rogue agents and act towards the objectives of foreign and estranged sources committed these criminal activities.[36]

Four members of the Intelligence Ministry were arrested, and the ring leader was identified as the deputy, Sa'id Emami. Khatami demanded the resignation of the actual Intelligence minister, Qursan-'Ali Durri-Najafabadi and went on to purge the Intelligence Ministry of about 80 per cent of its staff who had connections with state terror.[37] This was the high point for the Reform movement, it truly seemed the ship of the revolution was turning, and it was happening mainly because of the courage of the press.

Fearing revulsion over the murders could bring people onto the streets, the Supreme Leader had not intervened to stop Khatami's purge, but on 10 January he made a speech with a familiar argument – 'I cannot accept that these murders took place without a foreign scenario behind them. This is impossible . . .'[38] Taking up this cry conservative voices highlighted the fact that Sa'id Emami had been to university in the US where no doubt he had been recruited for the CIA. Though only the faithful believed this contention, it became impossible to disprove when it was reported in June 1999 that Emami had committed suicide in prison by drinking hair removal cream. Many found this suspicious,[39] but nevertheless Emami's death drew a line under the case as those questioned could always point to the dead man as the one who knew the answers. Badly wounded by the serial murders, the conservatives now fought back against the Reformist press with new vigour. In February the unknown cleric Mohsen Kadivar was sent to prison for 18 months for writing in the paper *Khordad* that the Islamic Republic was similar to the monarchy; in April the *Zan* magazine was closed for mocking the fact that in Iran's courts a women's value is worth half a man's; in May the managing directors of *Iran*, *Arya* and *Neshat* were arrested and only released after an exorbitant bail was paid, some of the funds actually coming from the Ministry of Culture; on 16 June the editor of the reformist weekly *Hoviyat – e Khich* was arrested; and then on 7 July the conservative parliament accepted a severe draft law against press freedom which would force journalists to reveal their sources and on the same day the judiciary closed down the very popular daily *Salam*, arresting one of its journalists and charging its director, Mohammad Khoeiniha.[40]

It was these arrests and the closing down of *Salam* that first brought a small group of students onto the streets in Tehran on 8 July. That night their dormitories were ransacked, students were beaten up and some were even thrown out of their windows. The next day Tehran and other cities erupted in the largest protests the regime had ever seen. At the heart of these protests was the issue of press freedom. Now the Supreme Leader and his allies made it quite clear that they were willing to use force to ensure their control of the papers. For all observers it was abundantly clear that this had nothing to do with religion, and everything to do with politics. For in response to the demonstrations several divisions of the Revolutionary Guards were stationed around Tehran and other major cities. All now depended on Khatami. If he spoke up for the students – and a free press – he would have been signalling for the whole Reform movement to be ready to fight. Knowing the crucial role he could play 24 senior leaders of the Revolutionary Guards sent President Khatami a letter, published in the regime's paper *Kayhan* advising him not to take any 'revolutionary decisions' but to 'act in accordance with your Islamic and national mission'. It also warned that their 'patience was exhausted'.[41] Khatami was not a Cromwell or a Lenin and faced with the choice of either a bloody civil war with the hard-liners, who controlled all the instruments of organized violence, or siding with them against the students, he chose the latter. On 16 July he denounced the demonstrators, and on 17 the ordinary police – not the Revolutionary Guards – moved in decisively and arrested over 1,000 protesters.

Though the Reformists went on to win the parliamentary elections in 2000, their movement and support for a free press never recovered from the defeat of July 1999. The conservatives now knew the reformists did not have the stomach for bloodshed. And to make sure President Khatami had no illusions regarding their own willingness to shed blood Said Hajjarian, Khatami's close adviser and director of the paper *Sobh-e Emrooz*, was gunned down on 12 March 2000. His assailants were riding a 1,000 cc motorcycle which only the security services were allowed to use. Hajarian survived, but was crippled: the conservatives wanted to make sure it was the same – metaphorically – for the rest of the reform movement, especially the newspapers. Already in the run-up to the February Majlis elections, the reformist press had faced constant intimidation with leading conservatives such as Ayatollah Misbah-Yazdi accusing the editors of receiving millions of dollars from the CIA, then in April the Supreme Leader joined in the accusation. Speaking at Tehran's Grand Mosque before thousands of supporters he said –

> There are ten to fifteen papers writing as if they are directed from one centre, undermining Islamic and revolutionary principles . . . unfortunately the same enemy who wants to overthrow the (regime) has found a base in the country . . . Some of the press have become the base of the enemy.[42]

By the end of the month 30 publications had been closed down,[43] and some of Iran's most famous journalists such as Mashallah Shamsolvaezin and Akbar Ganji sent to prison. In early 2000 Iran had a president and a parliament that wanted a free press, but the politics of force had given the last word. The press was muzzled, the buzz from the news-stands was no more; and people again relied on foreign radio and satellite TV stations for their news – and the internet.

Blogging

Conservative Muslims in Iran, following Ayatollah Khomeini, are always keen to stress that Islam supports scientific and technological progress. So there has been no hesitancy on the part of the regime to encourage the use of the internet. Many senior government leaders and Ayatollahs have their own websites, and libraries in Qom are available through the net to millions of Shias around the world. It is estimated that at least 5 million people[44] have access to the internet in their homes, and everyone can use the thousands of internet cafes in every town and village in Iran. Though the internet is the ultimate in freedom of expression the government to date has not ordered any blanket crack down. With emails the sheer number involved makes it practically impossible for the government to control, so this has meant that opposition groups can coordinate their activity, unless they come to the notice of the security forces. Then their computer can become a great information liability. However with websites the censor is constantly active. Again given the avalanche of material there is no attempt to block every website which presents women who are not wearing good 'hijab', however the government do heroically try and block pornographic sites. And any site that is perceived to be a political threat is blocked by the regime. This has led the censor directly to the world of web blogs.

With the clamp down on the printed press, web blogs swiftly became the nation's new public notice boards.[45] Some of these are featured in Nasrin Alavi's fascinating book *We Are Iran* where the bloggers lambast the government for its oppressive policies, indeed the hostility of some is more vitriolic than any printed article would ever be. It was unlikely the government was going to sit idly by while its reputation was shred apart in cyber space and in April 2003 Iran became the first country to imprison a web blogger – Sina Motallebi. Since then Ayatollah Shahrudi, the head of the judiciary, has decreed that all material in cyber space that undermines the government or Islam was a crime, and predictably the conservative paper *Kayhan* said that the anti-government blogs were a 'network led by the CIA conspiring to overthrow the regime.'[46] In 2004 there were reports of at least ten bloggers either being arrested or imprisoned, all for political reasons.[47] In 2005 Arash Sigarchi was sentenced to a 14 years imprisonment for criticizing the regime, the harsh punishment interpreted by many as being a warning to others, as typically he was later released on bail, but then in early 2006 he was imprisoned again for 3 years. Clearly signalling it wanted more control of cyberspace, the cabinet in November 2006 decreed that all news sites dealing with Iran had to register with the government.[48] This has not been possible to implement fully, but the government did begin to block a much wider range of websites in 2006, including the BBC Persian site and continues its intimidation of bloggers. It has also ordered all service providers to limit online speeds to 128 kilobits per second, so making access to all websites slow, and watching films on the net tortuous.

Irritatingly frightening

The slowing down of the internet is an irritation to most people, as are most of the cultural laws the Islamic state imposes on them. As seen they can get round most restrictions, and even when the authorities detain people, they often release them after one or two nights in prison. It is as if the strict schoolmaster has decided to teach some naughty children a lesson. Much of this legislation then is demeaning, rather than devastating. However a longer stay in Iran's judicial system can be very bleak. As well as having to deal with grim living conditions, the 'best' cell for Shirin Ebadi was 'covered in filth and the sink had no running water . . .',[49] there is often no access to any legal representation and sometimes the accused have to face long hours of interrogation and the possibility of solitary confinement or other forms of torture. In recent arrests a number of journalists and bloggers, including satirist Nabravi, writer Massound Behnoud, and the blogger Kinaoosh Sanjari have talked about the horror of solitary confinement –

> You have never been this close to walls in your life. You don't want to sit, because it is chalk, and you are not used to sitting on chalk. You stand. You pace. You start to get dizzy. After you get dizzy, you lean on a wall. After three or four hours, your legs get tired, and you sit. And then you scream and no one hears you.[50]

And throughout the ordeal there is complete uncertainty as to what the final judgment from the Revolutionary Court will be: for this court can pass the sentence of execution on anyone found guilty of 'enmity with God' or being 'the corrupt of the earth', crimes only the court can define. Since the massacre of Mojahedin sympathizers executed in 1988, the present regime to date has not sentenced any of its reformist political opponents to death. Nevertheless there have still been plenty of executions. Iran (with the US) is usually in the annual top five countries for executions: according to Amnesty International there were 177 in 2006, and by September 2007 there had already been 210.[51] Though most of these executions are for recognized crimes such as drug smuggling, murder and armed robbery, a few are killed for cultural crimes, such as consuming alcohol, adultery and homosexuality, all of which are illegal in Iran. In June 2005, a Kurd, Karim Fahimi, was condemned to die for drinking, and is still on death row.[52] In 2006 nine women and two men were sentenced to death by stoning for adultery,[53] and in July 2007 there were reports that the adulterer Jafar Kiani had been stoned to death in Takestan (Qazim province). His wife, Mokkaraham Ebrahimi, has been sentenced to the same punishment.[54] In 2005 two young men in Mashad were hung, officially for raping a 13-year-old boy, but others believe it was because they were homosexual, and claim the regime has executed many others.[55]

The fact that the state can execute people for their private behaviour or expressing a political opinion gives a frightening edge to all Iranians who have dealings with the judiciary. Not surprisingly, many are cowed by the danger and try to assure the government that they will no longer misbehave. So Ibrahim Nabavi, a satirical journalist said after being released from solitary confinement, 'From now on I will write my subjects concisely, well-calculated, and with wisdom and cleverness.'[56] Once cowed into submission they join the ranks of the majority who just have to tolerate all the irritating intrusions into their private life which over the years they have learned to live with and which since 2005 have been enforced with new vigour.

To date the hard-liners in the government have made sure that their cultural values have been upheld, and that alternative political views are muffled. Despite the overwhelming mandate from the electorate that people wanted more personal freedom and political debate, due to the Supreme Leader keeping control of the judiciary, the initial restrictions introduced by the revolution are still in place. It would seem that life will go on as normal in the Islamic Republic, but it might well be that a price will be paid. For the right of the state to constantly interfere in people's personal lives breeds resentment, picked up the most casual reading of Iran's blogs.

In one we read –

Have you not noticed that everything that Iranians do is considered illegal? In reality, everything is outlawed . . . Listening to music or watching a film. The clothes you wear, what you drink, the games you play, the conversations you have and what you discuss. What you read and write. What you do on the Internet, keeping a blog . . . all are illegal.[57]

This entry, titled 'An Illegal Existence' highlights a dangerous tension the cultural and political policies of the revolution have brought about. Before the revolution nearly everyone was ready to call themselves a Shia Muslim, and behave as they wanted in their personal lives. Since the revolution the government has tried to make people live like proper Shia Muslims and this has resulted in some calling their existence illegal. Confronted with the demands of their national religion, millions have concluded they are out of step with the reality of their life. Yet they are still aware that they are heirs of a rich spiritual inheritance. And so this constant controlling of culture and politics by the government has ironically caused some to seek for a legitimate existence elsewhere.

Notes

[1] Khomeini began this work in exile in Turkey and then completed it in Najaf. As well as covering spiritual topics such as praying and fasting, it also stipulates for

areas like business contracts and very personal matters, such as how one should defecate and urinate. For samples of the work see – www.al-shia.com/html/eng/books/fiqh&usool/islamic-laws/tahrir/01.html [last accessed 6 June 2008].

[2] This explains the importance in the East that the bride is a virgin whereas fewer questions are asked about the groom – she is the one who will bear the son. For more on this and the whole question of how female chastity is a measure of male honour see Dr. Arley Loewen's 'The Sound of Battle?' unpublished paper, March 1998, Middle East Civilizations, University of Toronto.

[3] Shirin Ebadi, *Iran Awakening*, Random House, New York, 2006, p. 51.

[4] See Part Three of *The Economy of Iran* edited by Parvin Alizadeh, I. B. Tauris, 2000.

[5] As in all cultures the issue of dress at times was also a focus for class hatred, with the aspiring middle class ladies tending to be more fashionable, and the poorer being more conservative. So when disputes flare up about more practical matters, such as parking or a traffic accident, working class people have been known to insult middle class women who show some of their hair by calling them *lokht*, naked.

[6] See Nasrin Alavi's *We Are Iran*, Portobello, London, 2006, p. 32. In a 2004 edition of the official paper of Iran's Hezbollah, the Yas'Saratal-Hussein, the editorial calls on readers to defend the country's honour against what 'American war ships cannot even imagine creating in Iran – the control of this country and its youth – the bare arms, the nude legs, the immoral made up faces and bare heads . . .'

[7] See 'Crackdown in Iran over dress codes' by Frances Harrison http://news.bbc.co.uk/1/hi/world/middle_east/6596933.stm [last accessed 6 June 2008]. You can also watch how the police caution women on YouTube – www.youtube.com/watch?v=Jcz3TYqWpwc [last accessed 6 June 2008].

[8] Iranian TV claimed that 85 per cent of people in a poll they conducted supported the crackdown, see http://news.bbc.co.uk/1/hi/world/middle_east/6596933.stm [last accessed 6 June 2008]. An Iranian business man wrote in the BBC with this – For women, since we live in an Islamic country, they should wear something polite and modest and respect Islamic rules. But I do not believe in police enforcing these rules! Also see Robin Wright's *The Last Great Revolution*, Random House, New York, 2000, p. 153. 'I've also talked to with dozens of regime women who honestly prefer the physical safety of Islamic dress . . .'

[9] See Alavi's *We Are Iran*, pp. 24, 26, 30.

[10] See 'Iranian women put on their running shoes' 1999 by Siavosh Ghazi, journalist in Teheran, Iran, www.unesco.org/courier/1999_04/uk/dossier/txt12.htm [last accessed 6 June 2008].

[11] For arguments for the ban see www.inter-islam.org/Prohibitions/Mansy_music.htm; and against see www.submission.org/music.html [both last accessed 6 June 2008].

[12] See 'A Topic of Dispute in Islam: Music' by Mustafa Sabrihi, copyright anadulo 1995, www.wakeup.org/anadolu/05/4/mustafa_sabri_en.html [last accessed 6 June 2008].

[13] See Alavi's *We Are Iran*, p. 114.

[14] For example the now classic film 'Bashu, The Little Stranger' was banned in Iran from 1986–1989 because of the prominent role given to the lead actress Susan Taslimi.

[15] All TV and radio stations are controlled by a special committee made up of representatives from the elected President and the Majlis (Parliament), and from the unelected head of the judiciary. Crucially the head of the organization responsible for all TV and Radio is appointed – and can be sacked – by the Supreme Leader. See Article 175 of the Iranian Constitution.

[16] See Middle East Watch, *Guardians of Thought: Limits on Freedom of Expression in Iran*, Human Rights Watch, New York, 1993, p. 66.

[17] Discussed in Chapter 2, p. 33.

[18] Examples would be Mehrjui's 'Hamoon' (Bath) and Ejareh Neshinan (Tenants), Ali Jakan's 'Madiyan' (Mare), Rahman Rezai's 'Mada Basteh' (Closed Circuit) and Kimiai's 'Goruhban' Sergeant. Mohsen Makhmalbaf's films in the 1980s like the Baysikel Ran (Cyclist) which depicted extreme poverty were also heavily criticized, but given the director's then impeccable revolutionary credentials they were allowed.

[19] See Middle East Watch, *Guardians of Thought*, p. 108.

[20] See Middle East Watch, *Guardians of Thought*, p. 66.

[21] 'Iranian state TV channels are very boring. The music is always dull, there are no dances and the news is always censored', said a young college student who rued the thought that he would not be able to watch his favourite channels – see 'Crackdown on Satellite TV taken stoically' by Kimia Sanati. http://ipsnews.net/news.asp?idnews=34407 [last accessed 6 June 2008].

[22] www.worldproutassembly.org/archives/2006/08/crackdown_on_ir.html [last accessed 6 June 2008].

[23] See Middle East Watch, *Guardians of Thought*, p. 33.

[24] See Middle East Watch, *Guardians of Thought*, p. 47.

[25] For a very clear analysis of the main political groupings at work in modern Iran see Chapter Two of Ray Takeyh's *Hidden Iran*, Times Books, New York, 2006, titled 'Conservatives, Pragmatists, and Reformers'.

[26] Ebadi, *Iran Awakening*, p. 148.

[27] See 'The Press under President Khatami', Human Rights Watch http://hrw.org/reports/1999/iran/Iran99o-02.htm [last accessed 6 June 2008].

[28] See Behzad Yaghmaian's *Social Change in Iran*, State University New York Press, Albany, 2002, p. 129.

[29] See 'The Press under President Khatami', Human Rights Watch.

[30] See Yaghmaian's *Social Change in Iran*, p. 126 and 'The Press under President Khatami', Human Rights Watch.

[31] See 'The Press under President Khatami', Human Rights Watch.

[32] The public were shocked at the way this couple had been murdered. Daryush had been tied to a chair which was set to face Mecca, and stabbed 11 times; his wife 24 times. Both their bodies were mutilated. See *Iran Awakening* by Ebadi, p. 137.

[33] See *Iran, Islam and Democracy: The Politics of Managing Change* by Ali Ansari, Royal Institute of International Affairs, London, 2006, p. 177.

[34] See *The Persian Puzzle* by Kenneth Pollack, Random House, 2005, p. 330.

[35] See *Iran, Islam and Democracy*, by Ansari, p. 180.

[36] www.iranmania.com/news/currentaffairs/features/dissidentmurders/default.asp [last accessed 6 June 2008].

[37] See *The Persian Puzzle* by Pollack, p. 331.

38 See Yaghmaian's *Social Change in Iran*, p. 133.
39 The human rights lawyer Shirin Ebadi doubted this story, not least because all the hair removal cream available had 'no arsenic' written on it. She even wondered whether Emami had died, but when she went to the mourning reception and offered her condolences to his wife she, 'took one look at her red rimmed eyes, felt her unsteady hand in mine, and knew that her husband was dead'. Ebadi, *Iran Awakening*, p. 139.
40 See www.cpj.org/attacks99/mideast99/Iran.html [last accessed 6 June 2008].
41 See *The Persian Puzzle* by Kenneth Pollack, p. 333.
42 See 'Iran: The Press on Trial' by Joel Campagna, New York, 5 May 2000 – CPJ Press Freedom Reports from around the world. www.cpj.org/attacks00/mideast00/Iran.html [last accessed 6 June 2008].
43 For a full list see www.cpj.org/attacks00/mideast00/Iran.html [last accessed 6 June 2008].
44 See CIA World Fact Book 2007.
45 Hossein Derakhshan is often credited as the father of Persian blogging when he set up an easy 'how to blog' in Persian in September 2001.
46 See Alavi's *We Are Iran*, p. 3.
47 See www.rsf.org/article.php3?id_article=11978 [last accessed 6 June 2008].
48 For more detail on the government crack down on bloggers and all journalists visit the Middle East Section of the Reporter Sans Frontiers website – www.rsf.org/article.php3?id_article=23780 and see their archived reports on Iran [last accessed 6 June 2008].
49 Ebadi, *Iran Awakening*, p. 164.
50 Interview by Human Rights Watch with Masssoud Behnan in London 20 December, 2003. For more detail see – http://hrw.org/reports/2004/iran0604/5.htm#_ftn56 [last accessed 6 June 2008].
51 See 'Iran: Amnesty International appalled at the spiralling numbers of executions', 5 September 2007, web.amnesty.org/library/Index/ENGMDE131102007 [last accessed 6 June 2008].
52 See 'Iran: Death penalty/imminent execution: Karim Fahimi', web.amnesty.org/library/Index/ENGMDE130692005 [last accessed 6 June 2008].
53 'Iran: Stoning for "adultery" – a women's issue', www.wluml.org/english/ [last accessed 6 June 2008].
54 See Amnesty International web.amnesty.org/library/Index/ENGMDE130842007 [last accessed 6 June 2008].
55 The homosexual magazine 'Outrage' puts the number at 4,000, see 'Iran – The State-Sponsored Torture & Murder of Lesbians & Gays Men New evidence of how the clerical regime frames, defames and hangs homosexuals' by Simon Forbes, April 2006 UK, www.petertatchell.net/international/iranstatemurder.htm [last accessed 6 June 2008].
56 See Yaghmaian's *Social Change in Iran*, p. 127.
57 See Alavi's *We Are Iran*, p. 333.

Conclusion to Part Two

In the conclusion to Part One it was said that though there are elements in the Iranian Identity which would be in sympathy with some of the tenets of Christianity, this observation was just academic, as since 1501 Iran has never seen to be remotely interested in abandoning Shia Islam as its national religion. The fortunes of her kings have waxed and waned, but the permanence of her religion had stayed, and then when seemingly threatened by a cultural invasion from the West, it was the call of Shia Islam that brought millions to the barricades. At heart the revolution was all about an entire nation rejecting one vision for a new modern secular identity offered by the Pahlavis, and embracing an older, religious one, offered by Ayatollah Khomeini. Since 1979 it would seem Shia Islam and Iran have been one and there is no room or need for another religion, unless the people have been traumatized by the experience.

And in this section it is fair to conclude that overall the experience of Iran being ruled in the name of Shia Islam has been traumatic. First Iranians experienced the trauma of deceit. Ayatollah Khomeini promised freedom, but all along he planned to establish a religious dictatorship which is exactly what he did; this was followed by the trauma of a civil war which saw thousands of teenagers imprisoned for showing the slightest interest in the Mojahedin. Many were later executed in 1988. And then there was the much greater horror of the unnecessary war with Iraq which resulted in half a million casualties and not a millimetre of extra territory for Iran. Historically wars can so scar society that they bring in major social changes. So it was that the religious wars in Europe in the seventeenth century opened the way for the enlightenment which cautioned against allowing theological dogma a place at the table of the elite; so too it was that the First World War was the catalyst for the Russian Revolution; and so too there is a clear link between the impact of the Second World War and the decline of the church in Europe in the second half of the twentieth century. As yet there is no such result in Iran – but there is no doubt that the scar of war is still very open. There is also the trauma of economic decline. Millions have seen their incomes plummet, bread winners needing two jobs, pensioners not being able to retire and workers' rights being curtailed. Yet the clerical elite have grown fabulously wealthy, so spreading a sense of injustice. Finally there is the trauma of cultural and political control. Despite people clearly voting for more freedom, the judiciary has continued to maintain its right to intrude into people's private lives, and has waged a successful war against the press.

There is no doubt that the overall impact of this trauma has been to bring about a dislocation of varying degrees of intensity between many Iranians and Shia Islam. It would be naïve to assert that this dislocation is going to bring about the imminent downfall of Shia Islam as Iran's national religion as some writers have claimed.[1] Historically nations only abruptly change their national religion when invaded by an army committed to imposing another faith, such as the Arab armies were in the seventh century. No such army threatens Iran today. However this dislocation has impacted Iran: there is increasing apathy and nominalism towards religion; intellectuals have issued a call for a reformation of Shia Islam; and there has been an upsurge of interest in other religions, including Christianity. Disillusionment does not always bring a decisive break with a religion, but it often brings nominalism, indifference and apathy. In Iran this apathy is not hard to detect. In conversation many people are quick to say they are not 'Hezhbolli', i.e. not committed Shia Muslims; it is clear that the city youth culture largely ignores a religion that calls most of their activities 'illegal';[2] and the rise of prostitution and drug use[3] is evidence that at a practical level people are not following the tenets of Islam. The impact of this dislocation on intellectuals has been very clear. Led by thinkers such as Abdolkarim Soroush, Akbar Ganji, Mohammad Shabestari and Mohsen Kadivar[4] there is a significant movement that questions the theological position of the Supreme Leader and calls for dogmatic Islam to withdraw from the political domain. Some commentators are calling Soroush the Martin Luther of Iran and are hoping for a reformation within Islam similar to that experienced in Christendom in the fifteenth century. And certainly this dislocation has increased people's interest in other religions. While some students have been attracted to Hinduism and Buddhism, there has been particular interest throughout the country in its ancient religion, Zoroastrianism,[5] because it is pre-Islamic.

Another religion that has definitely gained ground as a result of this dislocation is Christianity. It is important to stress here that no argument is being made that Christianity is going to oust Shia Islam from being Iran's national religion. The argument is that in this more questioning atmosphere brought about by the impact of the revolutionary regime Christianity could expand its foothold in Iran. As seen in Part One there are a number of key bridges in the Iranian Identity which relate well to Christianity, but were irrelevant as long as the country's religious identity was solidly Shia. Now the impact of the revolution has damaged the integrity of Shia Islam, and these bridges have become very important. As well as these links Christianity has two other characteristics that increase its attraction for Iranians. First in Iran, where there is instinctive respect for age, and the Christian faith there has had a long continuous historic presence for nearly 2,000 years. And secondly, the witness of the church in Iran's history has generally been positive. It is to this history of Christianity in Iran before 1979 that we now turn.

Notes

[1] For a typical example of such material see 'The Coming Fall of Islam in Iran' by Reza Safa, Frontline, Florida, 2006.
[2] See Chapter 7 'Cultural and Political Authoritarianism' p. 128.
[3] See Chapter 6 'Economic Hardship' pp. 107–108.
[4] For more on these thinkers and their impact on Christianity in Iran see Chapter Nine, 'The Regime and the Church'. For a more general treatment about these intellectuals see – *Islam and Christian–Muslim Relations*, 13, 1, 2002, 'Coming to Terms with Modernity: Iranian Intellectuals and the Emerging Public Sphere' by Mahmoud Alinejad, especially pp 36–41. Also see Nikki R. Keddie's *Modern Iran*, Yale University Press, 2002, pp. 305–311.
[5] A Mr Mistree from Mumbai takes Parsis (Zoroastrians) to Iran to visit the religion's ancient sites and there found out that many Iranian Muslims were also coming to discover their roots. See http://news.bbc.co.uk/1/hi/world/south_asia/4675343.stm [last accessed 6 June 2008].

Part Three

Christianity

Chapter 8

Christianity Before 1979

Christianity in Iran is not new; indeed its history stretches back almost to the days of Jesus. There is a noble tradition that the Magi, whom many think were Persians,[1] were the first to bring the good news of Jesus to Iran. This might be legend, but we know that Parthians, Medes and Elamites, three tribes from Iran, were in Jerusalem on the day of Pentecost, and could have brought back Peter's message to their homeland. We also know that Christianity was established in Edessa, capital of the buffer state Osrehoene separating Iran and Rome by the end of the second century as 'between 180 and 192 a cross appears on the head-dress'[2] of their king. The faith was allegedly brought there by Addai, one of the 72 apostles,[3] and then strengthened when Christians had to scatter after Stephen's martyrdom (AD 37) and again during the siege of Jerusalem (AD 68–70). On the silk route, yet officially beyond Rome's rule, it was a natural place to flee to.[4] Edessa came under the patriarch of Antioch, whose liturgy was in Aramaic, the language spoken by Jesus.[5] The literary language is known as Syriac which was used later by Christians throughout the Eastern Church, including Iran. Four hundred miles further East than Edessa, near the Tigris, the much disputed *Chronicle of Arbela* traces its line of bishops back to AD 104[6] and claims that in 117/118 its second Bishop Semsoun was martyred by the Zoroastrians[7] who were outraged at his evangelistic success. A little more reliable is the evidence of the inscription on a monument possibly erected in the mid-second century, in honour of Bishop Abercius of Hierapolis who wrote his own epitaph. Referring to some of his travels he writes – 'And I saw the land of Syria and all [its] cities Nisibis [I saw] when I passed over Euphrates. But everywhere I had brethren.'[8] This might mean he always travelled with fellow Christians, or more likely, that there were Christians already living across the Euphrates, i.e. in Iran.

Growth and persecution

It is 'Tatian the Assyrian' (110–180) who gives us the first definite historical evidence about the church in Iran. Born in Mesopotamia he came to Rome in about 150 and became a pupil of the church father Justin Martyr who was executed in 165. A few years after this Tatian returned to Assyria, 'in between the rivers', which probably meant Arbela where he started a Christian community. He also discovered that people were reading many dubious Gospels and Acts and determined to address this danger to orthodoxy by publishing the *Diatessaron*, which literally means 'through four'. It was a harmony of the Gospels which wove the four separate accounts into one compelling story. Though there is debate about as to the language it was originally written in,[9] there is no doubt that Tatian wanted it to be in Syriac, the *lingua franca* of that region, as he was 'emphatically and unashamedly Asian'.[10] So by the last quarter of the second century[11] we find the *Diatessaron* circulating in Syriac which became the official language of the Asian Church, and spreading Christianity into the countryside. As well as establishing Syriac as the language of the Eastern Church, Tatian also marked the church with a radical asceticism. It is said he even taught that sex within marriage was sinful and his opponents in the West, most notably Jerome, accused him of being a 'violent hiersarch' and the 'father of the Encratites', who practised the most extreme forms of self-denial such as chaining themselves to rocks, walling themselves up in caves and only eating uncooked grass.[12]

After Tatian, it is the clear the church east of the Euphrates, which was the then border with the Roman Empire, continued to grow. From Bardaisan, a Christian writer and prominent member of the court at Edessa in the early 200s, we learn there were Christians in Pars, Media, Kishin and Parthia.[13] We know that in 256 and 260 the Sasanian king, Shahpur, deported thousands of Christian prisoners of war from Antioch to Iran, thereby swelling the numbers of the church. Also 60 Christian tombs, dating from around 250, have been discovered on Kharg Island (in the Persian Gulf, 16 miles from the mainland), which indicates there was a significant church presence in Iran by the mid-third century.[14] And at Bishapur, on the border, there is the remains of a house church which dates to the same period, complete with a baptistery and 'wall paintings of Christ carrying the lost sheep and the three Marys coming to the empty tomb'.[15] The importance of the Persian Church is clearly underlined in 325 when we find a certain 'John of Persia of the churches of the whole of Persia and in the great India' in attendance at the Council of Nicaea, prompting the church historian Eusebius to note 'even a Persian bishop attended the synod'.[16] The full strength of the church in Iran becomes clear when it first tasted persecution. After suffering a humiliating defeat by Rome in 399/340 at Nisibis, Shahpur II (309–379) was easily persuaded by jealous Zoroastrian priests that the Christians were in league with the enemy, especially since 313 Christianity had become Rome's most favoured religion. Shahpur first ordered Bishop Simon of the Sassanid capital Seleucia-Ctesiphon, to collect double the normal tax from his church members. Simon refused saying he was 'no tax collector, but a shepherd of the Lord's flock'. In response Shahpur demanded the destruction of all churches and the execution of any clergy who refused to worship the sun. On Good Friday 344, five bishops and a hundred clergy were beheaded before Simon's eyes, before he finally gave his neck to the axe.[17] The persecution then continued for about the next 40 years, with one historian estimating that 35,000 Christians lost their lives,[18] another has 190,000.[19] The crime of the Christians is summed up by the Shah – 'These Nazarenes inhabit our country and share the sentiments of our enemy Caesar.'[20]

When eventually the persecution ended in around 401, the church had survived. In 409 Christians celebrated an edict of toleration issued by the new Shah Yazdegerd I who was pursuing a policy of peace with Rome, and in 410 their leaders gathered for the synod of Isaac in the capital Seleucia-Ctesiphon where they adopted the Nicene Creed, agreed to accept the Western dates for the great Christian festivals, and confirmed a hierarchical ordering of each diocese under one bishop. They were now an official organized national presence, linked to the rest of Christendom by an orthodox creed. The records of this Synod show exactly how far Christianity had spread throughout Iran by the early fifth century. According to the historian Christopher Buck there were at least 18 evangelized provinces out of 25 in the Sassanid Empire, with five archbishops (Metropolitans) and 38 bishops under the Patriarch in Seleucia-Ctesiphon. The most evangelized regions of the empire were the South West and West, while the least evangelized region was the North West. Significantly there was an established church in the Fars heartland in the South, and in and around Kerman in the South East. All of this means that the early church in Iran was very evangelistic. It was also missionary minded as we find there were dioceses in Central Asia – including Afghanistan.[21]

Unfortunately neither the church's position as an accepted national institution, nor its links with the rest of Christendom remained intact. In 420 the Zoroastrians petitioned the ageing Yazdegerd to move against the Christians alarmed at the hundreds leaving their faith to join the church, and furious that some fanatical Christians had attacked the fire temples. With Rome now more concerned about the northern European tribes, the politician Yazdegerd and his successors chose to please the Zoroastrians and another season of persecution began. Some Christians were flayed; some had their bodies torn with broken reeds; and others were thrown into pits to be eaten by starving rats. At Kirkuk one chronicler reported that ten bishops and 153,000 Christians were slaughtered, till the chief official, sickened by the blood, and overwhelmed by the faith of his victims, believed in Christ himself and was murdered.[22] In the midst of this horror, the bishops gathered for the Synod of Dadyeshe in 424 where, probably for political reasons, they loudly asserted that they were not subject to any other bishop in Christendom.

The Great Nestorian[23] Church

This independence soon became separation when the Iranian Church supported Nestorius, Archbishop of Constantinople, who was condemned as a heretic in 431 for denying that Mary was 'the mother of God' as it undermined the Biblical emphasis on Christ's humanity. This fiery argument was essentially a part of an ongoing feud between two Western churches: Antioch, renowned for its literalist interpretation of the Bible, and Alexandria, famous for its more philosophical approach. This Western dispute came to the Iranian Church through Edessa, the original missionary station for Christianity's launch into Asia, and home to the college for Iranian clergy, the School of the Persians, which had always looked to Antioch for inspiration. As soon as Nestorius was condemned, Edessa divided sharply. Its bishop, the Syrian Rabbula, burnt the works of the esteemed Antioch theologian, Theodore of Mopsuestia, seen to be the father of Nestorianism and drove the translator of his works, Hiba, into exile. When Rabbula died in 437, Hiba returned, became archbishop of Edessa till 357 and taught his city, and its theological school, that the anathemas against Nestorius were invalid. So at least three senior future leaders of the Iranian Church who studied in Edessa became thoroughly Nestorian: Acacius, partriarch at Seleucia-Ctesiphon; Barsauma, bishop of Nsibis; and Narsai, principal of the School of the Persians. The position of the Iranian Church became official in 486 when a synod convened by Acacius drew up its own creed that rejected both Monophysitism (Christ has one divine nature) and the Council of Chalcedon (Christ's two natures united), and asserted that Christ has 'two natures, divine and human . . . without confusion in their diversity'. The Iranian also diverged from the Western Church at this Synod by officially allowing clergy to marry, as, according to one historian, 'The virtue of virginity irritated the Persians.'[24] In 489 the Monophysite bishop of Edessa closed down the Nestorian School of the Persians which retreated East to Nisibis where its former Iranian pupils, Narsai and Barsaum turned it into the most important Christian training centre in Asia. With the Bible, radical discipleship and mission at the heart of the curriculum this school grew to have about 1,000 students by the mid-sixth century.[25]

The church had survived outright persecution, constant intimidation from Zoroastrians, and great hostility from other Christians, especially the Monophysites to emerge in the sixth century as dynamic influence in Iran. This is clearly seen in the way the Zoroastrians, always nervous of losing their status, tried to rid the church of one of her greatest patriarchs, Mar Aba (540–552). They discovered their word was not final. While the Shah, Khosrow I, was away at war they arrested him and accused him of being an enemy of their religion. He was an apostate; a proselytizer; and he publicly condemned their morality, especially the way they married close relatives. Mar Aba gladly accepted all the charges and should have been killed, but the Shah, who respected Mar Aba, and whose favourite wife, chief physician and many other courtiers were Christian, changed the punishment to prison and then exile in Azerbaijan. Here the Zoroastrians tried to assassinate him, and so in protest Mar Aba returned to Seleucia-Ctesiphon where the people poured out into the street in support to demand justice from the king. The Shah could have easily had Mar Aba executed for coming back from exile, but only had him imprisoned – and then later released. The Zoroastrians tried once more to get rid of Mar Aba when the Shah's son of his favourite wife not only followed his mother and became a Christian, but thinking the king had died away at war, proclaimed himself monarch. The king had not died, the prince's dreams came to an abrupt end, and the Zoroastrians gleefully claimed Mar Aba was at the heart of the conspiracy. He was duly sentenced to death, but it was discovered the claims were false, and the ageing Patriarch was yet again released. Even in death, Mar Aba had the last word. The Zoroastrians had demanded that his body be thrown to the dogs, but instead crowds of Christians poured out onto the streets of the capital and defiantly carried the Patriarch's coffin past the Shah's palace to its final resting place in a monastery outside Seleucia-Ctesiphon. No attempt was made to stop them. Mar Aba's life and death proves that the Iranian Christians were not just a tiny, insignificant minority, but a national movement that threatened the religious establishment and had sympathizers very near the throne.[26] Though the church suffered disunity when Monophysitism attracted support in the mid- to late sixth century, her influence and numbers continued to grow. There is no doubt about influence: in 590 Khosrow I's son, Homizd declared, 'My throne stands on four feet, not two. On Jews and Christians as well as on Magians and Zoroastrians.'[27] And when in the early 630s an unstable royal throne felt threatened, the Shah turned to the authority of the patriarch and sent him to sue for peace with Constantinople. As for her numbers, the church had certainly been growing: as seen in 410 the church had 44 bishops; in 650 there were 106.

It is thought that a part of the reason for the church's evangelistic success was her willingness to use the vernacular. So though Syriac, the language of the first missionaries to Iran, remained the church's official language, and though much of the historical record is in Syriac, nevertheless given the large numbers of native Iranians converting to Christianity, it was inconceivable that their mother tongue would not have made its mark. And indeed it did, so Christopher Buck writes – 'Discoveries of Nestorian texts in different Iranian languages (Middle Persian, Sogdian, New Persian) have proven conclusively that Syrian was not the exclusive language of liturgy and instruction in the Persian Church.'[28] There are fragments of the Persian liturgy used for celebrating the Feast of Epiphany in both the Assyrian and Chaldean churches; the story of John of Daylam who told his monks to build two monasteries, one for Syrian, the other for Persian worship; Acacius in the fifth century translated a summary of the Christian religion from Syriac into Persian and gave it to the Shah; Bishop Mana, also in the fifth century, wrote his own material in Persian, and translated the works of famous theologians such as Theodore of Mopsuestia into Persian. It is widely assumed that Bishop Mana was working on the church fathers because sufficient Scripture had already been translated, an assumption supported by the late fourth-century Patriarch of Constantinople, John Chrysostom who wrote that 'the teachings of Christ had been translated into the language of the Syrians, the Egyptians, the Indians, the Persians, and the Ethiopians.' And it is partly proved by the discovery of fragments of the Psalms in Persian in a monastery in China Turkestan dating back to the fifth century.[29] The fact that Persian was almost certainly used was not just a key to evangelistic success, but surely also played a crucial role in enabling Christians to form a strong, national church which earned the respect of the Shahs.

This church never lost touch with her early roots which were heavily marked by asceticism. This is seen in the abundance of monasteries found in Iran, so one historian writes that in the mid-fourth century, the way to India was 'strewn . . . with monasteries'.[30] The asceticism of the monasteries was felt across the wider church where there were strict rules about dress, marriage, children, and deacons had to see that during church meetings 'no one whispers, falls asleep, laughs, or make signs'.[31] The asceticism was also reflected in the character of the college at Nisibis which according to Moffett 'more resembled a monastery than a school'. Students had to study from dawn to dusk; take vows of celibacy while there; hand over all their possessions; and from August to October work for their keep. Unlike the asceticism of the Egyptian deserts the spiritual severity of the Iranians was outward looking. The Christian was called to deny himself, not for the sake of it, but to advance the kingdom. 'Its monasticism was . . . missionary through and through', writes David Bosch, 'to make it the missionary church "par excellence"'.[32] So it was the Iranian Church that sent missionaries to Central Asia, India, China and even England. In Central Asia they led thousands to Christ among the Huns in Transoxiana, the Keraites of Mongolia and the Onguts from near the Yellow River.[33] And, presumably following the model that had been successful in Iran, they immediately tried to produce Scriptures and liturgical material in the local language. In India they established congregations in Ceylon, along the Malabar Coast, and probably near Madras where there are crosses with inscriptions in Persian on them.[34] And in China there is the testimony of the famous Sian Fu stone, a 9-foot-high block of limestone now in the Vatican museum. This extraordinary monument tells the story of how the Iranian missionary Alopen brought the Christian message to the court of the Emperor Tai Tsung in 635 and how the faith flourished till 800.[35] Regarding England, there is a legend that a Persian missionary came to East Anglia in the seventh century and the town of St Ives is named after him. There is nothing inherently impossible about this.[36]

Decline under Arabs and Mongols

It is this strong, growing, dynamic, missionary minded church that suddenly faced the invasion of Arabs and their new religion in 642. There was no horrific violence: indeed one Patriarch praised the respect the Muslims showed the Nestorians.[37] However slowly but surely, though missionary work continued, the growth of the church began to weaken. The policy of the new rulers was to respect Christians as people of the 'book', but turn their communities into a Dhimmitude, a religious ghetto, which had to pay twice as much tax, have less legal rights than Muslims, no right to public office and face severe restrictions on their public worship.[38] There was a lot of incentive for non-Muslims to convert, and then the church found that it was much harder to evangelize adherents of the new faith, as the new rulers were much stricter about enforcing their law against apostasy. Despite this the church more than survived:[39] education especially helped the Christians and most Caliphs always had Christians as their personal doctors. Though there were no general persecutions as under the Zoroastrians, the Christians were always vulnerable. So under the Caliph Mahdi monasteries were attacked as a part of his campaign against the Manis; under Harun al Rashid Christians had to wear special clothes, and his successor al Mutawakkil ordered that Christian graves be desecrated. The Christians managed to live with this periodic intimidation, but as one of their own confessed in a debate with a Muslim apologist in the ninth century – 'But now the monks are no longer really missionaries.' The Nestorian Church had settled for a policy of survival.

It was not Muslims who decimated the Iranian Church, but Mongols. When they became the new regional rulers in the twelfth century,[40] there was at first a real hope they might support Christianity. Hulego (1256–1265) whose princess Dukas was Christian, were favourable to the faith, as were his successors, but the defeat of the Crusaders at Acre in 1291 swayed the Mongols away from the Christians to favour an alliance with the Muslims. Ghazan (1291–1304) took power in Persia as a Muslim and ordered the destruction of all churches. Persecution now became the norm, and in 1369, with the arrival of Tamerlane, 'The Scourge of God and Terror of the World', the church was completely swept away.[41] The remains of the Nestorian Church retreated to its heartlands around Urmia in the north-west of Iran. Due to the intensity of persecution normal church procedures had become impossible, and so the Patriarch, leader of the Nestorians, began to be chosen from within the family, which sadly led to division among this remnant. In 1551 Simeon VII Bar Mama appointed his nephew, but the bishops of Arbil, Salamas and Aderbaidjan did not accept him, appointed their own Patriarch, a monk called John Sulaqa, and the church split. Though initially the Sulaqa line of Patriarchs were friendlier to Rome, it was in fact the old Simeon line that was eventually recognized by the Pope in 1830 and are known as Chaldean Catholics.[42]

Roman Catholics' early attempts

The Roman Catholic Church had tried earlier to establish more of a presence in Iran in the early sixteenth century, but it was short-lived. It began when the Portuguese captured the island of Hormoz in the Persian Gulf in 1507, slowly followed in the 1570s by a group of Augustinian missionaries, whose leader Simon Morales was sent to the Safavid capital in Isphahan as the ambassador for the King of Spain and Portugal in 1582. Here he established a mission in 1602 and in 1607 these Dominicans were joined by the Carmelites, whose leader Father John Thaddeus became a friend of the Shah and 'even borrowed his spectacles on occasions'.[43] It seemed the Roman Catholics were set to establish a strong presence in the heart of Iran. But it all came to look less promising in 1622 when the British and the Safavids drove the Portuguese from Hormoz. With their political protection gone, the Portuguese missionaries and their converts soon faced the wrath of the ageing Shah Abbas (1587–1629) who had become increasingly paranoid towards the end of his reign.[44] Five Iranian converts were tortured and martyred,[45] and the Portuguese missionaries were expelled.[46] The Roman Catholic mission tried to soldier on. A French Carmelite, Father Bernard de Sainte Therese, built a cathedral in Isphahan in 1640, but there were no funds to maintain it and so after about 25 years it fell into disrepair. In 1653 the first Jesuits arrived in Isphahan, followed in 1656 by the Capuchins, monks linked to the Franciscans, who came to Tabriz and Isphahan, and in 1695 the Dominicans dedicated a church in Isphahan that still stands today. Despite this activity the Roman Catholic missionaries were never able to make any serious headway in Iran and by the end of the eighteenth century a Dominican in Julfa gloomily wrote that he only knew of 25 Catholics in the whole country. It was the same story in the nineteenth and twentieth centuries. A few heroic Catholic missionaries would try and start a work, but it always fizzled out in disappointment. There was little support from Europe, even less in Iran, and plenty of hostility from Muslims, who saw Catholics as foreigners threatening their culture.

The Armenians

There was also hostility from Armenian Christians who had prospered in Iran. Armenians had long been wandering over the less than definite border in the north of the country and establishing a life for themselves in Iran. Then in 1604, fighting against the Ottoman Turks in Armenia, Shah Abbas was forced to retreat to Azerbaijan. Following a common practice he captured around 300,000 Armenians to keep them from his enemies. They were settled in different parts of the country, while the wealthy ones, mainly from a thriving trading town called Julfa, were brought to the outskirts of the new capital Isphahan. Here they built New Julfa where under the benevolent protection of Shah Abbas they prospered. They were allowed to build churches, elect their own mayor, have their own courts, wear their own style of clothing and even make wine.[47] In 1617 the newly arrived immigrants won the auction of the Shah's silk monopoly which underpinned their trading houses which soon stretched from Europe to the Far East.[48] This established rich Armenians as the natural middlemen for the Shah to use in diplomacy against his Ottoman enemies, and later for Europeans seeking to influence Iran. Shah Abbas both enjoyed visiting his Armenian friends in their luxurious Julfa homes where food was served from gold plates; and he also enjoyed receiving their poll tax the mayor had to collect from every adult male. However his main reason for favouring the Armenians was political: he wanted to stop any of the ambitious Persian feudal lords in his court gaining dominance.[49]

Being so favoured it is no wonder that these Armenians opposed Roman Catholicism. They enjoyed the protection of the Shah, and had nothing to gain by joining Catholics who were his potential enemies: they also did not want the King to have another outside Christian group to threaten their place in his affections. They made their feelings clear in 1653 when Jesuits settled in New Julfa, demanding that the Shah expel all foreign missionaries. The Iranian kings were not to be disappointed by the Armenians: they proved themselves to be loyal. In the early eighteenth century when the Ottomans had invaded the north of Iran, the three Armenian 'Meliks' (military leaders) kept them out of Karabagh and Siunik for a decade and the whole community was honoured by Nader Shah (1736–1747) who invited their patriarch to his coronation and gave them tax exempt status.[50] Such treatment meant Iran became a natural place for Armenians to come to, especially when war was the norm in their own country. It is thought that as many as 200,000 arrived[51] in the eighteenth century, further strengthening the Armenian presence in the country. As the power of the Christian West and Russia increased in the late eighteenth century and nineteenth century, so did the status of the Armenians in Iran. Their wealth, international trading networks, linguistic skills, excellent education – and their Christianity – made them the natural interpreters between Iran and the West. Nasr al Din Shah (1848–1896) used them as envoys throughout Europe, and in turn they brought back Western culture and fashions to Iran. They pioneered technological innovations such as printing,[52] photography and built some of Iran's first theatres.[53] They also brought back new political ideas, especially from fellow Armenians in Russia who experienced revolution in 1905. In 1906 Armenians stood side-by-side with Iranians and successfully demanded a written constitution from the Shah, which they then helped fight for again in 1909.[54] Both in the mid 1890s and from 1915–1918 the dying Ottoman Empire committed genocide against the Armenians in their territories, killing at least 1.5 million.[55] Of the 600,000 to 1 million who escaped, thousands came to Iran, and so further strengthened the Armenian communities there.

Here the modernizing Reza Shah was more than ready to let the well-connected, educated, Christian Armenians help build his new technological state. So we find Armenians in senior positions in the oil, caviar, car, photography and other industries.[56] The Second World War further increased their importance as the Allies used Iran as a supply route to the Soviet Union and so the Armenians on both sides were the natural intermediaries. Armenians continued to prosper under Mohammad Reza Shah who continued his father's modernizing agenda, and drew even closer to America where after the genocide there was a very large Armenian community. So, the king 'trusted and liked his Armenian subjects'[57] and as Iran's wealth grew in the 1960s and early 1970s, so did that of the Armenians, seen in the schools, churches, clubs, libraries and cultural centres they built in most major cities. As they had been ever since their arrival en masse in 1604, the Armenians had remained a very definite presence in Iran.

And these Armenians are very proud of their Christian inheritance. They sincerely believe that they are an Apostolic Church claiming the Gospel was brought to them by Thaddeus and Bartholomew.[58] This is a tradition, but it is historical fact that in 301 Armenia was the first nation in the world to become Christian, after their pagan king was converted by Gregory the Illuminator, an aristocratic Armenian brought up in Caesarea. The Armenian Church was originally in communion with all other churches, immediately coming under the archbishop of Caesarea, fully accepted the decrees of the first three great councils of the church (Nicea, Ephesus and Constantinople), and subscribed to the Nicene Creed. However, like other Eastern churches, the Armenians rejected the decrees of the Council of Chalcedon in 527 which had condemned the teachings of Monophysitism, that Christ has one divine nature, a doctrine the Armenians were sympathetic to. Since then they have been known as Gregorians,[59] after the Illuminator, and have remained independent from all other churches ever since. They are sometimes misleadingly referred to as Orthodox which is only true in so far as their faith is orthodox according to the decrees of the early church, but they have no official ties with the Greek or Russian Orthodox Church. Though both Rome and Constantinople can find similarities with their own liturgy, it is uniquely independent and Armenian. Such though are the blessings of independence that they are overseen by five *catholicoi*, or supreme heads.[60]

Their devotion to Christ's one divine nature meant a theological, as well as a racial divide, separated the Armenians in Iran from the Assyrians, who as followers of Nestorius asserted Christ's humanity. Language was another dividing factor, for while the Assyrians remained with Syriac, Gregory taught in Armenian and in the late fourth century the ascetic scholar Mesrob invented the Armenian alphabet and by 411 the Bible had been translated into the vernacular. However both churches do share a great emphasis on monasticism and asceticism. Gregory set the example for the Armenians with long fasts, and ending his days in solitude. A monastery was built in Thortan, near where he died.[61] Mesrob too was renowned for his asceticism – wearing hair shirts, sleeping on mud, eating only vegetables and spending whole nights in prayer. It was this inheritance that the Armenians brought to Iran in the early seventeenth century and Iranians soon discovered they were fiercely loyal to their Christian religion. As seen, in the last year of his reign Shah Abbas (1629) turned against Christians and passed a law described as 'the edict which did more than any other single act to blight the chances of Christians in Persian'.[62] To encourage apostasy it gave all Christians who became Muslims the right to claim the property of their relatives going back seven generations.[63] Thousands of Christians duly followed their love of money and apostatized, but 'not the Armenians'.[64] They refused to recant, and their faith was further strengthened when that same year the radical reformer Moses of Datev became the Patriarch at Etchmiadzin, then in Iran, and brought strict discipline back into Armenian monasteries and seminaries. Their devotion to their Christian faith is seen in the report of the Jesuit missionary traveller, Alexander Rhodes, who in 1647 reported on the crowded ornate churches of New Julfa.[65] And as they built more and more churches throughout Iran, so they have remained crowded ever since.

Though it is true the Gregorian Armenians have made no recorded attempt to convert their Muslim neighbours, it is nevertheless a mistake to view their contribution to Christianity in Iran as being insignificant. Their presence has been hugely important – and still is. First of all Armenians established themselves in all of Iran's major cities, and so not only does every Iranian Muslim know about their Christian faith, but in the cities at least nearly everyone has had some contact with them. Secondly the impression the Armenians have given their Muslim neighbours over the years has been positive. So Syed Mohammad Ali Abtahi, journalist, broadcaster and politician in an interview specifically drew attention to 'the gentleness and the kindness of Armenian Christians in Iranian history'.[66] Thirdly with their church inheritance stretching back to the early fourth century, the Armenians, like the Assyrians, are a constant reminder to Iranians of Christianity's ancient roots. Fourthly, though, unlike the Assyrians, they remind Iranians that Christendom is worldwide. Ever since their arrival Armenians have had close contact with their fellow countrymen, initially in Russia and Europe, and then latterly in the USA, and indeed a part of their role was to introduce Iran to these other cultures. Fifthly, while connected to the wider world, the Armenians have also shown Iranians that the Christian faith can be fully integrated with a national culture. For their church is neither an imitation of Catholicism, Greek Orthodoxy or European Protestantism: it is uniquely Armenian. So teaching any Iranian who wants to become Christian that their church too does not have to imitate other cultures. Finally the presence of the Armenian Christians in Iran has been hugely important, especially in recent years, because they have shown that it is perfectly possible to be both Christian and Iranian. Armenians in Iran consider themselves to be Iranian and though since 1979 the official tone has not been so friendly, nevertheless they have always been loyal to their country proved by the high numbers who were ready to die in the war with Iraq.

Protestant missionaries

While the witness of the Gregorian Armenians has been more of a distinctive presence, the approach of the evangelicals was much more direct: they wanted to convert all – Muslims and Jews, nominal Armenians and Assyrians. Some of them, such as the first Protestant missionaries to Iran, the German Moravians[67] Hoecker and Rueffer, were heroic – but not very effective. On their way to Isphahan in 1747[68] they were robbed of all they had, including the donkeys they were riding, and had to walk some of the way. After a short stay in Isphahan, they headed south, again were robbed, and that was the end of their mission to Iran. Rueffer never recovered from the experience and died the next year. Other heroes who had adventures without making a lasting impression on Iran include Joseph Wolff, the son of a Bavarian Rabbi, who travelled throughout Iran in 'the full canonical dress of a clergyman of the Church of England' and preached in six languages; and Jacob Samuel, a missionary to the Jews, who went to Iran where he hoped to discover the ten lost tribes of Israel.[69]

Other nineteenth-century Protestant missionaries though had much more impact. One was the English Anglican missionary, scholar and linguist, Henry Martyn, who bequeathed Iran the first New Testament in Persian. He arrived in 1811 from India where he had worked on translating the Bible into Bengali with William Carey, the father of Protestant mission. Seeing the influence of Persian in Indian languages he determined to start work on a Persian New Testament and settled in Shiraz to check his translation. He kept a detailed diary[70] and as well as translating he spent a lot of time disputing with local mullahs which eventually led them to petitioning the local government to expel this sincere and argumentative Englishman. In February 1812 the New Testament was completed and by May beautifully written out by calligraphers. Martyn set out for Tehran where he tried to personally present a copy to the Shah, but his Vizier, 'treated him with contempt'[71] and dismissed him. So Martyn went on to Tabriz where he gave a copy to the English ambassador, Sir Gore Ouseley, who promised to give it to the king. Henry Martyn left Tabriz in September to travel to England by land, but only got as far as Tokat, just past the Turkish border. Here he died of a fever, aged 31. Just before his death, though very ill, he had visited the Armenian Patriarch at Echmiadzin as he had great respect for the Gregorian Christians. A young monk there described him as 'having a very delicate frame . . . with a countenance beaming with some much benignity as bespeaks an errand of divine Love'.[72] On his gravestone in Tokat there is this inscription – 'He will long be remembered in the East, where he was known as a man of God'.[73] It seems this was so for nearly 10 years later a Captain Gordon was distributing Christian tracts in Tabriz and urged others to join him in this work, writing, 'you little think how generally the English mullah Martyn is known throughout Persia and with what affection his memory is cherished'.[74] Christians certainly remember him for his translation work. Ouseley did give his New Testament to the Shah who promised to read it 'from the beginning to the end'.[75] Nobody knows if he did, but Ouseley made sure copies were given to the Russian Bible Society in Saint Petersburg who were the first to print them and make sure they were sent to Iran. There have been five other translations[76] of the New Testament since then, and all are indebted to Henry Martyn.

In 1817, just a few years after Henry Martyn's death, another missionary arrived in Iran from the British Isles. The report of the Edinburgh Missionary Society said that Dr William Glenn was to 'devote himself chiefly to the Persian language',[77] which is exactly what he did in order to finish off the work begun by Martyn and translate the whole Bible into Persian. When fellow missionaries from his Society withdrew from Iran in 1827, he remained and in 1846 as a result of his efforts the first whole Bible was published by the United Synod of Scotland. Two German contemporaries of Glenn, Pastors Pfander and Haas also made an impact. Pfander was a 'fearless preacher',[78] who wrote many popular tracts, including *Mizan-ul-Haag* (The Balance of Truth), that was used for over a hundred years, and Haas, as well as pioneering school work, played a crucial role in helping to introduce the two most important Protestant missions to Iran, the American Presbyterians and English Church Missionary Society.

The forerunners of the American Presbyterians came to Iran under the auspices of the interdenominational American Board of Foreign Missions founded in 1810 and inspired by stories from missionaries based in Turkey that the Assyrians around Urmiah were 'the Protestants of the East', who when revived would be a dynamic force for the cause of Christ throughout the region. And so in October 1834 we find Pastor Haas accompanying Justin Perkins, the founder of the American mission to Iran, on a visit to Urmiah and introducing him to a Nestorian bishop. Perkins and his wife successfully established themselves among the Nestorians and as well as starting schools, made a major contribution by providing the largely illiterate Assyrians with an alphabet for the modern Syriac they spoke. In 1841 the first book, *On the Necessity of a New Heart* was printed on a press the mission had set up,[79] and in 1845 Perkins gave the Nestorians a New Testament in this modern Syriac. Meanwhile another missionary, Dr Grant, engaged in much needed medical work, while his wife started a school for girls. The ministry of the Perkins and Grants epitomize all that was great about many nineteenth-century Protestant missionaries. They were brave, self-sacrificial activists, determined to give their lives to spreading the Gospel and improving the lives of the people among whom they lived. So Samuel Moffett writes of Perkins –

> For the next thirty six years, translating the Bible, preaching two of three times on Sundays, Perkins lived, talked, and almost looked like a native in his great two-foot-high sheepskin hat. So popular did he become that sometimes when he approached a village the people would march out en masse and bring him in to the sound of drums and trumpets.[80]

Their ministry though also illustrates the negative tensions that zealous but naïve foreign missionaries can create. The much publicized activity of the Americans inevitably attracted other missions who saw the poor and illiterate Nestorians as exotic and easy converts. The Lutherans, Baptists, Methodists, Congregationalists, and others, all descended on Urmiah, and by the end of the nineteenth century there were nine separate organizations 'all struggling to get prominence among these few people.'[81] This of course created sad tension among the missionaries, something of a spectacle for onlooking Muslims, and an easy way to make money for cunning and enterprising Assyrians.[82] Not surprisingly it was the Roman Catholics who created the most angst among the Protestants, especially the pioneers. In the early 1840s Perkins wrote that he had opened half his schools because he was 'impelled to do so by the presence of the enemy' and even travelled to Tehran to protest about the 'scourge' of the Catholic presence. So intense did this rivalry become that 'at one stage the Persian government had to intervene and forbid proselytizing between different Christian sects.'[83]

The ugly competition among Christians to win Nestorian souls was doubly negative. It displayed the crudity of Christian disunity, and for many Muslims it must have seemed as if these Western Christians were racists. For if Christians have the unique message of eternal life, why are they only going to the Assyrians? Most of the answer to this is not that the missionaries were racists, but they preferred the easier option of working among nominal Christians, a pattern that has remained in a lot of mission work in Muslim countries. However there was some romantic racism involved, for Dr Grant and many other missionaries at that time believed that the Nestorians were one of the lost tribes of Israel, and this partly fuelled their zeal to work among them, rather than the Muslims.

Much more dangerous than inter-missionary rivalry, this naïve obsession with the Nestorians also caused a catastrophic political storm. For while the arrival of the Americans greatly enhanced the status of the poor Assyrians, their presence created suspicions among both the Persian Muslims, and especially the Kurds, who shared some of the mountainous areas with the Nestorians and were officially their overlords. When Dr Grant built a medical outpost in Ashitham, a Kurdish area, which looked alarmingly like a fortress, he blithely told the Kurds he was not interested in politics. The Kurds drew their own conclusions and in 1843 carried out a massacre on the Nestorians. They retaliated in 1846, leading to another 10,000 being killed.[84]

Finally the American missionaries also caused division in the very church they had come to revive. Initially the Perkins and those who joined them tried to worship with the traditional Nestorian Church, but having come from an American Church strongly impacted by New England's second 'Great Awakening' Perkins was soon writing that these Christians, illiterate and given to long bouts of drunkenness, were 'a pitiful skeleton . . . (in) a valley of dry bones'.[85] First the missionaries began to gather to celebrate communion according to their own Low Church traditions which attracted Assyrians, and then from 1846 for about 15 years there was a great emphasis in their schools and wider ministry on the importance of personal conversion and revival. Not surprisingly the implicit suggestion that some of his people were Christians while others were not enraged the Nestorian Patriarch and in 1848 he publicly opposed the 'reformers', and demanded all Nestorians to stop working for the mission schools. The revival continued, and though Perkins, like Wesley's devotion to the eighteenth-century Anglican Church, refused to countenance official separation it inevitably happened. In 1855 the first 'revivalist' congregation was formed, and in the year after his death in 1869, this church, renamed 'Reformed' Nestorian Church came under the Presbyterians who had taken over all the mission work in Iran from the American Board.

The heroic Justin Perkins' dream of a revived Nestorian Church flooding Iran with Christian light had foundered on the usual hard rocks of race and culture. However his sincere and passionate work had not been in vain. Just 15 years after his death the new church born of his preaching was a strong institution. In 1884 it had four presbyteries with thirty-six ministers, trained in their own seminary, who were supervising twenty-five congregations totalling about six thousand who were meeting in forty-eight different buildings.[86] And free from a formal partnership with the Nestorians they had already set about working in new fields, determined to bring the Gospel to the majority Muslim population, an ambition shared by many zealous missionaries, but previously not acted upon out of respect for the Nestorians, wary of antagonizing their neighbours. And so throughout the twentieth century these Presbyterians, largely backed by US funds, established typical missionary work in Tehran, Tabriz, Hamadan, Mashad, Resht and Kermanshah. Similar to other Christian endeavour in Asia and Africa at the time these missionaries excelled in their educational and medical work, which they established in all these places. By the mid 1930s about 2,000 Iranians were being educated in Presbyterian schools, Alborz College[87] being the most famous. Thousands more were treated in their six hospitals. And their congregations also grew, usually made up of converts from Armenian, Assyrian, and a few from Muslim and Jewish backgrounds. In the late 1930s the nationalism of

Reza Shah turned on the Presbyterian schools and all but one had to be sold to the government.[88] After the Second World War, the medical work also declined, not because of government intervention, but because funds and staff were not forthcoming from America. The congregations also suffered because of its multiple ethnic make-up, and lack of national leaders, but were still very much a going concern. In the late 1950s the Presbyterians had over 60 missionaries, including the valiant William Miller[89] who as well as being an intrepid personal evangelist, also established a very successful summer training school in the north of Tehran, known as 'The Garden of Evangelism',[90] which is still used by Assyrians and Armenians. As we will see the Presbyterians more than survived the Islamic Revolution.

The other great Protestant mission work of the late nineteenth and twentieth century in Iran is that of the English Church Missionary Society (CMS). Inspired by the life and early death of their fellow Anglican Henry Martyn, Persia held a special place in the minds of evangelical mission minded Anglican Christians. Again we find Pastor Haas involved at the start of their story in Iran. In 1870 the CMS missionary Robert Bruce arrived in Isphahan on his way to India when the city was in the grip of famine. He immediately began looking after up to 7,000 victims and one of the people who sent funds was Pastor Haas, who had retired to Stuttgart. The next year Haas sent a further £1,700 for Bruce to start an orphanage, which he duly did. In 1875 this almost accidental but welcome birth of missionary work was officially approved by CMS, and missionaries began to arrive. They were not welcomed either by the Muslims, the Armenians or even the English government, one diplomat in 1897 calling them 'a dreadful thorn in our side . . . owing to their tactlessness and desire to proselytize among Muslims'.[91] However they rose to the challenge and established medical work in Yazd, Isphahan, Shiraz and Kerman; influential secondary schools in Isphahan (Stuart Memorial College and Carr School); and primary schools in Yazd and Kerman. They only operated in the south after agreeing with the Presbyterians in 1895 to leave the north as their preserve.[92] Their hospitals and schools flourished, but in the 1930s they were restricted by government interference, and they also suffered from a lack of support in the 1950s. They also saw small congregations come into being, but though they also had a number of converts from among the Armenians, Assyrians and Jews, the Anglicans had relatively more from a Muslim background, though not in huge numbers: in 1936 there were just 350 according to Waterfield.[93]

And like the Presbyterians, CMS had her fair share of self-confident heroes. There was Dr Carr who became famous as a physician in Isphahan in the 1880s and built the hospital there; in the 1890s Mary Bird, who referred to herself as a quack, but handed out basic medicine and preached to the poorest, provoking furious opposition from the mosques which she ignored;[94] the church's first bishop J. H. Linton who insisted that the future of the church rested with national leaders; Revd Sharpe, renown for his church architecture, music and knowledge of the Pahlavi script; and in the 1950s there was Dr Coleman, who ran the Christian hospital in Shiraz. He was once accompanied by the author Wilfrid Blunt to one of his village clinics –

Coleman had a kindly word, a friendly smile, a hand-on-shoulder greeting for everyone. One and all they adored him . . . We returned to Shiraz . . . and as we journeyed, I remembered in deep humility, what I had seen that afternoon. Such selfless devotion is true Christianity.[95]

Unlike the Presbyterians, the Anglicans never had any formal links with the Nestorians or any other historical church. Not having the initially large number of converts from other Christian denominations as the Presbyterians started with, the Anglican congregations were always smaller, as was their funding. This was one reason why the Presbyterians were reluctant to unite with the Anglicans when the idea was mooted at a conference in 1923. However this also meant their focus was always primarily on the majority Muslim population, and though the numbers were small, the Anglicans did have a relatively high number of Muslim converts by the 1960s, and most of their clergy in the 1970s apart from one ex-Jew, were Iranians from a Muslim background. These Iranians priests, led by Bishop Hassan Dehqani-Tafti, were very concerned to indigenize Christianity, and this was especially seen in the Persian liturgy, hymns and references to Iran's poetry produced by this church. Unfortunately both in the early 1950s and then later with the coming of the revolution these Iranian Christians suffered from the church's association with the English who were seen by others as the arch imperialists. After the revolution they paid a very heavy price for this association.

Though both the Presbyterian and CMS missionaries made mistakes, and shared a confidence in the superiority of Western culture that irked some Iranians, nevertheless the overall impression they left was overwhelmingly positive. For throughout the country thousands of ordinary Iranians experienced the kindness of Christians in excellent schools, hospitals and numerous village clinics. In their minds the work of these missions was not primarily associated with the machinations of Western governments, but with Christians wanting to help them. This point is made very clearly by an Iranian writer – 'These missionaries contributed significantly to Iranian life . . . the impact of (their) work was humanitarian and was strongly felt in the fields of education, public health, charity work, and social change.'[96] And though in all their charity work the missionaries gave Muslims an opportunity to hear the Gospel – there are no reports of them ever complaining of the Christians being aggressive or insensitive in their evangelism, and there was no backlash attacking missionaries as enemies of the national culture, as there was in China. The Anglicans were especially careful to make sure their liturgy and public buildings were beautiful to the Persian ear and eye. So though in the 1970s some Westerners appeared to be trying to impose on Iran modern and vulgar fashions, it was generally recognized by Iranians that this was not the work of the missionaries. They had served Iranians and with people like Norman Sharp who ended up lecturing in Shiraz University on the ancient Pahlavi text and building beautiful churches[97] completely Persian in style, they were also friends of Iran's culture. It is also important to note that at the start of their missionary work, both the Presbyterians and Anglicans, worked very closely with Nestorians and Armenians respectively, and so for many Muslims it must have seemed that these missionaries had come to strengthen their co-religionists, who represented an ancient institution in Iran, not import a new alien faith.

Roman Catholics try again

Though the Roman Catholics were never as prominent as the Presbyterians and Anglicans, nevertheless they also eventually managed to establish a similar, though smaller, witness to Christ in the nineteenth century. As seen the Catholic mission to Iran had really dwindled to very little by the eighteenth century, but it was revived again by the Lazarists, a French Catholic mission movement. In 1838 a French civil servant and fervent Catholic, Eugene Bore, founded two schools for Armenians in Isphahan and Tabriz and two for Assyrian Catholics in Urmieh and Salmas which were then manned by the Lazarites. Once the French had established a permanent representative at the Qajar court who happily gave the Lazarists permission to spread their mission, their work expanded, despite Protestant complaints. As well as the schools, the Roman Catholics operated a college for boys, a college for girls, three hospitals and one orphanage.[98] They also expanded the denomination's administrative structure. From the sixteenth to the eighteenth century the Catholics only managed to found two dioceses, one at Isphahan in 1609 which followed the Latin rite, and one at Salmas in 1709 which followed the Nestorian rite. The Lazarites and those who followed after them established three more dioceses in the late nineteenth century. In 1850 they created a diocese in Isphahan to follow the Armenian rite; and in Tehran (1853) and Urmieh (1892) they established dioceses for the Chaldeans, the Nestorians who had joined with Rome in 1830. Much later in 1966, they created a diocese at Ahwaz, again for the Chaldeans who had moved south for economic reasons.[99] This administrative structure has remained, but the social work was, as with the Presbyterians, taken over by the Pahlavis. Though their work was smaller, nevertheless for the orphans and sick people helped, this Catholic mission, just like the Anglican and Presbyterian mission, left a positive impression in people's mind about Christianity. And the fact that the Roman Catholic Church, Christendom's oldest and largest denomination, had an official link with Iran was not to be without significance after the 1979 revolution.

The Pentecostals

The first Pentecostal Church in Iran was founded in the early twentieth century among Assyrians in Urmieh, the favourite destination for missionaries. By the 1920s they had a church in Tehran and other major cities. This church though only operated in Assyrian which limited its appeal. The other Pentecostal Church in Iran, the Assemblies of God (AOG), which always used Persian, was to have a much wider impact. Ironically a major part of the early story of this church belongs to a Brethren Church. In the 1920s Dr Sayeed Kurdistani,[100] a Kurd and former Muslim from Sanandaj in the West of Iran started a church in Tehran with some Armenians. It became known as the Brethren Church[101] and in 1933 a young Armenian who did not believe in God began to attend the church and after one service sensed that 'the God of the entire universe' was challenging him to give Him his whole life. This man then went home and read the New Testament through at one sitting and posted a copy to his fiancé, writing on a note that this would be the foundation of their marriage. Seth Yeghnazar became a faithful member of the Brethren Church and developed a reputation as a man determined to be separate from the world. In the mid 1950s he had an overwhelming experience of the Holy Spirit and undertook a long fast of 42 days when he drank only water. His devotion and insistence of the need for a holy life caused uneasiness in the fellowship and Seth Yeghnazar heard that some wanted him to leave. So at the end of one meeting he stood up and said that if there were two people in the congregation who would prefer him to leave, then they should say so. Two ladies put their hands up: so he left with his family. Shortly afterwards he began a prayer meeting in his own house that continued every night for 4 years (1956–1960). Many Armenians experienced the new birth and had an experience with the Holy Spirit. As the meetings grew in size Seth Yeghnazar decided to add an extra storey to his house for the fellowship which was turning into a church.

However in 1959 two Armenian brothers, Haizak (aged 28) and Hrand Catchatoor (aged 18), came to Iran from England where they had been for their further education. While in England they had become members of a Pentecostal Church in London and they arrived back in Iran convinced God had called them to plant Persian speaking Pentecostal Churches throughout the country. As they began contacting like-minded Christians such as the Assyrian Pentecostals, so they met Seth Yeghnazar's group which then graciously decided to support the vision of the brothers. They also met John Bohlin, a Swede working with the United Nations as a technical assistant, who was a member of the 5,000 strong Philadelphia Church in Stockholm[102] who became a board member. Due to the contact with John Bohlin the new church was then known as the Philadelphia Pentecostal Church. With great energy the two brothers rented a basement that had been used a cello kebab restaurant in Pahlavi Street and transformed it into a Christian sanctuary. They made sure there was an easy to use baptistery, because when they started meetings in June 1960, they would immediately baptize everyone, Armenian, Assyrian or Muslim, who responded to their altar calls. The brothers were very active together, and soon around one hundred were coming to the evangelistic meetings on Friday. There was also a strong emphasis on healing, with many sick being prayed for, and some claimed they were cured. Though Bible studies continued in Seth Yeghnazar's home for a while, these eventually stopped, and the benches he had purchased for his own home meeting were given to the new fellowship. Keen to plant new churches, the brothers had started a meeting among Armenians in the Tehran suburb of Majidieh. They had soon raised funds to rent a property to transform into a church – again with a good baptistery – and the opening night was set for early December 1961. A few days before this opening, the Catchatoor brothers had driven to Kermanshah to bring back a young Assyrian Pentecostal Christian, David Thomas, to join them in the ministry, and to especially help with translation as neither of the brothers spoke Persian. Determined to make sure they were back for the opening of the Majidieh Church, the brothers did not stay an extra night in Kermanshah. On their way back to Tehran, on the night of 3 December 1961, their van crashed into the back of an unlighted parked vehicle. The two brothers lost their lives, while David Thomas and his wife were badly injured. The church was stunned, many had their faith shaken and others left all together. However Levon Hyrapetian and Tateos Michaelian, two men from Seth Yeghnazar's fellowship, stepped into the leadership position of the church, and were joined by David Thomas once he had recovered from his injuries.

Both the Central and Majidieh Church grew and by the late 1960s they were pioneering work in Namaak, another Armenian suburb of Tehran and in Isphahan and Gorgan. They were also ready to build their own church near Tehran University. As Pentecostals they had attracted the interest of the AOG Churches, the fastest growing denomination in the world, and as early as 1963 missionaries had come from the USA. They helped the church to start a Bible School[103] and a correspondence course was started using material from the International Correspondence Institute. These courses[104] soon had 10,000 students. They also helped raise funds for the new church building which opened in 1972. The energy of the new church continued into the 1970s with a strong emphasis on evangelism and discipleship. Seth's youngest son, Luke, began publishing books and opened a shop in the foyer of the church. Though the church never thought of imitating the Anglican or Presbyterian with their hospitals and schools, one of their elders, Yusef Nazanin did start an effective ministry among drug addicts in Tehran.

As the teaching of the church was the same as the worldwide AOG denomination, and as they were helped by their missionaries, it was natural that when the church needed a formal constitution, it adopted an AOG one. And though some people continued to call it the Philadelphia Pentecostal Church, most were soon calling it, as it was named on all its official documents,[105] 'Jammatt-e-Rabani', the AOG. Abroad too the church is seen as being a part of the wider AOG family, and Iranian ministers attended international AOG conferences. For some involved in the early days of the work this has given the unfortunate impression that the church was started by missionaries, when in fact it was founded by Pentecostal Armenian Iranians.

Though the church was always giving altar calls, which never happened in Presbyterian or Anglican services, and though there was a lot of street and door-to-door evangelism – still very few Iranian Muslims became Christians during the 1960s and 1970s. Some were baptized, but they would then move on: only a few actually joined the hundred or so mainly Armenian members of the Central Church in Tehran. Despite this lack of impact on Muslims, there was no lack of faith. They believed and prayed fervently, sometimes all night, that hundreds if not thousands of Muslims would turn to Christ. So this passionate church was excited at the opportunities they might have to preach the Gospel. They were not to be disappointed.

A familiar scent and strong roots

When the Islamic Revolution swept through Iran in 1979 the casual observer might have thought the churches would not really survive. Their numbers were insignificant, and their faith often identified with the now hated West. However as seen in this chapter the roots of Christianity in Iran were deep and extensive and the scent of her roses familiar to Iranians. Indeed so familiar that twice (seventh century, and thirteenth century) Christianity nearly became Iran's national religion. In 1979 the Assyrian Nestorians, mainly in the North West, were a constant reminder of the church's age. The Armenians, with very visible communities in every major city, were an influential minority and their many international connections showed the extensive reach of Christendom. And with their well-known hospitals and schools throughout the country, the Anglicans and Presbyterians proved that Christianity was about serving the needy. Despite the slur from some politicians that these churches were lackeys of the imperialist West, generally they enjoyed a good name among Muslims throughout Iran. Before 1979 the AOG were little known among Muslims, but as an indigenous church with no links with any imperialistic power, and a passionate fervency to see their fellow countrymen turn to Christ, they were more than ready to stand with Iran's historic churches to defend the rights of Christians and share the Gospel with all.

The church in 1979 then had roots – the question was whether they would be strong enough to deal with a regime that was fanatically committed at home to seeing Iran coming under Islamic law and abroad defying the 'Christian' West.

The next chapter will show that the roots were not only healthy enough to survive the rule of radical Islam, though there was a price to pay, but also see many new shoots grow from its ancient branches.

Notes

[1] The main argument is that in Zoroastrian Iran the Magi were a set of priests responsible for guarding the sacred and eternal fire; it is also likely there was a Jewish community there who had heard about prophecies regarding the Messiah. And when the thirteenth-century traveller Marco Polo went through Iran he found villages that claimed the Magi as their own. Arabia and Babylon are other places where they are thought to have come from. For a full discussion see – 'We See Three Kings', www.iac.es/galeria/mrk/Magi.html [last accessed 6 June 2008].

[2] See Robin Waterfield's *Christians in Persia*, George Allen and Unwin, London, 1973, p. 16.

[3] See Shawqi Talia, 'From Edessa to Urmia', *Bulletin of the Royal Institute for Inter-Faith Studies*, 7, 2, Autumn/Winter 2005: 39.

[4] See Samuel Hugh Moffett, *A History of Christianity in Asia Volume 1*, Orbis, New York, pp. 51–69 for a full discussion on Edessa, including the remarkable legend about a letter from its king to Jesus asking for healing as recorded by Eusebius.

[5] Dr Mark Roberts writes 'Aramaic was an ancient Semitic language related to Hebrew much as French is related to Spanish or as Cantonese is related to Mandarin. Though Jews had once spoken Hebrew as their primary language, this changed when Israel was overthrown, first by the Assyrians in the eight-century B.C. and then by the Babylonians in the sixth-century B.C. By the time of Jesus Aramaic was so common among Jews that the reading of the Hebrew Scripture in the synagogue was accompanied by translation into Aramaic.' The direct evidence that Jesus spoke this language is in the Gospels – *Talitha cum* (Mk 5.41, 'Little girl, get up!'); *Abba* (Mk 14.36, 'Father'); *Eloi, Eloi, lema sabachtani?* (Mk 15.34, 'My God, my God, why have you forsaken me?'). For more see Dr Roberts' very useful article –www.markdroberts.com/htmfiles/resources/jesuslanguage.htm [last accessed 6 June 2008].

[6] See *Spirituality in the Land of the Noble* by Richard Foltz, Oneworld, Oxford, 2004, p. 80.

[7] See Moffett, *A History of Christianity in Asia Volume 1*, p. 72.

[8] For different translations of the inscription and scholarly discussion see www.earlychristianwritings.com/abercius.html [last accessed 6 June 2008].

[9] Most scholars think it was originally written in Syriac, but some such as Harnack argue it was written in Greek and then translated into Syriac. See www.newadvent.org/cathen/14464b.htm for a full discussion [last accessed 6 June 2008].

[10] Moffett, *A History of Christianity in Asia Volume 1*, p. 74.

[11] See the very full note about this in Moffett, *A History of Christianity in Asia Volume 1*, p. 89, note 102.

[12] For a fuller discussion on Tatian and his asceticism see Moffett, *A History of Christianity in Asia Volume 1*, pp. 72–80.

[13] See 'The Universality of the Church of the East' by Christopher Buck, *Journal of the Assyrian Academic Society*, X, 1, 1996: 57. For more information about Badaisan, see the New Advent website, www.newadvent.org/cathen/02293a.htm [last accessed 6 June 2008].

[14] See 'The Universality of the Church of the East' by Buck, 59.

[15] See Moffett, *A History of Christianity in Asia Volume 1*, p. 93.

[16] See 'The Universality of the Church of the East' by Buck, p. 61.

[17] See Moffett, '*A History of Christianity in Asia Volume 1*, p. 140.

[18] Buck gives this figure in 'The Universality of the Church of the East', p. 60, relying on Sebastian Brock's information in 'Christians in the Sasanian Empire: A Case of Divided Loyalties'.

[19] See Moffett, *A History of Christianity in Asia Volume 1*, p. 145.

[20] See Waterfield's *Christians in Persia*, p. 19.

[21] For a detailed breakdown see 'The Universality of the Church of the East' by Buck, pp. 62–69.

[22] See Moffett, *A History of Christianity in Asia Volume 1*, pp. 160–161.

[23] Though the great historian of Asian Christianity Samuel Moffet describes the Assyrian Church that spread in Iran as the Nestorian Church, there are others who object. They say firstly though sympathetic to Nestorius, the Assyrians actually subscribed to the position of Babai the Great; secondly this implies their church started with Nestorius; and thirdly they dislike the innuendo they are heretical. However this author stays with Moffet as Church of The East is rather general.

[24] A. Voobus, quoted by Moffett, *A History of Christianity in Asia Volume 1*, p. 199.

[25] See Moffett, *A History of Christianity in Asia Volume 1*, pp. 200 ff.

[26] For more on Mar Aba see Moffett, *A History of Christianity in Asia Volume 1*, pp. 217–229 (Chapter 11).

[27] See Moffett, *A History of Christianity in Asia Volume 1*, p. 236.

[28] See 'The Universality of the Church of the East' by Buck, p. 55.

[29] See 'The Universality of the Church of the East' by Buck, pp. 88, 87, 82, 83, 84, and 85.

[30] See A. Mingana, 'The Early Spread of Christianity in Central Asia and the Far East', 1929.

[31] From 'The Teaching Of The Apostles', a 3rd Century Manual For the Church. See Moffett, *A History of Christianity in Asia Volume 1*, p. 94.

[32] See David Bosch 'Transforming Mission' 1991p.

[33] See Waterfield's *Christians in Persia*, pp. 39–40. Moffett also points out, p. 209, how the Nestorians were joined by a Monophysite Armenian who got on very well with them on the mission field.

[34] See Moffett, '*A History of Christianity in Asia Volume 1*, pp. 266–271, chapter 13.

[35] See Moffett, *A History of Christianity in Asia Volume 1*, pp. 288–323, chapter 15.

[36] See Waterfield's *Christians in Persia*, p. 46.

[37] This was Yeshuyab III 650 – 660, see Moffett, *A History of Christianity in Asia Volume 1*, p. 339.

[38] For an excellent overview of restrictions facing non-Muslims in their newly conquered territories see *The Decline of Eastern Christianity under Islam*, by Bat Ye'or, Associated University Press, New Jersey, 1996, Chapter Three.

39 'The Church of the East remained a vibrant and dynamic community with its own Syriac language and ecclesiastical autonomy.' See Talia, 'From Edessa to Urmia', 39.

40 See Chapter 3, p. 50.

41 For more on the destructive rage of the Moguls see Chapter 3 p. 50

42 For more details on this split see *A History of Christianity in Asia Volume II*, by Samuel Moffett, Orbis, 2005, pp. 196–197.

43 See Waterfield's *Christians in Persia*, p. 66.

44 See Chapter 3 for more about Shah Abbas and how he treated his sons.

45 One was disembowelled, another 'wrapped in a donkey's skin' and 'impaled on a stake'. The others were stoned to death. It seemed the government thought they were spies. See Waterfield's *Christians in Persia*, p. 68.

46 See *A History of Christianity in Asia Volume II* by Moffett, p. 198.

47 See 'Armenians in Iran (*ca* 1500–*ca* 1994)' by George A. Bournoutian, www.iranchamber.com/people/articles/armenians_in_iran1.php [last accessed 6 June 2008].

48 See *The Oxford Book of Entrepreneurship*, OUP, 2006, Chapter 22, 'The Migration of Entrepreneurs' by Andrew Godley, p. 601.

49 See Godley, 'The Migration of Entrepreneurs', p. 601.

50 See Bournoutian, 'Armenians in Iran (*ca* 1500–*ca* 1994)'.

51 See *A History of Christianity in Asia Volume II* by Moffett, p. 202.

52 They set up the first printing press in 1628 in New Julfa, the first in the Middle East. The first book printed were the Psalms in Armenian.

53 See Bournoutian, 'Armenians in Iran (*ca* 1500–*ca* 1994)'.

54 For more on this story, and especially the link between the Armenians in Russia with those in Iran see *Armenians and the Iranian Constitutional Revolution, 1905–1911: The Love for Freedom Has No Fatherland* by Houri Berberian, published by Westview Press, 2001.

55 See *The Decline of Eastern Christianity under Islam* by Ye'or, p. 197. For a thorough treatment of the massacre see Arnold Toynbee's essay at www.armenian-genocide.org/toynbee.html [last accessed 6 June 2008].

56 See Bournoutian, 'Armenians in Iran (*ca* 1500–*ca* 1994)'.

57 See Bournoutian, 'Armenians in Iran (*ca* 1500–*ca* 1994)'.

58 See 'A Brief History of the Armenian Church' by Archak Sahakian, www.saint-sarkis.org/Armenian_Church.htm [last accessed 6 June 2008].

59 They are also known as the Armenian Apostolic Church, and sometimes loosely just as Orthodox, though this is completely misleading as they have no links at all with the Byzantine Church.

60 The original one is based in Sis in Cilicia, then there is one based in Aghtamar, an island in Lake Van now in Turkey, one in Jerusalem, one in Constantinople and the most powerful in Etchmiadzin in Greater Armenia.

61 For more detail on Gregory see the outstanding New Advent website – www.newadvent.org/cathen/07023a.htm [last accessed 6 June 2008].

62 See Waterfield's *Christians in Persia*, p. 69.

63 See *A History of Christianity in Asia Volume II* by Moffett, p. 198.

64 See *A History of Christianity in Asia Volume II* by Moffett, p. 201.

65 See *A History of Christianity in Asia Volume II* by Moffett, p. 202.

[66] Quoted by Sasan Tavassoli in 'Muslim–Christian Engagements in Post-Revolutionary Iran: The Encounters of Iranian Thinkers with Christian Thought'. Page 50 in unpublished thesis submitted to the University of Birmingham, UK, May 2006.

[67] The Moravians were founded by the reformist John Hus in Bohemia in the late fourteenth century and experienced revival under Count Zinzendorf in the eighteenth century which led to missionaries being sent out, some of whom were famously involved in the conversion of John Wesley.

[68] See Waterfield's *Christians in Persia*, p. 88.

[69] See Waterfield's *Christians in Persia*, pp. 95–98.

[70] See *Journal and Letters of the Rev. Henry Martyn, B. D.*, ed. S. Wilberforce, M. W. Dodd, New York, 1851, 466 pp. available online at www.missionaryetexts.org/#m-martyn [last accessed 6 June 2008].

[71] See Waterfield's *Christians in Persia*, p. 93.

[72] See Waterfield's *Christians in Persia*, p. 94.

[73] George Smith, *Henry Martyn Saint and Scholar: First Modern Missionary to the Mohammedans 1781–1812*, Religious Tract Society, London, 1892, p. 530, quoted in essay by Brian Stanley, www.martynmission.cam.ac.uk/CBStanley.htm#_edn62 [last accessed 6 June 2008].

[74] See Waterfield's *Christians in Persia*, p. 99.

[75] See *A History of Christianity in Asia Volume II* by Moffett, p. 377.

[76] The Glenn and Burns version, the Old Version, the Good News version, the Living Bible and the Millennium version.

[77] See Waterfield's *Christians in Persia*, p. 99.

[78] See Waterfield's *Christians in Persia*, p. 99.

[79] See *A History of Christianity in Asia Volume II* by Moffett, p. 379.

[80] See *A History of Christianity in Asia Volume II* by Moffett, p. 378.

[81] Robin Waterfield quoting an historian John Joseph, see his *Christians in Persia*, p. 130. The missions were: the United Lutheran Church of America; the Evangelical Association of for the Advancement of the Nestorian Church; The German Orient Mission; Plymouth Brethren from England; Drunkards; Holiness Methodists; Southern Baptists; Northern Baptists; and English Congregationalists.

[82] According to Waterfield numerous Assyrian envoys presented pleas for orphanages and famine relief and other good causes to naïve Western donors whose money was rarely spent on these 'projects'.

[83] See Waterfield's *Christians in Persia*, p. 110.

[84] Dr Grant never knew about this as he had died of typhus, contracted while serving the sick in Mosul, in 1844.

[85] See *A History of Christianity in Asia Volume II* by Moffett, p. 378.

[86] See *A History of Christianity in Asia Volume II* by Moffett, p. 406.

[87] Alborz College was founded by Samuel Martin Jordan (1871–1952) another larger than life missionary figure, who has been called the 'most influential American in the history of US relations with Iran'. He arrived in Iran in 1898 and became Principal of the Presbyterian Boy's School which he expanded to include the whole high school curriculum. In 1913 he purchased 40 acres outside Tehran's northern gage and here built what first became the American College of Tehran, and later in the early 1930's, Alborz College. Dr Jordan's commitment to education

exemplified all that was inspiring about his generation of missionaries. Seeking out future leaders, he aimed to instill in them not just academic knowledge but a vibrant set of values taught though manual work, sport, and a strict enforcement of the principles of equality not just for all races and religions – but also both genders. Jordan's wife, Mary, was an active presence in the school and her motto – which she made the girls learn by heart was – 'No country rises higher than the level of the women of that country'. When Alborz College was taken over by the Iranian government in 1940 it had 850 students and had awarded 20 BA degrees. Famous old students include Ali Hekmat who was the Minister of Education 1933–38; Lofti Zadeh who developed 'fuzzy logic', and Sattareh Farman Farmaian, a leading social worker. Jordan played a key role in US–Iran relations during World War 2, which included two audiences with Mohammad Reza Shah in 1945. Much of this information was gleaned from a soon to be published article by Michael Zirinsky which he kindly sent the author. The article will be in the Encyclopaedia Iranica, published by Columbia University.

[88] The one school that was exempted from the general decree issued in 1939 demanding the closure of all foreign schools was the Community School in Tehran which was meant to provide education for the children of the international community. Mohammad Reza Shah was more amenable towards the Presbyterians and it seems they were allowed to again have some limited involvement in education, and so open new schools. The exact status of these new schools though is not clear. For more on the whole subject see 'Render therefore unto Caesar the things which are Caesar's: American Presbyterian educators and Reza Shah' by Michael Zirinsky, Iranian Studies, Volume 29, Issue 1, 1996, pp. 337–356

[89] For a full account of his work in Iran see his 'My Persian Pilgrimage', William Carey Library, Pasadena, CA, 1989.

[90] For more on the Presbyterians in Iran see Waterfield's *Christians in Persia*, Chapter 12.

[91] See *The English amongst the Persians* by Dennis Wright, Heinemann, 1977, p. 120.

[92] See *The English amongst the Persians* by Wright, p. 119.

[93] See Waterfield's *Christians in Persia*, p. 171.

[94] For more on Mary Bird see *Religious Feminism in an Age of Empire* by Gulnar Francis-Dehqani, University of Bristol, 2000, where all of chapter five, pp. 84–113, is dedicated to this remarkable lady.

[95] Wilfrid Blunt, *Persian Spring*, James Barrie, London, 1957, pp. 65–66. Dr Coleman became very well known in Shiraz and was later made an honorary citizen.

[96] Robin Waterfield quoting Heravi Iranian American Diplomacy, *Christians in Persia*, p. 143.

[97] Wilfrid Blunt mischievously suggests Sharp's church in Shiraz was a rival to Persepolis on the tourist's agenda. See *Persian Spring*, p. 49.

[98] See 'A Brief History of Christianity in Iran' by Massoume Price, December 2002, Iran Chamber, www.iranchamber.com/religions/articles/history_of_christianity_iran2.php [last accessed 6 June 2008].

[99] For full details about all the Roman Catholic dioceses in Iran see www.catholic-hierarchy.org/country/dir.html [last accessed 6 June 2008].

[100] Dr Sayeed Kurdistani features in a well known book by the American Presbyterian missionary, William Miller, called 'Ten Muslims Meet Christ'. His autobiography in Persian has been widely distributed. There is a biography of his life in English called *The Bitter and the Bold* by Jay M. Rasooli and Cady H. Allen, published by Good News Publishers, Westchester, IL, 1964.

[101] This is probably because Dr Kurdistani had grown very close to a Brethren Assembly in Croydon, England, when he went there for further medical studies, see chapter five of *The Bitter and the Bold*, details in footnote 95.

[102] The church was called the Philadelphia Church not because of any link with America, but because it once met in a hall called the Philadelphia Hall in Uppsala Street in Stockholm. For information on the fascinating story of this church whose name enters Iran see www.pri.pingst.se/english/pethrus/dates.html [last accessed 6 June 2008].

[103] The Assemblies of God missionary Mark Bliss was closely involved in helping the church in Tehran with training. Tragically in 1969 he and his wife Gladys lost three of their children in a car accident. Revd. Haik Hovsepian-Mehr and his wife Takoosh also lost their first child in the same accident.

[104] Another mission agency, International Mission, also operated a Bible Correspondence Course in the 1960's and 1970's and they had 30,000 students.

[105] For the churches official documents with the government they were not allowed to call themselves the Assemblies of God, so they added an h to the name and called themselves, Jammatte Rahbanni which means, the People of Monks.

Chapter 9

The Church and the Islamic Republic

On 1 February 1979, Christians, like most other Iranians, hoped Khomeini's revolution would bring freedom from dictatorship. The xenophobia did not alarm them since they had adapted to the Pahlavis[1] and as for the Islamic fundamentalism, they had long got used to Muslim sensitivities. And when the new constitution was ratified, Article 13 recognized Christians, along with Jews and Zoroastrians, as a legitimate religious minority, free to practise their faith; Article 14 guaranteed that their human rights be respected; and most important of all Article 23 promised freedom of belief. It stated – 'The investigation of individuals' beliefs is forbidden and no one may be molested or taken to task simply for holding a certain belief.'[2] Moreover the Assyrians were to have one representative in parliament, and the Armenians two.

It seemed Christians would still be the protected 'Dhimmitude' in Iran, living under Islamic rule, but able to practise their religion in peace. The major new restriction facing them was a law against proselytizing Muslims, who would then face a possible death sentence, according to Sharia law, if they converted.[3] It was also stipulated that though church buildings could be repaired, no new ones could be built. Given that few Muslims had become Christians in Iran, and they had often faced hostility from their own traditional families anyway, this danger surrounding Muslim evangelism was not new. And the church buildings for all the denominations were sufficient. So for many Christians there was no immediate, catastrophic change. However, as seen in Chapter 5, there was a large unofficial side to the Islamic Revolution manned by thousands of fundamentalist volunteers who took their orders from self-appointed committees with opaque links to the religious establishment. They saw historic Christianity as an inferior religion and the modern missionary movement as a dangerous tool of the West. Indeed Khomeini had publicly said that missionaries were 'the agents of imperialism . . . with propaganda centres set up for the sole purpose of luring the faithful away from the commandments of Islam.' And he went on to ask, 'Is it not our duty to destroy all these sources of danger to Islam?'[4] This was the spirit that inspired the volatile and fervent side of the revolution who were more than ready to take the law into their own hands. Their zealous violence was soon felt by the Anglican Church who produced most hatred among revolutionaries: they saw the church as the owner of prominent properties, a child of the imperialists, and worst of all, a home for Muslims converts.[5]

Anglicans suffer

On 19 February 1979 just 1 week after Khomeini had secured power two men purporting to be interested in Christianity came to visit Revd Arastoo Sayyah, the Anglican priest in Shiraz. When he did not appear for lunch, his eldest son went to call him. Entering the parish office, he found his father with his throat cut. Though the chief mullah in Shiraz told Bishop Hassan Dehqani-Tafti the murder was the work of 'counter-revolutionaries',[6] though nobody was ever arrested, many Christians still assumed Revd Arastoo Sayyah died because he was an apostate from Islam. If true this meant the lives of many others in the church, including her priests, were also in danger. Despite this Bishop Hassan Dehqani-Tafti, himself an apostate, ruled that all the churches should stay open, and public worship continued – as did the intimidation. In late February a group of men from Isphahan's self-appointed Revolutionary Committee confiscated all the Christian material at the Christian hospital in Isphahan. These men, well-known activists for the Islamic Propaganda Society, also demanded a room so they could 'supervise' the hospital's activities. In fact they 'were slowly drawing the Iranian staff over to their side and inciting rebellion'.[7] On 11 June the rebellion was successful. One hundred workers demonstrated outside the hospital, demanding that the foreign medical missionaries go. They did leave; the hospital was taken over by the Revolutionary Committee; and it was officially declared 'a first class spy base of the West'.[8] One month later the Christian hospital in Shiraz suffered the same fate, as did a school for the blind and their training farm in Isphahan. It seemed that Khomeini's wish for the destruction of the Christian 'propaganda' centres was being fulfilled. Bishop Dehqani-Tafti wrote letters of protest regarding all these incidents, but to no avail.

When the revolutionaries searched through all the files connected to the Shiraz Christian hospital, they discovered the church had a Trust Fund which held both savings for major projects, and the pensions for over two hundred church employees. They immediately demanded that Bishop Dehqani-Tafti hand the fund over: He refused, and later explained his reasons very bluntly. 'They had trespassed on church property. Now they were asking for money which did not belong to them. They were nothing but greedy usurpers.'[9] This refusal probably spurred the revolutionaries to step up their intimidation. On 29 August a group of 30 men ransacked the Bishop's house, burnt some files and took away photograph albums and lists of people he had confirmed. On 1 October the importance of this fund became very obvious. Revolutionaries arrested the ex-head of the Christian hospital in Shiraz and 6 days later they released him – on the condition he persuaded the Bishop to hand over the fund. Again the Bishop refused, again he was warned. On 8 October he himself was arrested for a few hours, and then on 22 October it became clear that now this intimidation was not just the work of a few volatile fanatics, but closely linked to the separate revolutionary organizations that Khomeini was establishing alongside the normal offices of government. For Bishop Dehqani-Tafti had to appear before a Revolutionary Court presided over by a Religious Judge and face a barrage of accusations that he was running a 'nest of spies'. Bishop Dehqani-Tafti defended himself well and was released. But on 26 October three armed assassins broke into his house at dawn and shot six bullets at almost point-blank range at the sleeping bishop. Miraculously he survived.[10] Four bullets made 'four neat holes in a semi-circle round where my head had been'; another went under the bed, and one into the hand of his wife, Margaret, who had flung herself over her husband to protect him. In early November the Bishop left Iran for prearranged meetings in Cyprus and England where he was persuaded to remain by the argument that 'A live dog is better than a dead lion'.[11] With the four holes in his pillow case, and no arrests of the assailants, there was little doubt he would have been 'a dead lion'.[12] All of the Bishop's family were able to travel freely and joined him in England – apart from his eldest son Bahram. Ominously he was not able to get his passport. When he went to see an official at the Revolutionary Court he was told – 'We have nothing against you. It's your father who is causing all the trouble.'[13]

Throughout the winter there were slanderous articles in the press and then in the spring of 1980 the violence began again. On 1 May the secretary to the Diocese, 58-year-old Miss Jean Waddell was tied up, beaten, and shot in her flat in Tehran. Miraculously she too survived. Five days later Bahram Dehqani was less fortunate. Returning from teaching in the afternoon his car was forced off the road by another vehicle. A man got into the passenger seat with a gun and told Bahram to drive to a lonely spot near Evin Prison in the north-west of Tehran. A shepherd boy later told police that he had seen two cars, men talking, and then the sound of gun shots. The brutal murder of Revd Arastoo Sayyah at the start of the revolution might have been the work of zealous fanatics: this was a carefully planned professional execution, cruel punishment meted out to an 'apostate' father who had refused to either deny his church, or hand over her money.[14] Grieving in England the Dehqani family did not succumb to bitterness, but instead the Bishop wrote a poem that continues to inspire Christians to forgive. It ends with these memorable words –

O God,
Bahram's blood has multiplied the fruit of the Spirit in the soil of our souls;
So, when his murderers stand before thee on the day of judgement
Remember the fruit of the Spirit by which they have enriched our lives,
And forgive.[15]

After this awful event Bishop Hassan Dehqani remained in England in exile, where he served as the Associate Bishop of Winchester, and gave himself to writing till his death[16] in April 2008. He is recognized as Iran's greatest Christian author, his Magnus Opus being a three volume study of Jesus Christ in Iranian history and literature.[17]

The persecution continued after Bahram's murder. In August Revd Iraj Mottahedeh (who was to succeed Bishop Dehqani-Tafti as diocesan bishop in 1986), Revd Nosratullah Sharifian, Revd Coleman and his wife Audrey, Jean Waddall and Dimitri Bellos, the church administrator, and another church member were all arrested, imprisoned and charged with spying: a charge that carried the death sentence. They were held for over six months and then released, possibly as a result of the intervention of Terry Waite, the Archbishop of Canterbury's special envoy. The foreign missionaries came home to England, the Iranians stayed and continued to lead the congregations in Tehran, Isphahan and Shiraz. There was no priest for the church in Kerman. The Anglican Church has never really recovered from this attack in terms of becoming a growing church as it had been before 1979. However brave members of the community, led from 1986–2004 by Bishop Iraj Mottahedeh, have still kept the doors of their services open for all. The present leader, Bishop Azad Marshall is from Pakistan and has not been given permission to live in Iran, so limiting his ministry there.

The Ethnic Christians leave

Once it became clear that Ayatollah Khomeini was going to successfully set up a Muslim religious dictatorship, both Assyrians and Armenians swiftly came to the conclusion that Iran was not the place for them. Their historic churches did not face any outright persecution from the government, they are truly the protected Dhimmitude who can freely worship and have Scriptures in their own separate languages. However five things soon became clear. First of all there was no long-term financial security for their children, especially since it was virtually impossible for a non-Muslim to find employment in the ever increasing state sector of the economy. Secondly the new regime ruled that only Muslims could lead a government organization, which included Assyrian and Armenian schools. This caused intense resentment. Thirdly their legal status seemed more vulnerable as till 1991 non-Muslims were awarded less compensation (blood money) in death or injury cases.[18] Fourthly Islamic rules were to intrude into their customs regarding dress, entertainment and socializing. And finally, with relatively wealthy communities abroad, and evidence they were a persecuted minority, both Armenians and Assyrians had an escape route out of Iran. So they left the country – in their hundreds of thousands. Between 1979 to the mid 1990s about 100,000 Armenians left Iran, and in the early 2000s the United Nations Special Envoy estimated about 15–20,000 were emigrating every year.[19] The exodus of the Assyrian community was even more intense. According to the official census their numbers dropped by 80 per cent between 1956–1986: from 100,000 to 20,000. Now it is less than 15,000[20] and the numbers are still falling. Both the Nestorian Assyrian Church and the Gregorian Armenians continue to worship in Iran, as they have done for hundreds of years, but as fewer and fewer families gather, there is an unspoken anxiety as to whether the next generation will keep the witness of these historic churches burning.

Pentecostals preach

While for the Anglicans the arrival of the revolution had turned into a night-mare, for the relatively newly formed Assemblies of God (AOG) it was an answer to prayer. This church was praying expectantly for Muslims to come to Christ, but before the revolution there was little spiritual interest. Indeed when Luke Yeghnazar first approached the elders about setting up an evangelistic Christian publishing and book distribution ministry – 'They told him it was a noble cause, but that people in Iran were not reading Christian books.'[21] And they had cup-boards filled with literature to prove it. But as soon as the revolution got under way with its calls for freedom, years of demand for uncensored ideas burst onto the streets. In Tehran 'Communists, secularists, democrats, Islamic Marxists, Zoroastrians, Bahai's and others set up stalls to sell their materials.'[22] And Luke Yeghnazar knew he had been right to set up his literature ministry. For 5 years, 6 days a week, from early morning till 6 or 7 in the evening he and his teams sold Christian literature to the public in Tehran, all the other major cities, and many small towns. In the early days of the revolution they would stand in the streets and shout 'The Gospel of Jesus Christ, the Gospel of Love!' and people would eagerly take the literature. Luke Yeghnazar estimates that during these 5 years over a million Scripture portions and evangelistic booklets were distributed.[23] In the year of the revolution 30,000 of the new Living Bible New Testament was published: they all went out that year.

The prayers of the AOG Churches were not only answered by this massive increase in literature evangelism, but also by more Muslims attending their churches, especially the Central Church in Tehran. Indeed during the 1980s and early 1990s the whole make-up of the church changed. In 1984 there were 150 official members, with a few ex-Muslims – there were always many more in the main meetings; by 1987 there were 250 members and by the early 1990s the church had 350 members, many more came to the services, and 80 per cent of them were Iranian Muslims.[24] The church also grew outside Tehran, and during the 1980s they planted nine new fellowships throughout Iran in different pro-vincial towns,[25] and all of these had Muslim converts in them. Literature had clearly played a part in this growth, and there were claims that 'In the early 1980's eight out of every ten people who were being baptized attributed their conversion to reading Christian material.'[26] There were other factors too. Most important of all was the general disillusionment which set in as soon as the regime clearly became a religious dictatorship towards the end of 1980. This dis-appointment with the revolution especially impacted the idealistic young and it was they more than any other age group that came to the church wanting to find out about Christianity. And when they fully understand the Christian message it often, in the words of one priest, 'made sense to them'. Another factor why the disillusioned made their way to the church is, as one church leader emphasized, the almost instinctive attraction Iranian Muslims have for Jesus Christ. This is surely related to the Iranian identity discussed in Part One. During the 1980s some Christians (from all backgrounds) began to seek asylum in Western countries on the basis of religious persecution, and it might be that a very small minority of those who came to the church, though attracted to the faith, also hoped Christianity would open doors to give them a better future outside Iran.

Pentecostals suffer

In 1985 serious shadows began to appear on the open season the AOG evangelists had been enjoying. First local officials forced all book vendors off the streets, so bringing to an end the direct literature evangelism. This was probably more due to pressure from the bookshop owners who resented the fact these stalls stole their business, rather than any political motive. Luke Yeghnazar and his teams were not disheartened and started to sell their stock directly to these established bookshops who knew there were customers for Christian titles.[27] In October 1985 there was a development showing that the authorities were concerned about the church's activities. A letter came from the Ministry of Information demanding the leaders stop all attempts to proselytize Muslims. Haik Hovsepian-Mehr, the superintendent of the church, ignored the request, and ministry continued. In 1988 things became more serious. In February the Ministry of Information summoned Haik Hovsepian-Mehr, and his brother Edward, also a pastor, and again demanded that the church stop preaching to Muslims. Again the brothers refused, a decision the government took note of. A few weeks later their other brother, Rubik, was arrested in Ahwaz where he was pastoring a new church and working as an evangelist. He was kept in solitary confinement for a month. It seemed the AOG Churches were being warned of what might happen if they did not stop reaching out to Muslims. And, from the tragic story of the Anglican Church, it was well known how far the enemies of the church were prepared to go. Haik Hovsepian-Mehr was an exceptional Christian leader whose gracious lifestyle attracted many to the church.[28] He was also a very brave man, and when confronted with this choice, he was determined to preach Christ. This resolve was soon to be tested. In October 1990 the pastor of their small church in Mashad, Revd Hossein Soodmand, was arrested 'on charges of "apostasy"' from Islam, propagating Christianity, distributing Christian literature and setting up an illegal church'.[29]

The 55-year-old Revd Soodmand had been a Christian for many years. He had come to faith through a Pentecostal Armenian friend while doing his military service in Ahwaz. When he arrived home at Mashad a Christian his family rejected him, so he went to Isphahan to find his Armenian friend who arranged work for him at the Anglican Christian hospital. Here he met and married his wife who is blind. When the hospital was taken over after the revolution, Hossein Soodmand was sent by the AOG to be a pastor in Mashad where he started a small church in the basement of his house which brought about his arrest. In response to this Revd Edward Hovsepian-Mehr from the church in Tehran came to Mashad and pleaded with the judge to have mercy, given that Revd Soodmand's wife was blind. The judge agreed as long as the court was given the title deeds to the Soodmand house. This was arranged and Revd Soodmand was released. He then tried to go to Gorgan in the north of Iran to work as a pastor, but the authorities did not allow this. Having seen the size of his file in the court, Revd Haik Hovsepian-Mehr suggested to Revd Soodmand that it was perhaps safest for him to leave Iran, even if this mean losing his property. However Revd Soodmand believed it was God's will for him to stay, and was concerned about the example he would set. His response was – 'I am the shepherd: I must not leave my sheep.' So he resumed his pastoral work in Mashad: in late November was arrested again and on 3 December he was hanged. Revd Soodmand is buried in a part of the city's main cemetery separate from the other graves in an area reserved for the 'cursed'. Here no memorial stones are allowed, but somebody has scratched a cross on his grave.

The ferocity that had earlier struck the Anglican Church for welcoming Muslim converts had now claimed the first martyr for the AOG Church. The church was shocked – but Haik Hovsepian-Mehr was not willing to back down, even though a new confrontation was looming with the authorities regarding another long-standing Muslim convert. In 1953 Mehdi Dibaj had become a Christian by reading a simple Gospel tract. He was just 14 years old and when his family discovered his new faith he had to leave home. He came to Tehran where he worked at a Christian bookshop and later attended the meetings held in Seth Yeghnazar's home.[30] When this fellowship joined the new Philadelphia Church founded in 1960 this became his denomination. Mehdi Dibaj was a radical Christian. He gave away over 50 per cent of all his income, was a fearless evangelist, and after receiving theological training in India, Beirut and Switzerland, he began work as a missionary in Afghanistan where he translated the *Gospel of Mark* into Dari. After a return visit to Iran he was refused entry into Afghanistan, so he settled in Babol on the Caspian Sea where he taught English at the university, and also contributed to a Christian evangelistic radio station.[31] Though Dibaj's clear Christian witness had already raised eyebrows in conservative Babol, his first serious brush with the government came in 1983 when someone close to him showed a letter to the local revolutionary authorities claiming that it slandered Ayatollah Khomeini. He was arrested and imprisoned for 68 days[32] and was then released on bail after the court had received the title deeds to a piece of land in Sari the AOG had purchased to build a church on. About a year later a church official and Mehdi Dibaj approached the authorities for these deeds which were handed back: but the court asked Mehdi Dibaj to stay for further questioning. His family expected to see him after a few hours, but he never returned from that police interview, and remained in prison for the next nine years. Though the letter was eventually dismissed as a forgery, the court authorities refused to ignore the issue of his apostasy against Islam. After gentle persuasion failed[33] and he refused to sign any document suggesting he was mentally weak, Mehdi Dibaj first faced physical beatings, mock executions and then 2 years of solitary confinement in a small unlit 3-yard cell. It should have been 'the eternity of the damned', but later Mehdi Dibaj bore witness that 'God had performed many miracles for him'.[34] In 1986 he was officially convicted of apostasy from Islam by a Revolutionary Court, but he appealed on the grounds that the Koran does not demand the death of an apostate. For the next 7 years there was little movement on the case.

In 1993 though it was clear the government wanted to appear tougher on the issue of Muslims converting to Islam. During Easter week officials from Ershad, the Ministry of Islamic Guidance, called in the Superintendent of the AOG churches, Revd Haik Hovsepian-Mehr, and bluntly told him to stop all the church's evangelistic activities, close down the Friday meeting, allow only Christians to their Sunday meeting and not add one extra Muslim convert to their congregation. To enforce this he was to give the officials a list of all the present members of the church. The officials at Ershad were told that these directives were impossible to obey as Christians had to preach the Gospel to all. The meeting ended and the Revd Haik Hovsepian-Mehr, and his brother, Edward, the pastor of the Central Church in Tehran, called the church to pray and fast that week. On the Friday, 25 April, about 15 officials arrived at 3 o'clock to stop the service; however Revd Edward Hovsepian-Mehr again insisted the church had to be open to all. The meeting started, and eventually the officials left. As the leader of his denomination and the Chairman of the Protestant Council, Haik Hovsepian-Mehr was becoming increasingly concerned about the hostility of the government towards Protestant Christians. He had been particularly distressed when the authorities had closed down the church he had started in Gorgan and when he had travelled there to complain, the officials had not just rejected his concerns, but mocked his faith. Also he knew Mehdi Dibaj's case was again due before the courts in Sari near Babol. So in early December Revd Haik Hovsepian-Mehr went to visit the Director for Minorities Affairs at the Ministry of Culture and Islamic Guidance. He wanted to share his concern over the government's general treatment of Christians, and to especially speak up for Mehdi Dibaj. Once there he reminded the Director that Iran had signed the International Covenant on Civil and Political Rights which declares that people can be free to change their religion,[35] and that the 1992 report by the UN inspector, Reynaldo Pohl, on Iran's Human Rights records showed the international community were aware and concerned.[36] The Director was not impressed by 'international accords, shaped as they are by Western hegemony', so to plead for Mehdi Dibaj, Revd Haik Hovsepian-Mehr was left to pointing out that he had become a Christian 45 years ago, 'when Iran was so different', implying how unfair it would be to apply later apostasy laws to him. Though the director bluntly stated that Dibaj had brought the danger on himself, nevertheless he still assured Revd Haik Hovsepian-Mehr that he would look into the 'new developments'.[37]

If the director kept his word, it did not have much impact. Dibaj was tried, found guilty of apostasy, and sentenced to death by the Sari Court in December. Tired of being under the constant threat of execution, Mehdi Dibaj welcomed the judgment and wrote a letter to the judge asking him to 'Expedite the process of carrying out the sentence'.[38] In the Sari prison where Mehdi Dibaj was kept there was an Armenian guard who was due to go to Tehran for Christmas leave. With this guard, Mehdi Dibaj smuggled out three important documents: the official sentence of execution which in writing stated that he was being killed for 'apostasy'; the letter he had sent to the judge with his final wishes; a copy of his defence before the court; and, his final testament, a moving and spiritual account of why he was a Christian, and why he must evangelize.[39] The guard arrived with his 'post' at the home of Revd Haik Hovsepian-Mehr on 21 December who immediately realized he had very little time to act if he wanted to save his friend's life. This would mean alerting the world which could be very dangerous. Revd Haik Hovsepian-Mehr decided he had to take action even if it meant dying as he saw no future if the church remained silent. So in the next few days he faxed out copies of Mehdi Dibaj's prison documents to friends in Europe who translated them and alerted others in the USA and South Korea. The story was soon picked up by the international press, and Bernard Levin, a famous UK columnist for *The Times*, had the whole of Dibaj's 'Final Testament' published in the newspaper. On 11 January 1994 Revd Haik Hovsepian-Mehr invited the El Salvadorian, Reynaldo Pohl, the UN Special Envoy, who had already written critically about Iran's human rights to come again to investigate the situation of Protestant Christians. Pohl immediately wanted to come, but the Iranian government refused him entry and to counter the adverse publicity the Mehdi Dibaj case was creating they asked all the Christian denominations to sign a declaration 'stating that they enjoyed full constitutional rights as Christians in the Islamic Republic of Iran'.[40] Revd Haik Hovsepian-Mehr refused to sign such a declaration. Meanwhile the Vatican had got involved and there were reports that Archbishop Romeo Pancivo, the Vatican's Ambassador to Iran, had appealed directly to the Supreme Leader for a meeting. It is also reported that during the meeting, where ambassadors from other European countries were present, Ayatollah Khamanei had denied the claim that Dibaj was going to be executed and declared there was freedom of religion in Iran. So the Archbishop produced a copy of the death sentence as faxed to them by Revd Haik Hovsepian-Mehr. Not surprisingly it is reported that Ayatollah Khamanei was very upset, and had no choice but to say he would look into the case. On 16 January 1994 it seemed that the campaign had been completely successful: the government said the local judge in Sari had made a mistake and Mehdi Dibaj was released. However just 3 days after Dibaj's homecoming, Revd Haik Hovsepian-Mehr was abducted on the way to the airport to pick up his sister-in-law. He was never seen alive again. The family waited 10 days for news, till eventually they had a call from the police in Tehran asking a family member to come and identify a photograph of a corpse which had been left beside one of their stations. The eldest son Joseph Hovsepian-Mehr[41] confirmed it was his father. He had been stabbed 27 times. The body had already been buried in a Muslim graveyard, so the family first had to get permission for it to be exhumed, some say after a special intervention from President Rafsanjani, before organizing a Christian funeral. It was held on 3 February and over two thousand 'stood for three hours in bitterly cold weather at the graveside to honour Bishop Haik including the ambassador of Norway and innumerable Muslims'.[42]

At the funeral Mehdi Dibaj had said, 'I should have died, not Brother Haik.' For, though the government insisted Revd Haik Hovsepian-Mehr had been killed by 'unknown assailants' most assumed he had died for publicizing the Mehdi Dibaj's death sentence. Now free, Mehdi Dibaj delighted in seeing the many Muslims in the church who had come to faith and spent many hours both in Tehran and beyond speaking at meetings. His activities did not escape the notice of the church's enemies, and in April a conservative newspaper wrote critically of his release from prison. One church leader noted that he had been given his passport, which was presumably a way of inviting him to go into exile. He was in fact planning to go to Afghanistan to resume his missionary work there, but first he wanted to spend more time in Iran. On 20 June he led a small conference in Karaj a suburb of Tehran, and on 24 June he set out for the city to attend his daughter's seventeenth birthday party. He never arrived and on 5 July his family was informed that they had found Mehdi Dibaj's body in a park. On the death certificate it was written he had been stabbed to death in the heart area.

The AOG was not the only church to suffer in 1994. On 29 June, just 5 days after Mehdi Dibaj was last seen, Revd Tateos Michaelian, pastor of St John's Presbyterian Church in Tehran, also went missing. On 2 July his family were asked to identify his body, which according to one report was riddled with bullets. Revd Tateos Michaelian had been a very influential Christian leader. He had been the Secretary of the Bible Society before it was closed down in 1990; the Executive Secretary of the Synod of the Presbyterian Church; and most importantly of all he was a prolific and very able translator. As well as being closely involved in bringing out the 'Good News' version of the New Testament in Persian, he had also translated over sixty other Christian books into Persian. He was also a very brave man and did not hesitate to speak out when he thought it was necessary. In the late 1980s a senior Muslim cleric said on TV that Christians, like pigs and dogs, were 'Najess', unclean. Revd Michaelian was furious and made sure an official at the Ministry of Islamic Guidance knew his views. He also complained bitterly over the closure of the Bible Society; and when a foreign newspaper reporter asked him at the funeral of Haik Hovsepian-Mehr who was responsible for the murder, he bluntly accused the regime. In May 1994 he attended an international church conference in Cyprus where he made a devastating attack on the Islamic government, accusing them of not keeping the spirit of their own constitution and being a 'religious dictatorship' which 'can be compared with the Middle Ages'. He also spelt out what this meant for Christians: they were unable to get government jobs, they 'are considered as second class citizens and even unclean', they 'are encouraged and even indirectly forced to become Muslim', they are not allowed to build new churches or publish Scriptures, and their leaders are killed. At the end he asked the World Council of Churches and the United Nations to put pressure on the Iranian government to ensure Iranians had religious freedom. When he sat down, a colleague leant over and told him he had signed his own death sentence.

As the news of Revd Tateos Michaelian's murder spread, so too did a rumour that there was a hit list for Christian leaders and some swiftly left Iran. One leader, whose name was reported to be on the list, was Revd Edward Hovsepian-Mehr, the brother of Haik. After much prayer he decided he should stay in Iran and serve as the new superintendent of the AOG Churches. In this role he was called with the other leaders of religious minorities to a special meeting hosted by the Ministry of Information in Tehran in the autumn of 1994 where government officials were very polite and respectful to their guests. Once all were gathered, two blindfolded young girls who belonged to the Mojahedin were ushered onto the stage.[43] The ministry spokesman, the Sa'id Emami who allegedly committed suicide in prison in June 1999,[44] then explained that these girls had confessed to the murder of Mehdi Dibaj, and Revd Michaelian and it could be assumed they were involved in killing the Revd Haik Hovsepian-Mehr. So he asked if the audience could now go and tell their congregations that they had seen the killers and emphasize that the government was not to blame for the deaths of the pastors. This version of events was not generally accepted by any of the religious minority leaders at the meeting as all of them knew that it was the government that had issues with the evangelical churches. Nevertheless by holding this meeting it seemed these officials wanted to draw a line under the events of 1994 and were being more conciliatory towards the religious minorities.

Still much interest in Christianity . . .

In the midst of this storm that had engulfed the evangelical churches in the early 1990s, ordinary Iranians continued to show interest in Christianity. As seen this was the time when the AOG Churches entered a new phase of growth and there were more Iranian Muslims in the church than Armenians or Assyrians. A new experience at this time would be that whole house or family groups who had become Christian completely separately from any church, often through a dream or a vision, would contact the church for help.

The AOG Churches were not the only denomination encouraging semi-separate house groups. Having so many ethnic Christians in their denomination, the Presbyterian Church was largely left alone after the revolution: the Assyrian and Armenian congregations continued to operate as normal, as did their two Persian speaking congregations at Emmanuel and St Peter's Church in Tehran. And when later the authorities began to intimidate the AOG Churches, the Presbyterian Church did not attract so much hostile attention as their style of working with Muslims tended to be quieter. Though quieter, it was still effective and they also benefited from the increased interest in Christianity brought about by the revolution. As well as seeing their two Persian congregations grow, they were also contacted by Muslims who had experienced Christ outside the church setting.

The interest in Christianity has also impacted the Roman Catholics. Though the Roman Catholics had six active dioceses in 1979, none of them followed a liturgy in Persian. At Isphahan one followed the Latin rite, while another followed the Armenians, and the other dioceses at Salmas, Urmieh, Ahwaz and Tehran followed the Chaldean rite. This meant that despite in theory the great suspicion the new Islamic regime might have for churches linked to the world's most powerful Christian denomination, the Roman Catholics were not the target for intimidation. However though their official liturgy is not in Persian and historically most of members of the Roman Catholic Church are from the Armenian and Assyrian communities, nevertheless they have been involved in translating Christian material, and have never forgotten the call of mission to share the Gospel with all people. This has inevitably engendered a negative reaction from the government and there are reports that one of their centres has been closed down. So they remained much more than just a functioning Christian presence in Iran. They have four bishops and a number of priests and though their own figures record a decline in numbers in Tehran, Ahwaz, Urmieh and Salmas reflecting the impact of the emigration of Assyrians, in Isphahan there has been a substantial increase, especially since 2000.[45] There is no doubt the Roman Catholics have benefited from the increased interest in Christianity that has been apparent since 1979.

Such has been the interest in Christianity that Muslims have even been knocking on the doors of the churches of the Assyrian Nestorians and Gregorian Armenians. In the 1990s a European Christian visited the beautiful Armenian Church in Julfa and got into conversation with the caretaker who told him of this interest. He said every day a Muslim would come into the church and ask if he or she could join; every day a Muslim would come into the church and ask for a Bible; and several times a week Muslims would come and ask if they could be baptized. This gives some indication of both the courageous interest that Iranian Muslims have in Christianity, and that they often first turn to the public presence of the historic churches.

It would seem clear then that in the 1990s every denomination, from the Pentecostal AOG through to the Gregorian Armenians bore witness to the phenomenon that Muslims were showing remarkable interest in Christianity. Over a period of nearly 10 years one Christian lady gave out around 1,000 videos or

DVDs of the *Jesus*[46] film: only two were handed back to her. The demand for
Scriptures and Christian literature tells the same story. From 1994 to 2004 just
one major interdenominational agency saw over 250,000 Gospel portions,
100,000 New Testaments, 100,000 whole Bibles and 50,000 study books taken
into Iran and distributed in 5 to 7 of the country's largest cities.[47] As has been
pointed out above, there was no such demand for Christian scriptures before
the revolution.

Dialogue?

With the election of President Khatami in 1997 there is evidence that this
interest in Christianity had reached even senior clerical figures in the religious
establishment. To counter the message of Samuel Huntington's influential
1996 book *The Clash of Civilisations*, Khatami famously made a call for a 'Dialogue
of Civilisations' which definitely needed the involvement of the major religions.
Khatami was very serious about this. As well as travelling to Rome (1999),
Canterbury (2006) and Washington (2006) to meet the Pope, the Anglican
Archbishop, and speak at Washington Cathedral, he also worked very hard in
Iran to promote dialogue between religions. He was very involved in setting up
the Organization of Culture and Islamic Relations in 1995, and later his government set up the International Centre for Dialogue among Civilizations in 1999.
And Khatami's Vice President Ali Abtahi established The Institute for Interreli-
gious Dialogue in 2001. Though in theory these organizations have been set up
to engage with all the world's major religions, nearly all their activity has been
directed towards Christians. As well as leading Shiites holding seminars with the
Orthodox, Roman Catholics and even Presbyterian Christian leaders, there has
also been a great surge of interfaith literature, some of it from these institutions.
Indeed from 2002–2005 Dr Sasan Tavassoli, author of a thesis titled 'Muslim-
Christian Engagements in Post-Revolutionary Iran', was able to purchase in
Iran 'over four hundred books and journals on various themes and topics
relating to this study'.[48] Historically this is unique: there has never before been
this amount of engagement between Christian and Shia leaders and is further
evidence of the increased interest there is in Iran in Christianity.[49]

More persecution

With all this dialogue activity and implied respect for Christianity one would
have thought the evangelical church leaders would have been very optimistic
about the prospects of the church under the Khatami government. After the
murders of 1994 there was an uneasy peace with the authorities, however this
came to an end on 28 September 1996 when the corpse of the AOG pastor
Mohammad Bagher Yusefi, known as Ravanbaksh (soul giver) was found hanging

from a tree in a forest near his home in Sari in the north of Iran. It was not difficult to see why 35-year-old Yusefi might have had enemies in fundamentalist Islamic circles. He was an apostate who had converted from Islam to Christianity when he was 24: worse, he was ordained a pastor serving the AOG churches in Mazandaran province, he was a successful evangelist and he hosted a house fellowship in his home. He was also a close friend of Mehdi Dibaj who had mentored him at the start of his Christian life and after Dibaj's murder Yusefi, with support from the church, had taken care of Dibaj's sons. Hearing the news of Pastor Yusefi's death Revd Edward Hovsepian-Mehr was deeply saddened – and angry when he saw reports that Yusefi had committed suicide. He and the rest of the AOG church were not able to accept this. Nor were they ready to write a letter confirming this assumption of suicide, especially when a few days earlier they had received a letter from Pastor Yusefi outlining plans for his future ministry.

The death of Pastor Yusefi in September 1996 obviously coloured the way Protestant church leaders viewed the election of President Khatami in May 1997. They hoped for change, but instinctively sensed intimidation would continue. As seen in Chapter 8, the brutal murder of dissidents in 1998, followed by the suppression of the student movement in 1999 proved their instincts right. The hard-liners refused to give up power, and for all his talk of wanting dialogue, President Khatami never even considered reforming traditional Islamic views on apostasy.[50] So Iran remained a very dangerous place for active Christians who wanted to share their message with Muslims. This is though exactly what keen Christians wanted to do especially because of the ongoing openness among ordinary people.

House churches

To avoid danger, continue normal Christian activity, and bypass the rule that a growing church could not put up new buildings, it seemed a number of church leaders decided in the late 1990s to encourage Christians to meet in homes. As these groups began to grow, soon there were other fellowships whose members had never been to an ordinary church and had no contact with official leaders. There are very strict rules about confidentiality, so there is very little information about these groups, but there is every reason to believe they have been growing. First of all there is this increased interest in Christianity. As well as reports from the overground churches and the demand for literature regarding this, there is now also the feedback from satellite broadcasters who have been beaming in Christian programmes since 2001. The agency SAT-7 says that in their first year they received 'a flood of letters, phone calls and e-mails from its Iranian viewers expressing thanks for introducing them to Jesus Christ'.[51] International Antioch Ministries reports that 250–300 Iranians phone in every month to pray to receive Christ after seeing their programmes. On the basis that many others are responding, but are not able to make the long-distance phone call necessary to contact the programme, International Antioch Ministries estimates that in fact 3,000 a month or more are turning to Christ just through their broadcasts.[52] Even if it is just 250–300 a month this is still very significant. Another popular Christian channel is 'Mohabat' (Love). They hired a professional company who carefully surveyed 1,500 people in three different cities and report that nearly 200 (over 12 per cent) watched the Mohabat programmes, and of these over 40 had wanted to experience the salvation in Christ they learned about, that is nearly 3 per cent of the people surveyed.[53] These figures from Mohabat are not estimates; it is solid evidence of the interest in Christianity in Iran. Secondly it is likely these fellowships are growing because they meet in homes and are extremely secretive. It is reported that members often use false names, and will rarely give out their contact details: so in any one city it is very likely that there are different groups who have no idea of the other's existence. This means that a new member can slowly get involved without risking his or her own security. With the normal church there is no hiding where the Muslim is going, but with this church they are just visiting a friend in an ordinary flat. Thirdly there is the spiritual strength of the underground church, for when there is a real risk of arbitrary arrest,[54] there is no room for the lukewarm. All those who have had contact with church members often comment on the freshness of their relationship with God and their fervency in prayer, fasting and evangelism. It would seem there is a great emphasis on 'hearing from the Lord' and already there are some remarkable stories of how God has supernaturally led these Christians to witness to unbelievers.[55] There are also reports of healings.[56] There is a fourth reason why the house churches have been growing and that is a shared sense of ownership, giving all the members a sense of responsibility. Due to the security situation there would be much less distance between leaders and the members than in a normal church situation. To avoid attention the groups have to be kept small so there is a sense of ownership of both the worship and the outreach. Together they must decide whether they can sing out loud at a meeting or whether it will risk the unwelcome curiosity of neighbours; together they must pray and plan their evangelism; together they must decide whether it is safe to bring in a new person to the group. So though these groups do receive outside pastoral support, they are in essence self governing, and as many studies[57] have shown this is a key element in bringing about growth.

There is a final reason why it is very likely these house churches are growing that brings us to the heart of our subject, the Iranian identity and Christianity. Like all great nations Iran is made up of a number of ethnic groups, but it is the Persians who have always been the majority; their culture that has absorbed others; and their history that stretches back 2,500 years. And though there have been occasions when there have been a significant number of Persian

Christians in the Iranian Church, most notably at the start of the seventh century, there has never been a time when the majority of the leaders and members of the whole church have been Persian. Historically the church has either been Assyrian, Armenian or closely linked to Western missions. It is true there were many Iranian Muslims in the Anglican Church, and in the 1990s many joined the AOG Churches, but still outsiders thought of these churches as being English and Armenian.

So throughout its long history the perceived identity of Christianity has been that it is not wholly Iranian: until now. For most of the leaders and members of the new house churches are not from ethnic Christian backgrounds, they are from Persian-speaking families. For students of church growth this is very significant. In his seminal work *Understanding Church Growth* Donald McGavran wiped away the super-spiritual language that many agencies used to cover up their failure to win people to Christ and showed by thoroughly researched case studies that there were understandable reasons why some churches grew, while others did not. In 1977 an occasional paper of the Lausanne Conference summed up the key principles for church growth as elucidated by Dr McGavran as follows. First of all people often reject the Gospel for sociological reasons, rather than theological ones. They fear that if they become a Christian, they will be betraying their culture. In McGavran's now well-known words, people 'like to become Christians without crossing racial, linguistic or class barriers'. Secondly therefore the evangelist must be able to identify with the listeners and his message must be 'contextualized in such a way that it communicates with them'. Finally, and most importantly, 'the church into which they are invited must itself belong to their culture sufficiently for them to feel at home'.[58] Here is the reference to McGavran's famous 'Homogeneous Unit Principle' which he defined as 'a section of society in which all members have some characteristic in common', his point being that people will much more easily both become Christians and faithful church members if they feel they are joining a group of people similar to themselves. If many join, then it becomes a 'people' movement, as for example happened to Hindu tribes in the Punjab at the end of the nineteenth century.[59] Though McGavran's thesis has had its critics, especially as it could undermine the church's overall unity in diversity, the overall emphasis of his thesis has been largely accepted, and indeed acted on with significant results.[60]

Obviously McGavran's insights are useful for the situation in Iran. Though it is not certain how much Persian influence there was on the early Nestorian Church, there is no doubt that Iranians who wanted to explore Christianity from the fifteenth century onwards had to cross 'racial and linguistic' barriers as there were no churches that were home grown. In McGavran's paradigm this would partly explain why there was no major church growth especially in the nineteenth and twentieth century, for there was no 'homogeneous unit' for ethnic Iranians to join. Indeed some congregations[61] were very diverse, made up of Jews, Armenians, Assyrians, as well as a sprinkling of ex-Muslims and often following a liturgy devised in England or America. Now though for the first time in modern Iranian history there is a church that is homogeneous in that both the leaders and members are ethnically from the same predominant Muslim Persian national culture.[62] At present there is not enough information to be able to say for certainty that the house churches are operating as homogenous subcultures, but there have been reports of instances when over thirty members of one family network have come to faith. This would indicate that people are reaching out, as one would expect, to people who are similar to them and they are responding. It would seem then that the house churches in Iran have all the characteristics that McGavran identified as being crucial for growth: no cultural barriers; evangelists who are of the people; and homogeneous fellowships. This growing church has been greatly helped by new technology. Satellite TV has not just brought people to faith,[63] but also hundreds of Christians look to their programmes for teaching. The internet has also proved crucial, enabling Christians to network and access both Scriptures and thousands of teaching articles from websites.[64] This and the support given by outside agencies[65] means it is less likely these house churches will fall into extremism or heresy.

There are then good reasons as to why these house church networks should be growing: increased interest in Christianity; security; spiritual strength; ownership; and homogenous units, all supported by new technology. Regarding actual growth, there are many estimates, but few hard facts. However there are a number of networks, and one of them grew from a few members to one thousand in 5 years, so there must be several thousand underground Christians, if not a lot more.[66]

The wisdom of house churches was more than proved in the autumn of 2004 when government officials arrested 80 leaders of the AOG Churches during the church's annual business meetings. All were imprisoned for 2 days for questioning and then released, except Hamid Pourmand who was imprisoned for nearly 2 years as he was both an apostate from Islam and a colonel in the army. During the questioning of the church leaders, the issue at stake was very familiar. The officials were intent on stopping the Christians proselytizing Muslims and before being freed all those arrested had to give assurances that they would not engage in this. Since the arrest all the leaders of this denomination have been under very close surveillance to ensure this stipulation is enforced.

If Iran had had no house churches at the end of the 1990s the new millennium would have ushered in depressing days for the history of Christianity in Iran, especially with President Ahmadinejad's promise to 'stop Christianity'[67] in his country. Unfortunately this was not rhetoric. In his mind-set Iran is no place for apostates, and, as has been the case ever since 1979, it is almost certain there will be periodic efforts to eliminate the house churches. Indeed both Iranian and general history would sadly expect that when the church grows, so does opposition. However, as a senior church leader has said, the Iranian government should not presume that it will be more successful than the Soviet Union or China in suppressing the Gospel of Jesus Christ.

Christianity alive and well

Christians then are still feeling the tremors of the earthquake of the Islamic Revolution. Unfairly perceived as being controlled by England, Anglican Christians were the first to taste the wrath of revolutionary anger and though they have continued to bravely worship under severe constraints, they have not been able to give the same service to Iran as they were doing before 1979. Meanwhile thousands of Gregorian Armenians and Nestorian Assyrians have sadly decided there was no future for their families in the Islamic Republic and started to leave Iran. The AOG used the Revolution's demand for freedom and preached the Gospel to thousands, mainly through literature distribution. This evangelism, combined with disillusionment with the regime, saw many Muslim converts come into their church which brought the sort of persecution the Anglicans had suffered. In response to the opportunities presented by the Revolution the Presbyterians adopted a quieter approach that has also been effective and has left them with considerable freedom to operate. With no official liturgy in Persian the Roman Catholic Church did not court the immediate attention of the regime, and so has not only survived, but seems to have grown.

In the face of ongoing hostility from the authorities, but evident interest from people, Protestant leaders in the late 1990s decided to focus much more on letting Christianity spread underground. For reasons outlined above and the few hard facts available it would seem this is certainly happening and so Christianity at the start of the twenty-first century is alive and well in Iran. Indeed it might be entering one of its most fascinating chapters.

Notes

[1] Shawqi Talia argues that due to this 'the position of Iran's Christian community was only slightly better under the Pahlavis than in the new Islamic republic.' See his 'From Edessa to Urmia', *Bulletin of the Royal Institute for Inter-Faith Studies*, 2, Autumn/Winter 2005: 50.

[2] See www.iranonline.com/iran/iran-info/Government/constitution-3.html [last accessed 6 June 2008].

[3] 'Apostasy' only became an official state crime in 1993. Since early 2008 there have been moves in the Iranian parliament for death to be the mandatory punishment.

[4] See Paul Hunt's *Inside Iran*, Lion Publishing, England, 1981, p. 107. Hunt is here quoting from Khomeini's 'Little Green Book'.

[5] Missionary Revd Paul Hunt once asked the Roman Catholic Archbishop in Iran why the Anglican Church had suffered so much, 'Yours is the church that has made the converts' was the reply. See Hunt's *Inside Iran*, p. 156.

[6] See H. B. Dehqani-Tafti's *The Hard Awakening*, SPCK, London, 1981, p. 38.

7 See Hunt's *Inside Iran*, p. 60.
8 See Hunt's *Inside Iran*, p. 108.
9 See Dehqani-Tafti's *The Hard Awakening*, p. 46.
10 For a full account see Dehqani-Tafti's *The Hard Awakening*, pp. 60–63. Paul Hunt notes that at the exact time of the attack there was an intense time of prayer for the Bishop in Ramsgate, Kent where the intercessors sensed they had to ask for protection. The organizers of the murder were so sure of success that someone arrived at the hospital in the morning asking for his corpse.
11 Dehqani-Tafti's *The Hard Awakening*, p. 68.
12 Given the international contacts Bishop Dehqani-Tafti had it is extremely unlikely that a group of vigilantes would have taken it upon themselves to have murdered him. It is much more probable that they would have first checked orally with seniors – hence the lack of arrests.
13 Dehqani-Tafti's *The Hard Awakening*, p. 65.
14 The Trust Fund is still in a bank in Iran and legally belongs to the Diocese.
15 Dehqani-Tafti's *The Hard Awakening*, p. 114.
16 As for many years Bishop Dehqani-Tafti was the associate Bishop of Winchester his funeral was conducted in Winchester Cathedral and he is buried in its grounds. On hearing in the early 1990's that this would be his final resting place he wrote back to the Cathedral authorities to thank them, and added with his characteristic humour, 'I am so excited, I can hardly wait to die.' Obituaries can be read . . . <http://www.timesonline.co.uk/tol/comment/obituaries/article3918778.ece>. <http://www.telegraph.co.uk/news/obituaries/1918728/The-Rt-Rev-Hassan-Dehqani-Tafti.html>.
   <http://www.guardian.co.uk/world/2008/may/21/anglicanism.iran>.
   http://www.independent.co.uk/news/obituaries/the-right-rev-hassan-dehqani-tafti-exiled-anglican-bishop-in-iran-832817.html
17 All of his books are available from Sohrab Books and Elam Ministries.
18 See www.state.gov/g/drl/rls/irf/2005/51599.htm [last accessed 6 June 2008].
19 See 'Minorities at Risk', Report on Christians in Iran, www.cidcm.umd.edu/mar/assessment.asp?groupId=63010 [last accessed 6 June 2008].
20 See 'Documenting the Crisis in the Assyrian Iranian Community', Dr. Eden Naby, www.aina.org/articles/dtcitaic.htm 2007, Assyrian International News Agency [last accessed 6 June 2008].
21 Unpublished paper by David Yeghnazar, 'AOG in Iran after the Revolution', Atlanta, p. 2.
22 Yeghnazar, 'AOG in Iran after the Revolution', p. 2.
23 Yeghnazar, 'AOG in Iran after the Revolution', p. 2.
24 2007: Interview with 1980's Secretary to the Directors of AOG Church.
25 Shahinshah, Ahwaz, Rasht, Bushehr, Arak, Shiraz, Jannat Abad, Karaj and Gonbade Ghaboos. Information from Yeghnazar, 'AOG in Iran after the Revolution', pp. 7–9.
26 Yeghnazar, 'AOG in Iran after the Revolution', p. 6. His statement is based on an interview with his uncle Luke Yeghnazar.
27 Yeghnazar, 'AOG in Iran after the Revolution', p. 6. His statement is based on an interview with his uncle Luke Yeghnazar.
28 For an excellent summary of his life see Karen Hatley's 'Biography of Haik Hovsepian-Mehr', *Truett Journal of Church and Mission*, 2, 1, Spring 2004: 43–57.

29 'Report on the Situation of Human Rights in the Islamic Republic of Iran' by
    R. Pohl, United Nations, February 1991, www.abfiran.org/english/document-
    182-373.php [last accessed 6 June 2008].

30 See Chapter 8, p. 155.

31 See 'Paying the Ultimate Price' by Catherine Butcher, Christianity October 2006,
    www.christianitymagazine.co.uk/engine.cfm?i=92&id=832&arch=1 [last accessed
    6 June 2008].

32 See 'Three Pastors Life, Death, and Religion in Muslim Iran' by Harold Fickett,
    Crisis Magazine 3 January 2007, www.crisismagazine.com/january2007/fickett.
    htm [last accessed 6 June 2008].

33 Once a prison guard said 'You are sixty, your hair is turning white, why don't you
    just say you are a Muslim and go home' to which Mehdi Dibaj replied, 'I have
    plenty of time till I am 120.'

34 See Fickett, 'Three Pastors Life, Death, and Religion in Muslim Iran'.

35 Article 18. Everyone shall have the right to freedom of thought, conscience and
    religion. This right shall include freedom to have or to adopt a religion or belief
    of his choice, and freedom, either individually or in community with others and
    in public or private, to manifest his religion or belief in worship, observance,
    practice and teaching. www.unhchr.ch/html/menu3/b/a_ccpr.htm [last accessed
    6 June 2008].

36 See www.unhchr.ch/Huridocda/Huridoca.nsf/(Symbol)/E.CN.4.Sub.2.1993.13.
    En?Opendocument [last accessed 6 June 2008].

37 For a full account of the interview see Fickett, 'Three Pastors Life, Death, and
    Religion in Muslim Iran'.

38 Fickett, 'Three Pastors Life, Death, and Religion in Muslim Iran'.

39 This final testament is now famous and is widely available on the internet. For
    example, see www.dohi.org/view_article.asp?id=348&cat=12 [last accessed 6 June
    2008].

40 'Interim Report on the Situation of Human Rights in the Islamic Republic of
    Iran, Prepared by The Special Representative of the Commission on Human
    Rights in Accordance with Commission Resolution 1994/73 and Economic and
    Social Council Decision 1994/263', www.unhchr.ch/Huridocda/Huridoca.nsf/
    0/74e1f21f50a70017802566fe005ba67c?Opendocument [last accessed 6 June
    2008].

41 Joseph Hovsepian-Mehr has become a film director and in 2007 released a film
    about his father's death – see www.hovsepian.com/products.htm [last accessed 6
    June 2008].

42 See Fickett, 'Three Pastors Life, Death, and Religion in Muslim Iran'.

43 For more detail on this opposition group see Chapter Five

44 See Chapter 7, p. 124.

45 The number on their website is 25,000, but those who know the situation think
    this is unlikely. See www.catholic-hierarchy.org/country/ir.html for more detail
    about Catholics in Iran [last accessed 6 June 2008].

46 This is the film produced by Campus Crusade For Christ based on the story of
    Jesus Christ according to Luke. It is the most seen film in the world.

47 Interview with senior agency leader, October 2007. After the closure of the Bible
    Society much Scripture for Iran was provided by Elam Ministries.

[48] The full name of the thesis which gives a detailed analysis of this topic is called 'Muslim–Christian Engagements in Post-Revolutionary Iran: The Encounters of Iranian Thinkers with Christian Thought' by Sasan Tavassoli. The thesis was submitted to the University of Birmingham, UK, May 2006. This particular quote is from p. 9.

[49] It is also further evidence of the main thesis in Chapter 1, that Christianity has much more in common with Shia Islam than with Sunni Islam.

[50] Dr Sasan Tavassoli gives an excellent overview of the topics discussed between Shia and Christian leaders in chapter four of his thesis, for title see above, but the issue of apostate's from Islam is never tackled directly.

[51] See 'Jesus TV breaks through barriers in Iran' by Michelle Vu, 16 October 2007, Christian Today, www.christiantoday.com/article/jesus.tv.breaks.through.barriers. in.iran/13957.htm [last accessed 6 June 2008].

[52] www.iam-online.net/Press_release_PDFs/IAMTVrelease_FINAL.doc%20 (Read-Only).pdf [last accessed 6 June 2008].

[53] These figures come from a confidential report produced by the Mohabat Channel.

[54] There are unconfirmed reports that in 2007 over hundred house church members were arrested for questioning. One man was unable to walk after his release.

[55] There is one story of two young girls who after praying and fasting believe they should try and share the Gospel on the inter-city busses. On the day they choose to go, the bus driver decides to show the film 'The Passion of Christ' on the coach TV. After the film the bus stops and people are milling around. The two girls then overhear a conversation between two men arguing about the historicity of the cross and expressing their wish to have a New Testament to study for themselves. At this point one of the girls interrupt and the story ends with these men being given New Testaments. There is another story of a Christian who shares the Gospel in a taxi with a woman who is deeply depressed because she has had to become a prostitute. The story ends with the Christian eventually being able to share not just with her, but the 'Madam' of the brothel who both accept Christ.

[56] One very moving story involves a female evangelist who visits hospitals to share the Gospel and was able to pray for the son of a woman very opposed to Christianity, but who was desperate for help. The son was healed.

[57] The importance of churches being self governing, self funded and self propagated was first articulated by the missionary strategist Revd Henry Venn.

[58] See 'The Pasadena Consultation – Homogeneous Unit Principle 1978', www. lausanne.org/pasadena-1977/lop-1.html [last accessed 6 June 2008].

[59] For a detailed analysis see *People Movements in the Punjab* by Frederick Stock, William Carey Library Publishers, Pasadena, CA, 1975.

[60] In the USA three pastors of mega churches, Rick Warren, Robert Schuller and Bill Hybels, would all acknowledge their debt to McGavran. See www.webtruth. org/articles/church-issues-30/the-purpose-driven-church-(a-critique)-59.html for a critical assessment of their ministries where the link is made clear [last accessed 6 June 2008].

[61] This is true of some of the Presbyterian and Anglican congregations.

[62] It is important to note that while these groups are made up of Muslim converts, nevertheless ethnic Christians have had a vital and much appreciated input into

a number of the underground networks, so showing that unity in Christ overrides racial divides.

[63] One mission leader with over ten years experience of working with the church in Iran has made the fascinating observation that in the 1990s people would often initially come to Christ through a vision or a dream and then seek out other Christians. Now there is much less reference to supernatural dreams, and much more to the impact of satellite TV.

[64] Though the government nobly tries to block pornographic websites, they will only block Christian ones if they become overtly political.

[65] As well as international agencies there are also a number of Iranian led ones which offer support to house churches. One of the earliest was Elam Ministries led by Samuel Yeghnazar, eldest son of Seth Yeghnazar, which has played a crucial role in providing training and resources to the church in Iran.

[66] One senior church leader says his most conservative estimate is 50,000 Christians in these networks.

[67] He made this promise at a meeting of provincial governors in November 2005. See www.compassdirect.org/en/display.php?page=news&lang=en&length=long &idelement=4090 [last accessed 6 June 2008].

Conclusion

Twice before in Iranian history the entire nation has tilted towards becoming a Christian country – first just before the Arab invasions in the early seventh century, and secondly during the early years of the Mongol invasions. There is absolutely no evidence now that there is even the slightest chance that Iran will become a Christian nation in the near or distant future. The country is solidly Shia. However two crucial things have happened in the past 25 years that might well mean the rapport between the Iranian identity and Christianity becomes more significant.

First, as demonstrated in Chapters 4 to 7 the Islamic Republic has wounded the country's relationship with Shia Islam. There has been a dislocation. This does not mean that every Iranian now wants to abandon their national religion. The First World War profoundly shook Europe's relationship with Christianity, but it still remained the national faith for most people in most of that continent[1]. However it is clear that some have been so disillusioned they are more than open to considering other faiths and as seen from Part One there is much in the Iranian identity that is naturally attracted to Christianity.

The second crucial thing that has happened, again ironically because of revolutionary Islam, is that there is a real possibility of a 'people' movement in Iran.[2] The hostility of the regime to the church has created house fellowships which are not just spiritually vibrant, but also probably made up of 'homogenous units', and so people do not have 'cultural or linguistic' barriers to cross. And there are no limits to this church. There are no buildings to construct (which is illegal anyway) or programmes to sustain for them to keep on expanding. It is just different groups of Christians meeting secretly in homes, so as long as there is a home to meet in, this church can keep on growing.

With the emergence of these house churches in Iran combined with what we have learned in Part One about the Iranian identity, it would be reasonable to conclude that the future of Christianity in the great land of Iran is truly intriguing.

Notes

[1] That did not remain the case after the Second World War when society increasingly rejected Christianity.

[2] If the figures from the survey carried out by Mohabbat TV (see Chapter 9, p. 177) were translated nationally, it would mean that 8 million people are interested in Christianity and nearly 3 million would actually want to become Christian. That would amount to a 'people' movement.

Bibliography

Ahmadi, N., and F. *Iranian Islam*, St Martin's Press, Basingstoke, 1998

Alavi, N. *We Are Iran*, Portobello Books, London, 2005

Alizadeh, P. (ed.). *The Economy of Iran*, I. B. Tauris, London, New York, 2000

Ansari, A. *Iran Islam and Democracy*, Chatham House, London, 2000

Arberry, A. *Sufism: An Account of the Mystics of Islam*, Dover Publications, New York, 1950

Banisadr, M. *Masoud*, Saqi, London, 2004

Behrooz, M. *Rebels With a Cause*, I. B. Tauris, London, New York, 2000

Blunt, W. *Pietro's Pilgrimage*, James Barrie, London, 1953

— *Persian Spring*, James Barrie, London, 1957

Boroujerdi, M. *Iranian Intellectuals and the West*, Syracuse University Press, Syracuse, 1996

Corbin, H. *Spiritual Earth and Celestial Earth: From Mazdean Iran to Shi'ite Iran*, I. B. Tauris, London, 1990

Dabashi, H. *Close Up Iranian Cinema*, Verso, London, New York, 2001

Dehqani-Tafti, H. *The Hard Awakening*, SPCK, London, 1981

— *Christ and Christianity in Persian Poetry*, Sohrab Books, Basingstoke, 1986

Donaldson, D. *The Shi'ite Religion*, Luzac, London, 1933

Edabi, S. *Iran Awakening*, Rider, New York, London, 2006

Fisk, R. *The Great War for Civilisation*, Harper Perennial, London, New York, 2006

Foltz, R. *Spirituality in the Land of the Noble*, Oneworld Publications, Oxford, 2004

Francis-Dehqani, G. *Religious Feminism in Age of Empire*, Bristol University, Bristol, 2000

Frye, R. N. *The Golden Age of Persia*, Phoenix, London, 1975

Hiro, D. *The Longest War*, Paladin, London, 1990

— *Iran Today*, Politicos, London, 2005

Humphreys, E. *The Royal Road*, Scorpion Publishing, London, 1992

Hunt, P. *Inside Iran*, Lion Publishing, England, 1981

Issa, R., and Whitaker, S. (ed.). *New Iranian Cinema*, National Film Theatre, London, 1999

Karsh, E. *The Iran–Iraq War 1980–1988*, Osprey Publishing, Oxford, 2002

Keddie, N. R. *Modern Iran*, Yale University Press, 2003

Lewis, B. *What Went Wrong*, Harper Perennial, New York, 2002

Mackay, S. *The Iranians*, Penguin, New York, 1996

Malm, A., and Esmailian, S. *Iran on the Brink*, Pluto Press, London, 2007

Middle East Watch, *Guardians of Thought*, Human Rights Watch, 1993

Milani, A. *Lost Wisdom*, Mage Publishers, Washington, DC, 2004

Miller, W. *My Persian Pilgrimage*, William Carey Library, Pasadena, CA, 1989

Moffett, S. *History of Christianity in Asia Volume 1*. Orbis Books, New York, 1998
— *History of Christianity in Asia Volume 2*. Orbis Books, New York, 2005
Moin, B. *Khomeini: Life of the Ayatollah*, St Martin's Press, New York, 1999
Mottahedeh, R. *The Mantle of the Prophet*, Oneworld Publications, Oxford, 1985
Nafisi, A. *Reading Lolita in Tehran*, Fourth Estate, New York, 2004
Nasr, V. *The Shia Revival*, W. W. Norton, New York, 2006
Nazir-Ali, M. *Islam: A Christian Perspective*, Paternoster Press, Exeter, 1983
Nima, R. *The Wrath of Allah*, Pluto Press, London, 1983
Pollack, K. *The Persian Puzzle*, Random House, New York, 2004
Rasooli, J., and Allen, C. *Dr Sa'eed of Iran*, Good News Publishers, Tehran, 1964
Sciolino, E. *Persian Mirrors: The Elusive Face of Iran*, Free Press, New York, 1997
Shah, I. *The Sufis*, Doubleday and Company, Garden City, NY, 1964
Takeyh, R. *Hidden Iran*, Times Books, New York, 2006
Waterfield, R. *Christians in Persia*, George Allen and Unwin, London, 1973
Whinfield, E. *Masnavi I Ma'Navi*, Yassavoli Publications, Tehran, 1999
Wright, D. *The English amongst the Persians*, Heinemann, London, 1977
Wright, R. *In the Name of God*, Bloomsbury, London, 1990
— *The Last Great Revolution*, Alfred A. Knopf, New York, 2000
Yaghmaian, B. *Social Change in Iran*, University of New York, London, New York, 2002
Ye'or, B. *The Decline of Eastern Christianity under Islam*, Associated University Press, New Jersey, 1996

Index

Abbas, Shah, Safavid king 52, 144, 147

Abu Bakr, first Caliph 4

Acacius, Patriarch of Seleucia-Ctesiphon 140

Ahmadinejad, President 2005– 109, 118, 180

Akhavan Saless, Mehdi, poet 33, 37

Al Adaqiyah, Rabia, Iranian mystic 12

Al Bistami, philosopher 11, 13

Al Din, Nasir, Qajar King 53

Al Din, Sheikh Safi, famous Safavid ancestor 50

Al e-Ahmad, writer 3, 7, 11, 74

Al Ghazali, philosopher 13–14

Al Mutawakkil, Caliph persecutes Christians 143

Al Naqi, tenth Imam 6

Al Suhrawardi, philosopher 14

Alexander of Macedonia, enemy of Iran 46

Ali, Muhammad's son-in-law 4, 5, 7, 8, 9, 74

Anglicans (Episcopalians) 148, 149, 152–4, 165–7
  beginnings 152
  focus on majority 153
  Marshall, Bishop Azad, present (2008) bishop of Iran 167
  Martyn Henry, Anglican missionary – see separate entry
  image, generally positive 153–4
  persecution 165–7

Aqa Muhammad, Shah 53

Arab invasions of Iran 28, 48–9

Arbela, early Christian centre 137, 138

Ardabili, Musavi, head of judiciary 1980s 105

Ardeshir, first Sasanian king 45, 46–7

Armenians:
  Apostolic Church 146
  arrival in Iran 52, 144, 145
  Bible 146
  cultural interpreters 145
  departure from Iran after revolution 167
  genocide of 145
  Pahlavis, treatment by 145, 146
  prosperity 146
  witness to Christ 147

Ashura, anniversary of Hussein's death 8, 72

Assemblies of God Churches (AOG)
  beginnings 155–7
  Evangelical success 168
  persecution 169–73, 176–7, 180

Assembly of Experts 84, 108

Assyrian (Nestorian) Christianity in Iran:
  asceticism and monasticism 142
  Assyrians' departure after revolution 167
  dhimmitude 143
  evidence of early origins 137–8
  growth 139, 141
  liturgy in Persian 141–2
  missionary success and decline 142–3
  persecution 138, 139, 143
  relationship with Shah 141

Ataturk, Kemal, inspires Reza Shah 54

Attar, poet 3, 16

Baalbeck, centre for Iranians in Lebanon 89, 90

Bakhtiar, Shapoor, Mohammad Reza Shah's last prime minister 78

Bakr, Abu, first Caliph who usurped Ali 4

Bani-Sadr, first elected president 81, 85

Bar Mama, 16th C. Church Patriarch 143

Barsauma, bishop of Nsibis 140
Bartholomew, apostle 146
bazaaris (merchants) 101
Bazargan, Khomeini's first
    prime minister 1981–1984 91
Beheshti, leader of Islamic Republic
    Party 83, 85
Beizai, Bahram, film director 119
Bellos, Dimitri, imprisoned church
    administrator 167
Bible/New Testament:
    Persian 148, 149, 168, 173
    Syriac 149
    Versions 161n76
Bird, Mary, Anglican missionary 152
blogging 118, 126
Blunt, Wilfrid, travel writer 52, 153
Bohlin, John, role in starting AOG
    Church 155
bonyads (charitable foundations) 101, 121
Bore, Eugene, Roman Catholic
    philanthropist 154
Borujerdi, Ayatollah 71
Bruce, Robert, Anglican missionary 152

Carr, Dr, Anglican medical
    missionary 152
Catchatoors, Haizak and Hrand, leaders
    of AOG Churches 155–6
Chahar-Shanbeh Soori, fire jumping
    ceremony 40
Chalcedon, Council of 146
Chaldean Catholics 143
China, evidence of Iranian missionary
    work 142
Christianity
    interest in 174–5, 176–7
    relationship with political theory 59–60
Church Missionary Society (CMS)–*see*
    Anglicans
cinema:
    censorship 119
    comedies 39
    New Wave 38–9
    rules of Islamic government 38
Coleman, Audrey, missionary wife 167
Coleman, Dr John, Anglican medical
    missionary 152, 153, 167

Constitution, on religious freedom 164
Council of Guardians, origin 84
Cyrus, Archamenian Shah 28, 45–6

Daqiqi, poet 29
Darius, Archamenian Shah 45, 46
Dehqani-Tafti, Anglican Bishop 153,
    165–6, 182nn10, 12
Dehqani-Tafti, Bahram, Christian murder
    victim 166
Dhikr, Sufi practice of remembering
    God 12
Dibaj, Mehdi, Christian murder
    victim 170–4, 177
drug addiction 107

Ebadi, Shireen, judge and author 87,
    114, 122, 127
Ebtekar, Massoumeh, government
    minister under Khatami 115
economy:
    Ahmadinejad's tinkering 109
    cause of social problems 107–8
    elite's wealth 108
    impact of revolution 100
    impact of war 102–3
    labour protests 105–6
    post-war recovery 103
    potential 104
Edessa, early centre of Iranian
    Christianity 137, 138, 140,
    158n4
Eisenhower, Dwight, US president 58
Emami, Sa'id, security officer 124, 174

Fadaiyan, Marxist-Leninist group 88
Fana, Sufi state of annihilation 12, 13, 21
Fardin, Ali, film star 38
Farrokhzad, Forough, poet 33, 37
fate, emphasis in literature and film
    29, 41
Fatimah, Muhammad's daughter and Ali's
    wife 4
Fatimeh, Imam Reza's sister buried in
    Qom 6, 54
Fadaiyan, Marxist group 88
Ferdowsi, real name, Abdul Qasim
    Mansur, poet 29–30, 35, 36

Fitzgerald, Edward, translator
    of Khayyam 30
football, women not allowed to watch
    men 117

Ganji, Akbar, journalist 123, 125
Gharebaghi, General, surrenders to
    Khomeini 79
Ghazan, Mongol ruler 143
Glenn, Dr William, Bible translator 149
Golpaygani, Ayatollah 72
Grant, Dr, Presbyterian missionary 149,
    150
Gregory, the Illuminator, apostle to
    Armenians 146

Haas, Pastor, German missionary 149, 152
Hafiz, poet 3, 18–20, 35, 36, 40, 78
Harun al Rashid, Caliph who persecutes
    Christians 143
Hezbollah, Party of God 83, 84
hijab, women's 54, 115, 118
Hilba, translator of Theodore of
    Mopsuestia 140
Hoecker, Moravian missionary 148
honour, male, importance of 113–14
Hormoz, island, Portuguese ousted 52, 144
house churches 177–81, 186
Hoveida, Amir Abbas, Shah's prime
    minister, execution of 82
Hovsepian-Mehr, Revd Edward,
    Superintendent AOG Churches
    169–71, 174, 177
Hovsepian-Mehr, Revd Haik,
    Superintendent AOG
    Churches 169–74
Hulego, Mongol ruler 143
Hussein, Muhammad's grandson, martyr
    of Karbala 6, 7, 8, 10, 85
Hussein, Saddam, Iraqi leader 77, 91,
    92, 93
Hyrapetian, Levon, Assemblies of God
    leader 156

Imams, the twelve 6
Imam Reza, shrine in Mashad 6, 101
inflation 100, 103
intellectuals, murders of 123

Iran–Iraq War
    Iranian children used 94
    Iranian invasion of Iraq 92
    Khomeini agrees to peace 93
    origin in Khomeini's mind 90–1
    Saddam's overtures for peace 92
    tanker war shooting down of flight
        IA 655 93
Iran Khudro, car manufacturer 105
Irfan, Sufi practice of seeking light 15, 21
Islam, political impact 49, 50, 51
Islamic Republic Party (IRP) 83
Ismail, founder of Safavid dynasty 4, 7,
    50, 51

Javadi, Fatimeh, deputy president under
    Ahmadinejad 115
Jesus Christ, treatment by poets 35–7, 41
John of Persia, at Nicaea 138
Julfa, New, Armenian suburb of
    Isphahan 144, 145

Karbala, site of battle and revolutionary
    icon 6, 8, 30, 51, 72, 77, 85
Karim Khan, Shah 53
Karimzadeh, Manouchehr, cartoonist 121
Kavadh, Shah 48
Kennedy, John F. US President 71
Khalkhali, first head of Revolutionary
    Courts 82
Khamenei, Ali, Supreme Leader 85, 122,
    124, 125, 172
Khan, Gengis, Mongol invader 50, 71
Kharajites, Muslim separatists 5
Khatami, Muhammad,
    President 1997–2005:
    Dialogue of Civilisation 176
    failure to support students 125
    opposition to security services 123, 124
    support for cinema 38
    support for free press 121, 123
    support for music 118
Khayyam, poet 30–1, 35
Kho'i, Ayatollah 70
Khomeini, Ayatollah Ruhollah, leader
    of Islamic Revolution
    accusations against him spark
        revolution 76

Khomeini, Ayatollah Ruhollah, leader
   of Islamic Revolution (*Cont'd*)
assessment of communism 88
attacks diplomatic immunity for US
   citizens 72–3
attacks Shah as the enemy of Islam
   71, 72
attitude to Christian missionaries 163
attitude to cinema 38
attitude to press freedom 121
attitude to Western imperialism 71
attitude to Zionism 70
author of Tahrir al-Vasilah 113
belief in divine authority 95
children to fight in war 94
condemnation of Mojahedin 85–6
condemnation of President Carter's
   hypocrisy 76
condemnation of Western music 117
dissimulation, use of 69, 72,
   74, 80
exile to Turkey 73
export of revolution to Gulf States 89
friend of bazaaris 101
hatred of Saddam Hussein 90–1
image of true Iranian ruler 75
invasion of Iraq 92
move to Najaf 74
move to Paris 77
New Year, bans celebrations 40
political theory 69–70
return to Iran 78
Velayat-e Faqih established 83–4
Khosrow I, Shah 47, 140
Khosrow Parviz, Shah 47
Kiarostami, Abbas, film director 38
Komitehs 83, 116
Konya, Rumi's home 16, 17
Kufa, early Shia centre 4, 5
Kurdistani, Dr Sayeed, founder of
   Brethren church 155

Lazarists, Roman Catholic mission 154
Lebanon, success of Iranian backed
   Hizballah 89–90
legal status, women 114–15
Linton, Bishop, first Anglican bishop 152

Loewen, Dr Arley, Persian literature
   scholar 19

McGavran, Donald, author of
   'Understanding Church
   Growth' 179
Magi, and Iran 137, 158n1 on tradition
   Magi from Iran
Mahdi, The Twelfth Hidden Imam 6, 9,
   10, 51, 70
Mahdi, Caliph, persecutes
   Christians 143
Mahmud, of Ghazna, regional ruler 29
Makhmalbaf, Mohsen, film director 38,
   119
Mana, bishop, Syriac to Persian
   translator 141
Mani, radical Zoroastrian preacher 48
manliness, in Iranian culture 113, 114
Mansur al Hallaj, philosopher 12
Mar Aba, 6th C. Church
   Patriarch 140, 141
Martyn, Henry, English missionary 148
Mazda, Zoroastrian god 45, 46, 47, 54
Mazdak, radical socialist Zoroastrian
   preacher 48
Mesrob, ascetic saint and inventor of
   Armenian alphabet 146, 147
Michaelian, Revd Tateos, murdered
   Presbyterian leader 156, 172–3
Miller, William, Presbyterian
   missionary 152
Millspaugh, Arthur, American
   economist 57
Ministry of Culture and Islamic Guidance
   (Ershad) 121, 171, 173
Mojahadin-e Khalq, Islamic socialists:
   alliance with Saddam Hussein 86
   beginnings 85
   character of, authoritarian and
     cultish 87
   fight against Imperial guards 78
   impact of their war with regime on rest
     of Iran 87–8
   invasion of Iran from Iraq 86
   Khomeini's opinion of 85
   leader–*see* separate entry for Rajavi

members imprisoned and executed 86, 87
war against Islamic Republic 85–6
Mongol invasions 16, 18, 50, 133
Monophysites, opponents to Nestorians 140
Montazeri, Ayatollah 86–7, 89
Morales, Simon, early Roman Catholic missionary 144
Moravians, first Protestant missionaries to Iran 148
Moses, of Datev, strict patriarch of Etchmiadzin 147
Mossadeq, Muhammad, prime minister 57–8
Motahhari, Morteza, Khomeini lieutenant 74
Mottahedeh, Iraj, Anglican priest and bishop 166, 167
Muawiya, founder of Umayyad dynasty 5
Muhammad Reza Shah, last Iranian King 56–9
  against bazaaris 101
  departure from Iran 69, 77
  devoid of charisma 56–7, 116
  dictatorship based on force 59, 73, 75
  image, luxurious and indulgent 75
  spectator during coup against Mossadeq 58
Muharram, month of mourning for Hussein 8, 71, 77
Mulla Sadra, philosopher 15, 95
music, gender segregation 117
Muslim, Ali's cousin 6

Nader, Shah, founder of Afshar dynasty 53, 145
Najaf, Ali's burial place, home for Khomeini 5, 51, 74
Nassiri, Colonel, sent to dismiss Mossadeq 58
Nassiri, General, SAVAK chief, execution of 82
Nasr al Din, Shah 145
National Democratic Front 84, 123
nationalization 100, 101, 109

Nestorian Church–*see* Assyrian Christianity
Nestorius, Archbishop of Constantinople 139, 140
New Year Festival 20, 40–1
newspapers:
  censorship and control 121
  dissident murders 123
  intimidation of 122, 123, 124, 125
  student support 124
Nisibis, Christian training centre 140, 142

oil, West's profits 57, 59
Ossanlou, Mansour, leader of 2005 bus strike 106
Ouseley, Sir Gore, English Ambassador 148, 149
Oveisi, General, attacks anti-Shah demonstrators 77

Pahlavi, ancient language of Iran 28
Peacock Throne, arrival from India 53
Perkins, Justin, Presbyterian missionary 149–51
Persepolis, site of Darius' palace and royalist celebrations 28, 45, 46, 75
Persian language, passion and origins 28–9
Pfander, German missionary and writer of tracts 149
pilgrimage, Shia 10
Pir, Sufi guide 11, 19, 20, 21, 26, 27
Plato, philosopher 14, 15
poetry, as indicator of ambivalence 35
Pohl, Reynaldo. UN human rights investigator 171, 172
Pourmand, Hamid, arrest and imprisonment 180
Presbyterians 149–53, 173, 181
  beginnings with Assyrians 149–51
  expansion despite intimidation 174
  hospitals and schools 151–2
  image, generally positive 153–4
  murder of leader, Revd Michaelian 173–4
privatization 103, 109
prostitution 107–8

Qajar dynasty 53
Qom, Shia centre 6, 7, 15, 71, 76

Rafsanjani, Faezeh, daughter of Hashemi
and activist 114, 117
Rafsanjani, Hashemi, President 1989–1997:
93, 103, 104, 105, 108, 109, 173
Rajavi, Massoud, leader of Mojahadin 85,
86
Revolutionary Courts 116, 123, 127, 171
Revolutionary Guards 83, 87, 116, 120
Rex Cinema, Abadan, its torching 76
Reza Shah (Reza Khan Mirpanj), founder
of Pahlavi dynasty:
dictatorial style 55
founder of modern economy 55
hostility to religious extremism 54
opposition to veil 54
support for Germany 56
wins power 53, 54
Rhodes, Alexander, Jesuit traveller 147
Roman Catholicism, link to Shia faith 10
Roman Catholics 143, 144, 150, 154, 175
expansion 154, 175
first mission, 16th c 143–4
Roosevelt, Kermit, organizer of 1953
coup 58
Rostam, hero of Shahnameh 29
Rudaki, poet 29
Rueffer, Moravian missionary 148
Rumi, poet 3, 16–18, 35, 36

Saadi, poet 31–2, 36
Sadr, Javad, Mohammad Reza Shah's
interior minister 72
Safavi, General of Revolutionary
Guards 122
Saladin, executor of Suhrawardi 14
Saless, Mehdi, poet 119
Saless, Sohrab, founder of new wave
cinema 39
Samuel, Joseph, missionary looking
for lost Jews 148
sanctions, US 100, 105
satellite television
Christian 176–7
general 120

SAVAK, Shah's security force 59, 73, 77,
82, 88
Sayyah, Revd Arastoo, murder victim 164
scarf, women's–*see* Hijab
Seleucia-Ctesiphon, old capital 6, 28, 29,
139, 140, 141
Sepehri, Sohrab, poet 33
Shahnameh, Ferdowsi's masterpiece
29–30, 41, 45
Shahrbanou, Iranian wife of
Hussein 7, 51
Shajarian, musician 117, 119
Shamlou, Ahmad, poet 32, 34, 35, 37
Shapur, Sasanian king 47
Shariati, Ali, writer 74
Shariatmadari, Ayatollah 70, 72, 77
Sharifian, Revd Nosratullah, imprisoned
priest 166
Sharpe, Revd Norman, Anglican
missionary and scholar 152, 154
Shiism:
background 3–7
Christianity, links with 9–11
Imams 6
Iran, successful national religion 7–9
Mahdi–*see own entry*
Shirin Ebadi, winner of Nobel peace
prize 114, 122, 127
Sigheh, temporary marriage 107–8
Simon, first murdered Bishop 138
Sirgachi Arash, imprisoned
blogger 126
Sohrab, slain son in Shahnameh 29
Soodmand, Revd Hossein, execution
of 169–70
sport, gender segregation 117
strikes 105–6
students, demonstrations 125
subsidies 102, 104
Sufism:
beginnings 11, 16
Christianity, links with 20–1
Khomeini's expertise 21
philosophers–*see* separate entries
for Al Bistami, Al Ghazali,
Al–Suhrawardi, Mansur al Hallaj,
Mulla Sadra

poets–*see* separate entries for Attar,
    Hafiz, and Rumi
Sulaqa, John 16th C. Church Patriarch 143
Sunnis, origins 6
Syriac, Assyrian language 137, 138, 141

Tamerlene, Mongol invader 50, 143
Tatian The Assyrian, Eastern Church
    Father 137–8
Thaddeus, apostle 146
Theodore, of Mopsuestia, Asian
    theologian 140, 141
Thomas, David, Assemblies of God
    leader 156
trade unions 105
Tudeh (Iranian Communists) 57, 58, 88

Umar, second Caliph who usurped Ali 4
Ummayads, wealthy Medina family 11
Uthman, third Caliph who usurped Ali 4, 5

Valerian, Roman emperor 47
Velayat-e Faqih, the rule of the
    jurisprudent 69–70, 81
Veramin, site of early pro-Khomeini
    protest 72

Waddell, Jean, secretary to Anglican
    bishop 166, 167

Waite, Terry, special envoy for Archbishop
    Runcie 167
Wakkas, Abu, military victor of Karbala 6
websites 126
weddings, issues of gender
    segregation 116
Wolff, Joseph, Anglican missionary 148

Yazdegerd I, policy towards
    Christians 139
Yazdegerd III, last Shah of
    Sasanians 8
Yazdi, Mohammad, threatens reformist
    press 122
Yazid, Umayyad opponent to Hussein 5,
    6, 72, 76
Yeghnazar, Luke, literature
    evangelist 168–9
Yeghnazar, Seth, founding
    member of Assemblies of God
    Church 155
Yusefi, Mohammad, 'Ravanbaksh'
    Christian murder victim 176–7
Yushij, Nima, modern poet 32–3

Zahedi, Fazollah, General, led coup
    against Mossadeq 58
Zoroastrianism 40, 47–8, 49, 137, 138,
    139, 140

Lightning Source UK Ltd.
Milton Keynes UK
UKOW03f1018030214

225761UK00001B/56/P